International Relations
Perspectives and Themes

Jill Steans and Lloyd Pettiford

PEARSON
Longman

Harlow, England • London • New York • Boston • San Francisco • Toronto
Sydney • Tokyo • Singapore • Hong Kong • Seoul • Taipei • New Delhi
Cape Town • Madrid • Mexico City • Amsterdam • Munich • Paris • Milan

Pearson Education Limited
Edinburgh Gate
Harlow
Essex CM20 2JE
England

and Associated Companies throughout the world

Visit us on the World Wide Web at:
http://www.pearsoned.co.uk

First published 2001

© Pearson Education Limited 2001

ISBN 0 582 32211 1

British Library Cataloguing-in-Publication Data
A catalogue record for this book is available from the British Library

Library of Congress Cataloging-in-Publication Data
Steans, Jill.
    International relations : perspectives and themes / Jill Steans and Lloyd Pettiford.
        p. cm.
    Includes bibliographical references and index.
    ISBN 0 582 32211 1
    1. International relations.   I. Pettiford, Lloyd, 1966–   II. Title.

    JZ1242 .S74 2001
    327—dc21   2001016447

10 9 8 7 6 5 4
07 06 05 04 03

Typeset by 35 in 10/12pt Sabon
Printed in Malaysia, LSP

For our parents

Contents

List of Abbreviations

CFC	Chlorofluorocarbon (ozone depeleting gas)
DDT	Popular pesticide of 1960s. Highly toxic
EPS	Project on Environment, Population and Security
FIFA	Federation of International Football Associations
GATT	General Agreement on Tariffs and Trade
IBRD	International Bank for Reconstruction and Development (World Bank)
IMF	International Monetary Fund
IPE	International Political Economy
IR	International Relations
ISA	Ideological State Apparatus
LIEO	Liberal International Economic Order
MNC	Multinational Corporation
NAFTA	North American Free Trade Agreement/Area
NIEO	New International Economic Order
NGO	Non-Governmental Organisation
OPEC	Organisation of Petroleum Exporting Countries
SAP	Structural Adjustment Programme
UN	United Nations
UNCED	United Nations Conference on Environment and Development
UNGA	United Nations General Assembly
USA	United States of America
USSR	Union of Soviet Socialist Republics/The Soviet Union
WST	World-Systems Theory
WTO	World Trade Organisation (formerly GATT)

Preface

This book is not simply a first introduction to IR. It is a second, third, fourth and fifth introduction too, and in writing it I have learned one or two things along the way also. In exploring a range of themes and perspectives we hope that all students will find our book not only useful, but also worth revisiting. We fully expect different students to take different things from our work; and our separate discussion of origins, assumptions, themes, criticisms and common misunderstandings (more fully explained in the introduction) are designed, not only to be clear, but also to encourage comparison and reflection. We do not aim or claim to do everything, but do seek a clear account of IR theory which is, at the same time, comprehensive and challenging.

There are two particular points about the text which are worth making from the outset. One about our approach to referencing and the second concerning the use of 'International Relations'/'international relations' and 'IR'. Both these questions, lest they be missed by the eager, are also included as 'boxes' in the introduction and are similarly explained. The use of boxes is an important feature of the book as a whole; they add to and break the text, but also provide important insights, information or clarification in their own right.

First then, referencing. Since we hope that many people will use this book, but particularly students of the discipline (and if this book provides some students with their first introduction) then it is important to emphasise some golden rules of referencing and to explain the approach we have taken here, since it may not meet with the approval of all scholars/tutors. First, we appreciate that students' work should be properly referenced using one of a number of accepted systems which can be learned by asking a tutor, consulting books or, perhaps, from a library and information service. Second, that work should always have a bibliography of all sources used (not just quoted) at the end.

In this context you may ask why have we kept referencing to a minimum whilst providing a bibliography in the form of further reading? Our rationale, which some accept and others query, is that in our experience, too few students consult original texts. Where introductory work *is* heavily referenced it is too often used in instrumental fashion to 'mine' key ideas and pad bibliographies. That said we have felt the need to refer to key authorities in each field so that the text does not unnecessarily take on the feel of the thoughts of Steans and Pettiford where, in fact, we are most often talking around existing ideas.

So, we want this text to help students understand key ideas which we introduce, but to use our work to enable them to *understand* some of the 'classics' of IR and valuable new works and departures in the field, rather than as a way of avoiding them altogether. This is not, we fully admit, an uncontroversial approach but *is* one based on extensive teaching experience, and one which seeks to address a perceived willingness to accept 'second hand' theory on the part of many of our students.

Turning now then to the distinction between various forms of spelling 'IR'. Though it is not used by all writers in the field, this book employs what we believe to be a reasonably accepted system for talking about IR: The Discipline. Where we use the phrase 'International Relations', we are referring to an academic discipline – to theory and study (and we similarly capitalise other disciplines). Where we use 'international relations' (or 'International relations' at a sentence's start) we mean the *practice* of world politics, economics and so on; what is happening. Whilst 'IR' can be used as an abbreviation for either, we will use this where we need to refer to both International Relations and international relations simultaneously. This distinction is, of course, normally quite evident according to context, and does not unduly affect the flow of one's reading. We mention it since it is a useful device, especially for students, to ensure clarity of meaning and understanding.

This book has a long history prior to publication, the idea dating back to my own time as an undergraduate and since then my own teaching in my first year at Nottingham Trent University, where Jill Steans was, for a while, a colleague. It is worth thanking various people who have helped the project along the way; indeed I should perhaps begin by thanking Alan Russell for giving me the opportunity to study such a fascinating subject in the first place! In the early days, Cedric Rawlings, Chris May and Nana Poku added to my own enthusiasm for such a book which was then taken up by Chris Harrison (now at Cambridge University Press). However, the project really took on its current form when Jill Steans agreed to co-author it; our styles and work have complemented each other well, and I would particularly like to thank her for her tremendous efforts towards this book. As well as writing, editing and so on she has also found time to encourage me and show faith in such a project when she had so many others in the pipeline clamouring for her attention.

We have both relied on the time and resources of family, friends and colleagues. First we would like to thank those people who have read drafts or otherwise assisted in the preparation of the manuscript: Tanya Matthewson, Cedric Rawlings, John MacMillan, Christopher May, Andrew Linklater, Stephen Chan, Caroline Arnold, Gillian Youngs, Mat Paterson, Eivind Hovden, Christopher Farrands, Hidemi Suganami, John Barry and Cindy Weber. In leaving this section until the end I am desperately hoping not to have missed a name! These people are at liberty to claim credit for the book's strengths, but should not be held in anyway responsible for its weaknesses.

There are many other friends (including family) who also deserve our thanks in terms of their encouragement and ongoing moral support. Jill's thanks are set out below. I would particularly like to thank Caroline, Mum and Dad, Owen, Karsten and Caroline, Peter Wilkin, Chris May, Jane McNeil, Melissa Curley and, of course, Matt Le Tiss! But at both home and work I rely on many more people than this. Thanks to all.

Finally, thanks should go to our publishers, and especially Emma Mitchell, for being enthusiastic about our progress, sympathetic about the other pressures we have faced and patient when our work has slowed.

Lloyd Pettiford, Clifton

In addition to the thanks offered above, I would like to thank my mum, Joyce, for her invaluable practical help during a very busy period, and Luke and Ria for their continual love and support. I would also like to thank Lloyd for his constant enthusiasm and good humour, which made working on the book a pleasure.

Jill Steans, Keele

Acknowledgements

The publishers are grateful for permission to use the poem 'Attack', from *Collected Poems of Siegfried Sassoon* by Siegfried Sassoon, copyright 1918, 1920 by E.P. Dutton. Copyright 1936, 1946, 1947, 1948 by Seigfried Sassoon. Used by permission of Viking Penguin, a division of Penguin Putnam Inc. and the Barbara Levy Literary Agency, London.

Introduction

The story of the origins of International Relations usually begins with an account of the Great War (1914–18), a war so horrific that many people believed it was the war to end all wars. The destruction and devastation, the physical and economic effort expended on killing and the horrific slaughter of an entire generation of predominantly young men, was on a scale few could have imagined before 1914. The study of International Relations grew out of the belief that war was the gravest problem facing humanity and that something must be done to ensure that there would be no more 'lost generations'.

The initial optimism that war could be prevented was short-lived. Just 20 years later the world was at war once again. In the wake of this Second World War, International Relations scholars continued to focus on the nature of international or inter-state relations, in their endeavours to understand the causes of war. In the aftermath of the conflict, there were renewed efforts to organise the peace, with the birth of the United Nations in 1945. However, the mood of the time was rather less optimistic. The order which emerged after the Second World War was very different from the world of the 1920s and 1930s. Germany was almost completely destroyed by the war, and other European powers, like Britain and France, required major assistance packages to rebuild their shattered economies and physical infrastructure. In contrast, the USA and USSR emerged from the war as 'superpowers' though the latter had suffered as much as perhaps any other nation. In an age characterised by caution, if not cynicism, many scholars formed the view that the elimination of war was impossible, and so focused instead on how best to limit and contain conflict. As relations between the two military giants deteriorated, in an atmosphere of suspicion and mistrust, and awareness of the awesome destructive potential of nuclear weapons grew, politicians, strategists and scholars alike, turned their attention to the urgent need to maintain what became known as a 'balance of terror' between the US and USSR, in order to prevent a Third World War and 'mutually assured destruction'.

WORLD EXAMPLE

The Bomb

On 8 May 1945 the war in Europe had officially ended. At the time of the German surrender, it was generally believed that the allies would eventually triumph over Japan in the Pacific. Very little was left of the Japanese naval forces and the Japanese air force seemed to be on the point of collapse. However, Japan had proved to be a resilient and formidable opponent, and it was by no means assured that victory would come quickly. At 8.16 am on the morning of 6 August 1945 an American bomber named Enola Gay dropped the first atomic bomb on the Japanese city of Hiroshima. Three days later a second atomic bomb devastated the naval port of Nagasaki. The dramatic impact of the use of the bomb on people's perceptions of war is illustrated by the extract below. In the longer term, the impact of the bomb was to transform thinking about the nature and purpose of warfare, strategy and diplomacy, and open up an impassioned debate about both the morality and efficacy of nuclear weapons.

> The initial flash spawned a succession of calamities. First came heat. It lasted only an instant but was so intense that it melted roof tiles, fused the quartz crystals in the granite blocks, charred the exposed sides of telephone poles for almost two miles and incinerated near-by humans, so thoroughly that nothing remained except their shadows burnt into the asphalt pavements or stone walls. (Extract from Fletcher Knebel and Charles Bailey, *No High Ground*, reproduced in Purnell's *History of the Twentieth Century*, London, Purnell Publications, 1968)

These events form the back-drop to the development of an academic discipline. However, much has changed since the Second World War. The Soviet Union has disintegrated, and ethnic and nationalist tensions have re-emerged across this vast region of the world, while Russia now stands on the verge of economic and political collapse. Much of the European continent has enjoyed a period of unprecedented economic prosperity, but now confronts the challenges of post-Cold War re-unification. The United States, which for so long has enjoyed a position of unrivalled influence in world affairs, now faces the prospect of being eclipsed by Japan, the newly industrialised countries (mainly in South East Asia), and, perhaps even China, as we enter the 'Pacific Century'. Africa has thrown off the yoke of formal colonialism, but continues to be dogged by problems of poverty and political instability. The Middle East has similarly emerged from a long period of colonial domination, but at the same time the rich oil reserves there mean that it remains of considerable strategic interest to the rest of the world, prompting intervention into the region's affairs which can exacerbate existing tensions (increasingly complicated by the politics of water scarcity). Many parts of Latin America have been brutalised by a succession of military regimes which have plundered national resources and abused human rights in the name of national development.

IR/ir?

Though it is not used by all writers in the field, this book employs a reasonably accepted system for talking about IR. Where we use the phrase 'International Relations', we are referring to an academic discipline – theory/study (we similarly capitalise other disciplines). Where we use 'international relations' (or 'International relations' at a sentence's start) we mean the *practice* of world politics, economics and so on. Whilst 'IR' can be used as an abbreviation for either, we will use this where we need to refer to both International Relations and international relations simultaneously. This distinction will normally be evident by context, and you should not let this unduly affect the flow of your reading, but we mention it in the event that you become confused by our exact meaning.

Today, the 'scourge of war' continues to blight the lives of many of the world's peoples. However, it is no longer just the spectre of war that is perceived to threaten the peace, security and stability of the world. The agenda of world politics has changed radically: population has grown exponentially, poverty has increased dramatically, technology has advanced in rapid and unexpected ways, economic relations have become globalised to the extent that recession in one country can reverberate across the world, sea-levels have risen as a consequence of global warming, while pollution and the rapid and indiscriminate use of the world's natural resources have prompted warnings of impending environmental catastrophe. At the same time, the language of human rights has become a global discourse, moving in to fill the ideological vacuum left by the end of the Cold War, and empowering workers, women, indigenous peoples, ethnic minorities and other marginalised groups with a powerful vocabulary in which to articulate their grievances and demands.

CONCEPT BOX

New World Order

This term was used after the First World War by both Woodrow Wilson and Lenin, each of whom, in their own way, envisaged the possibility of a universal world society. After the end of the Cold War, US President George Bush again invoked the term, in the aftermath of the Gulf War to suggest a future of peace and stability for all through the rule of international law, a system of collective security and the emergence of a global consensus on human rights. For many though, the expansion of Bush's liberal dream has been a nightmare and others (for example, the South Commission) have suggested different interpretations of what this 'new' world order might look like. See chapter 3.

It is not surprising then, to discover that in recent years, there have been challenges to a state-based, war-dominated understanding of the world. Just as International Relations in the earlier part of this century reflected the preoccupations and concerns of the time, the discipline has evolved and changed over time in response to what are perceived to be urgent and pressing concerns of humanity today. What this means is that the student coming to the study of International Relations for the first time, must not only grapple with the seemingly intractable problem of human conflict, but also develop an awareness of the changing nature of 'world order', the wide array of issues and concerns that have pushed their way onto the agenda of contemporary world affairs in recent years and be receptive to the many voices clamouring to be heard. Contemporary International Relations involves questions about the importance of the environment and economics, as well as war, peace and security. It means thinking about the needs, concerns and intrinsic value of different societies and cultures, as well as the actions and motives of the world's 'big players'. It means asking if we should think primarily in terms of globalisation and global processes, rather than a system or society of nation-states. It also demands that we confront the question of the nature and purpose of human knowledge and understanding. In summary, debates in the modern discipline concern: (1) what to focus on; (2) how to understand the world; and (3) what methods we should adopt in our study.

For example, should we endeavour to study the world 'objectively' and impassionately, in the same way that a physicist might study an atom? Or should we recognise that our values will *always* influence the way we view the world and so embrace a normative agenda, focusing, perhaps, on questions of inequality, justice and rights? At a time when many multinational corporations wield considerable power and influence over governments, should we continue to focus mainly on states, or should we also include a range of other 'non-state actors' in our purview? Posing the question, 'why do we study international relations?' encourages us to reflect on whether we are hoping to effect positive changes, or whether we can do no more than gain a better understanding of intractable problems endemic to the human condition.

Contemporary IR may be confusing to the student coming to it for the first time. It is certainly difficult and demanding, drawing upon and blending many disciplines and considering a whole range of issues and ideas which, while they have a global context, are very different from the discipline's original concerns. Students of IR today are faced with a much wider array of approaches than even 10 years ago and the discipline is virtually unrecognisable from that of 20 or 30 years ago.

About This Book

There are many fine introductions to International Relations but this one attempts to do something that other texts do not: provide a *first* introduction to the multitude of theoretical perspectives which have been brought to bear on international relations. Before we can begin to study international relations, we have to ask the question of what constitutes our field of study? That is, what actors, issues and processes do we regard as important or significant? The study of contemporary international relations is made even more challenging by the lack of consensus on these matters. A narrow definition of the subject might be that it is concerned with states (countries) and how they interact. This has the advantage of clearly identifying and limiting the subject matter and core concerns of the discipline, by concentrating on states as the central actors and limiting our study to how states conduct their relations with 'others', through foreign policy, diplomacy and war, for example.

However, this definition would not satisfy most IR scholars today, and would effectively exclude many issues and areas where new approaches and research agendas have generated fresh insights. A very broad definition of the subject might be that the discipline of International Relations is concerned with the human condition on a global scale. This definition has the virtue of being inclusive. It also demonstrates forcibly the value of International Relations as the only area of the social sciences which considers the world's peoples as a whole. On the other hand, it serves to blur the boundaries somewhat between the discipline of International Relations and other areas of the social and human sciences such as Politics, Sociology, Economics, History, Law and Geography. International Relations has always tended to be somewhat inter- (or at least multi-) disciplinary, including elements of Geography, Economics, History and Politics in particular.

Some scholars prefer to study the world by dividing it up geographically into clearly demarcated 'bounded spaces' such as nation-states and regions (for example Asia Pacific, Latin America, Eastern Europe) and make no real distinction between International Relations and Comparative Politics. Others argue that increasingly it is difficult to justify making such clear cut distinctions between the international, the regional and the national and prefer to employ the looser terms 'world' or 'global' politics to describe their realm of study. Still another way of approaching the subject is to concentrate on 'issues', for example, health, water, population, nuclear proliferation, trade and so on. There are also a number of distinctive sub-fields within International Relations such as Peace Studies, International Political Economy, Diplomatic History or Strategic Studies. As you can see, the range of issues, concerns and research orientations which can be incorporated into this field of study is, potentially, very wide indeed!

As well as deciding on *what* we are studying when we study International Relations, we also need to ask *how* we are to go about the task of understanding a complex world and, of course, why we are engaging in this activity in the first place. That is, we need to ask, what specific concerns and motivations inform and shape our activity? Once we begin to reflect on what we think is important or unimportant, significant or trivial, we are forced to ask a further question, on what basis do we make such judgements? For example, the call by some feminists for research on the political, economic and social status of women around the world, might be dismissed in some quarters as an indulgence. Feminists are, in turn, entitled to point out that women constitute over 50 per cent of the world's population and that the marginalisation of women and their lives is a consequence of the indifference and, perhaps, self-interest of the already powerful, who for the most part are men. Similarly, global warming might be regarded as an 'issue' in international relations which is slowly finding its way onto the agenda of international politics, but one which is at best a secondary concern for the world's great 'players' like the United States or Japan. However, global warming might be perceived as a pressing concern to people living in small island Pacific states, which are facing the threat of rising sea levels. In this case, global warming is likely to be viewed as a vital security concern.

Moreover, the world is likely to look very different to a politician or career diplomat than from the point of view of a poor woman living in a heavily indebted country, or a coalminer whose livelihood has been effectively wiped out by the economic whirlwind of 'globalisation'. Clearly, the same world can be viewed from a number of perspectives, or indeed, we might say that there are 'many worlds'.

REFLECTION BOX

What planet are you living on!

When we travel, we witness different cultures, practices and rituals which can seem strange, even nonsensical, when viewed from the 'outside'. We are even more at a loss to understand or explain stories of ancient civilisations (worlds) sacrificing babies to pacify the gods and prevent earthquakes. We live on the same planet but throughout history and across the globe, people live very different kinds of lives and, therefore, their ways of making sense of their world are quite different. Our experiences, modes of thinking and the language which we use to express our ideas, simply fail us in certain circumstances. Certain cultural practices are invested with symbolic meaning and significance which the outsider cannot penetrate. There is no common frame of reference, and so shared understanding is difficult or even impossible.

This notion of 'many worlds' does not just apply to the many and varied ways of life which exist across the globe. The insight that people draw from specific experiences and myths in order to give their actions meaning does not just apply to different countries and cultures. Even everyday speech can support the idea of 'many worlds'. People sometimes express incredulity, or even hostility towards those who have a radically different view or opinion on a matter, particularly if it is on a subject or issue that they feel strongly about. We have, perhaps, all experienced frustration, or even anger, because we feel that we are not being heard, or our point is simply not being properly understood or represented. Some feminists believe that women have very different ways of viewing the world and making sense of particular processes or events which are rooted in very different life experiences. Karl Marx famously employed the term ideology to describe the belief systems and world views of particular social classes. Poststructuralist thinkers (see chapter 5) argue that we can never completely grasp the essence or truth about the world; this is because we use language to invest our actions with meaning and to communicate with others, but language is 'unstable'; the meaning of words or terms – signifiers and symbols – is never fixed, but constantly shifting.

It is not entirely surprising to find, therefore, that International Relations has grown into a diverse discipline with a number of quite distinctive approaches, which in turn focus on particular aspects of the world, raise certain issues and are driven by particular concerns. This means, of course, that in addition to the wide-ranging nature of the subject, the student must also confront the broad and diverse range of theoretical perspectives which have been brought to bear on aspects of international relations. The perspectives in this book represent what might be said to be the established perspectives on International Relations and also, what we have identified as a number of relatively new but valuable 'departures' in the field. We are only too aware of the challenging nature of the subject and have tried to produce a book which steers a course between comprehensiveness, on the one hand, and accessibility, on the other.

The major aim of the book is to provide an introduction to a number of theoretical perspectives. A theory is an attempt to explain something – an event or activity. For example, a theory might attempt to explain the cause of a war, or why and under what conditions states engage in cooperative trade strategies. A theory is then a set of ideas, which are coherent, internally consistent and claim to have some purchase on the nature of the world and how it 'works'. A perspective is a particular representation of 'reality'. A theoretical perspective is, therefore, an attempt to construct a coherent explanation for a certain phenomenon, which in turn rests upon a wider belief system, or upon certain basic assumptions, about the nature of the world. It is not unusual to find students who are rather sceptical of the value of theory, believing that much of what we observe in the world is 'common sense' or that we should simply concentrate on the 'facts'. Whatever their feelings, students of International Relations are increasingly expected to relate their work to theory in order to achieve the highest grades. This provides one justification for producing a book of this kind and a possible motive for buying it! Despite such pragmatic motives, it is important not to lose sight of why you are being encouraged to think about theory in the first place. Basically, you cannot assume that the 'facts' speak for themselves in some way and, as for so called 'common sense', this can often be a 'smoke-screen' used to disguise an interested, particular or partial point of view.

ANALOGY BOX

I'd like to trust you, but . . .

Theory also matters because theory influences action or 'practice'. The way in which we understand and interpret the world has important consequences. The relationship between theory and practice is complex and will be dealt with in some depth in later chapters. However, at this stage, an example drawn from everyday life might be helpful. Suppose that, based on my previous experience of relationships, I am concerned that if I enter into a relationship with a person they will be unfaithful. I do, indeed, enter into a relationship, but my insecurities rooted in past experience cause me to behave in a very jealous fashion. As a result, the relationship ends.

Here the relationship between my 'theory' about human behaviour and my practice (action), were intimately connected and had particular consequences. Faced with a problem (the need to act in the context of uncertainty) I drew upon past experiences in order to help me understand the nature of that problem and how to act. My theory caused me to construct the root of the 'problem' as human inconstancy. Of course, I do not know for sure whether my theory was correct. I have to consider the possibility that the course of events resembled something of a self-fulfilling prophecy. Had my theory led me to believe that people can be trusted and respond well to trust, I might have constructed the root of the 'problem' as one of insecurity, rather than inconstancy. In such circumstances, my action would have been different and the outcome might have been very different in terms of a successful relationship.

At first sight, the insecurities, jealousies and calamities which sometimes characterise inter-personal relationships might seem a world away from international relations. International relations is a realm frequently presented as being characterised by tough-mindedness, rationality and the cool calculation of interests. We would also hope that theorists do not rely solely upon personal experience, when trying to identify the nature of 'problems' and how to respond. Nevertheless, a useful analogy can be drawn here. Some theories of inter-state behaviour are rooted in deep seated beliefs about human nature. Furthermore, the need to make decisions and act in the context of uncertainty, where levels of trust are minimal, is held to be a constant dilemma for states and, so, is a re-occurring theme in the International Relations literature. Suppose we are entrusted with ensuring that our country is secure from attack. We are in possession of weapons of mass destruction. However, this does not, in itself, guarantee our security, because other countries have a similar military capacity. We do not know for certain if these countries pose a real threat to us, but we cannot be sure that they do not. In such circumstances, a theory about the major processes and forces that motivate our behaviour and the behaviour of our potential adversaries is absolutely essential and, what is more, it is vital that we 'get it right'.

Suppose we believe that states are likely to behave aggressively, because this is 'human nature'. In such circumstances, we are likely to recommend a defence strategy that always enables our country to negotiate from a position of strength. The problem is, of course, that our action can then be interpreted as a form of aggression by our 'opponents'. In such circumstances, the relationship quickly degenerates into one of fear, mistrust and aggressive posturing. On the other hand, if our theory tells us that the real 'problem' is one of insecurity and mistrust, rather than real aggressive intent, our action will be very different. Rather than engaging in a build up of arms, we might open up diplomatic relations, negotiate arms control treaties and suggest various verification procedures or confidence building measures, which will help to strengthen the level of trust in the relationship.

ANALOGY BOX (continued)

We will not labour this point about the relationship between theory and practice here, suffice to say that, it is important to recognise that theories might not so much describe an unproblematic world 'out there' as construct 'reality' in certain ways. This has consequences for how 'problems' are identified and events interpreted, and this, in turn, has important consequences for how we act. Theoretical perspectives are themselves selective. They cannot include everything within their purview, nor can they explain everything. Theoretical perspectives necessarily give only a partial view, or representation of the world. Furthermore, it is possible that the resulting actions and re-actions will be interpreted selectively to provide 'evidence' to support our existing theory. It is important, therefore, to have a basic grasp of theories and the practical consequences of adopting certain perspectives rather than others, at the very outset of study.

The book, as the analogy box above suggests, employs an approach which is more theoretically focused than many introductory approaches. It is designed to help students cope with the theoretical deep-end of a rapidly changing discipline into which they will be thrown. This does not mean that students will be able to use this book without developing a general knowledge surrounding international affairs and a sense of the historical development of the practice of world politics. It is, accordingly, very much designed as a first introduction to the subject, aimed at first level students in particular but also useful as a reference/source of clarification for all students. While to some extent, we aim to encourage a degree of independent learning, this book is also designed to be used in conjunction with a programme of study. We hope, in particular, that it will allow you to make sense of unfamiliar terms which might emerge as part of that programme. To further assist you, we have included an extensive glossary of terms at the end of the book.

Perspectives and Themes

In order to make the task of a comprehensive introduction manageable and to aid understanding, the discussion of theoretical perspectives is organised around a limited number of key themes. In putting together a book intended as a first introduction, we also recognise that the activity of theorising is a complex process and that the resulting theories are often rather complicated. The theoretical perspectives which you will encounter in this book frequently employ an unfamiliar vocabulary, or assume more knowledge than is useful to the beginner. Some introductory textbooks similarly might confuse the reader in their attempt to tell a story of International Relations which includes all possible caveats and nuances.

Perhaps an appropriate analogy for our efforts here is that they are somewhat akin to a teach yourself language book. If you have ever tried to learn a language solely from a book, or even cassettes, you will realise that the real learning starts once you try to put your knowledge into practice. However, the initial stage of book-learning is very useful because it allows one to begin understanding and to start talking. Actual conversations will then introduce new vocabulary, often learned contextually, and one can also learn from mistakes that are made. International Relations theories have their own language, a specific vocabulary and a set of concepts, which are used to construct knowledge about the world. These theories could be said to be the difficult part of the language of International Relations and this book is designed to get you talking in this language.

As with a language (though the comparison is not exact) communication is the key. If you mistakenly learned 'Je voudrais *une* café' (rather than *un* café) this will not prevent communication; in time you will correct your error. Accordingly, we do not consider it a serious weakness, but rather a strength, that we seek to simplify International Relations so that you can begin to discuss it. By discussion, misunderstandings will become apparent, ideas will develop and further reading will then become intelligible and, in turn, contribute to your deliberations. This book introduces a limited vocabulary and explains a limited set of ideas, organised around a selective set of themes. We are attempting to convey something of the diversity and scope of International Relations, by offering you introductory chapters on a number of key perspectives, but which is characterised by a degree of simplification. It does not claim to capture the full richness of its subject. This is because just as too much vocabulary, and therefore constant references to a dictionary, would likely discourage the language student, we are looking to explain International Relations, which has its own language, in a way that will be clearly understood and encourage the student's first steps. Where a specific vocabulary is introduced it is clearly explained.

A second major objective of the book is to equip you with the knowledge and skills necessary for further study. By the time you reach the end of the text, we hope that you will have a sense of the richness, complexity and, yes, difficulty of International Relations, but that you will also feel that you have learnt enough of the language and gained sufficient understanding of the basic assumptions and guiding ideas of each major approach to undertake more in-depth study with confidence. In the concluding chapter, we return to questions regarding the nature and purpose of theory, but address these questions in more detail.

In the first instance, we would suggest that you read the chapters in this book sequentially. The various boxes have been devised on the assumption that you will, for example, familiarise yourself with the fundamentals of realism, before moving on to digest the basics of liberalism. However, we also hope, that having read the text through once, you will then be able to dip into it from time to time, just as you would a language book, to remind yourself of key discussions or in order to be assured that you are employing a term in the correct context.

When we learn even the basics of IR theories and attempt to engage in meaningful exchanges with others about the subject, we are drawing upon discourses about the world which have a distinctive language, which have a history, which draws upon particular intellectual traditions and which have been constructed in the context of specific interests and concerns. At this stage, our objectives are: to introduce and clearly explain the vocabulary of theories; consider their specific intellectual origins; outline the basic assumptions of each in an easily accessible manner; show how these differing assumptions lead us to different views of the key concepts and themes of the discipline; and sketch some of the ways in which each can be criticised (though you should not infer that the authors *necessarily* agree with all the criticisms offered).

Origins

Each chapter follows essentially the same structure. For the sake of clarity and simplicity, for the most part, we discuss realism or critical theory for example, as if there were no disagreement about their nature. Our justification in using this approach, is that we do not want anyone to find their first encounter with the various approaches to IR unnecessarily frustrating or complicated. So, for example, we frequently speak of liberalism as if there was only one version, whereas in fact there are many different strands. You should be aware that not all of the texts which you will encounter can be neatly 'pigeon-holed' or labelled as, for example, 'Marxist' or 'postmodern'. Also, in the literature, each perspective may be referred to using a number of different names. Where appropriate, in the relevant chapters, we shall draw your attention to different names and uses of terms. However, while essentially aiming to simplify theories, we also try to alert you to at least some nuances of each school of thought. This is best achieved by taking a brief look at the origins of the particular theoretical approach. This will also allow you to appreciate more fully the many 'strands' of feminist, or green thought and how they open up specific questions and areas of interest within the broader domain of International Relations.

Assumptions

All human action is based on certain fundamental beliefs about the nature of the world and the purpose of life. As Italian Marxist Antonio Gramsci famously held, all people are 'theorists'. In the course of our day-to-day lives, we endeavour to give our actions meaning by reflecting upon our particular motives for undertaking a course of action and what we aim to achieve. We will also, no doubt, weigh up the various obstacles to realising our objectives. However, for the most part our reflections will not extend to the fundamental assumptions we are making about the nature of the world and the purpose of human knowledge, preferring to leave the 'bigger questions' to the world's philosophers and great thinkers.

In contrast, theorists devote a great deal of their time and intellectual capacities to pondering these same questions. Each perspective is built upon a number of assumptions about the nature of world problems and, relatedly, prescriptions for how to overcome them.

Realists, liberals and Marxists, for example, have developed their own distinctive approaches to studying International Relations, mapping out the field conceptually, identifying who they each consider to be the main 'actors' and the big issues in international relations. Whilst there will be some differences in the way certain basic ideas are applied to IR within each perspective, all liberals or realists, for example, share certain fundamental assumptions. These assumptions represent the liberal or realist points of departure in explaining the world. In each chapter we highlight some of the basic assumptions which underpin perspectives in International Relations. To help you, we have tried to keep the discussion of assumptions fairly simple in the first instance. We divide up our assumptions into a number of categories:

1. Perhaps, the most basic assumption that each perspective makes concerns what constitutes human nature. That is, is human nature unchanging (immutable)? Or do beliefs and actions vary according to the wider social and cultural context and over time? For example, critical perspectives argue that what we often take to be unalterable features of human nature actually describe human behaviour at a specific period in history. So, given current experience we might believe that people are 'by nature' materialistic and greedy. However, critical theorists argue that people are conditioned to behave in a self-interested manner and to accumulate material possessions in excess of their basic needs because capitalism is a divisive social system that generates conflict, competition and insecurity. It follows from this that human nature is not immutable or fixed, but changes in accordance with the social and political conditions of any given historical period.

2. We also highlight the basic assumption that each perspective makes about the main 'actors' and 'processes'. For example, realists argue that a central process of international relations is the exercise of power. States use whatever power they possess to advance or protect the national interest. So, in realist thought, the state is a key actor and power is the main process while 'national interest' is a key concept. The liberal perspective highlights many actors, including states, non-governmental organisations (NGOs) and multinational corporations (MNCs), and stresses the fundamentally cooperative nature of international relations in a world which has become increasingly interdependent.

3. We might also ask: From any given perspective, is there a clear separation between the 'domestic' and the 'international' realms? So, for example, realists see the state as a territorially and nationally 'bounded' community with distinctive boundaries. The domestic (inside) is very clearly demarcated from the international (outside). Greens, on the other hand, argue that focusing on the 'artificial' political and territorial boundaries which exist in the world (though not visible from space!) detracts from the fundamentally interconnected and interdependent nature of all life (eco) systems on the planet.

4. Perspectives also understand the nature and purpose of human knowledge differently, so we might ask: Does this perspective claim to be 'value free' or impartial? Or does it claim to explain the behaviour/actions of all people at all times? (In other words are the claims which the perspective makes universal claims?)

5. We might also draw attention to the prescriptive implications of the perspective (what does it say should be done?). So, again, realists tend to have a very pessimistic view of the possibilities of creating a better world, and see 'theory' as essentially providing a guide to how states*men*, military leaders or diplomats should act in an insecure world. Their prescription, if they have one, is 'caution'. Liberals, critical theorists and feminists, on the other hand, argue that by gaining a better understanding of the human condition we are empowered to change it and frequently suggest how it should be changed.

6. Related to point 5, we will also occasionally touch upon the way in which each perspective views the relationship between constraints on behaviour and possibility of changes. We will ask, how does this perspective view the relationship between constraints on human action (structure) and possibilities for people to effect (bring about) changes in the existing 'order' and the way they live their lives (agency)? The prescriptive implications (in effect, recommendations) of a 'theory' might be revolutionary. That is, we might be forced to conclude that the only solution to the problems that beset humankind is fundamental change in the way societies – including societies of states – are organised, and a radical alteration in the way people behave. At the same time we might be forced to recognise that our action is constrained by the existence of concrete institutions and practices that support the existing order. This might lead us to conclude that while change is possible and worth struggling for, in any historical period there will be certain limits on what can be achieved.

These assumptions are really the key to understanding the different types or schools of theory which exist within the broad domain of International Relations. We will not attempt to delve into questions of 'objectivity' or 'subjectivity' or 'universalism' or 'particularism' at this stage. This is the difficult language of theory and cannot be tackled until you have picked up the basic vocabulary.

It is more appropriate to revisit these issues in the concluding chapter. Instead, we will confine ourselves to the less ambitious task of highlighting similarities and differences between perspectives as we work our way through the text and, from time to time, asking you to reflect on how certain interests and concerns shaped each school of thought. At the same time, we hope that from time to time you will step 'outside' of these particular debates and reflect upon the kinds of issues and concerns which are *neglected* by, say, realism, liberalism or structuralism. In this way you will become aware of the limitations as well as possibilities of 'explaining' and 'understanding' inherent in each perspective.

We would like you to be able to work your way through the various discussions of perspectives and themes, picking up the basic vocabulary as you go along, and getting a very general sense of the insights that they offer into, say, security or conflict. However, we also hope you will gain an understanding of the origins and assumptions of each because this enables us to compare and contrast common and divergent underpinnings and so prepares the ground for more in-depth study. Reflections on the basic assumptions of different perspectives are encouraged from time to time. You will find a number of reflection boxes scattered throughout the book.

Themes

Having outlined the origins and assumptions of each perspective, the discussion then moves on to the particular insights which they offer into various aspects of international relations. These discussions are organised around a set of specific themes. In concentrating on certain key themes, we are not claiming that we have identified the 'essence' of international relations. Structuring the discussion of theoretical perspectives around key themes is done more for pedagogic, than intellectual, reasons; that is to enable better learning and teaching rather than to capture every nuance. It enables you to make quick and easy comparisons and contrasts between different approaches and so aids learning. However, we have selected the particular themes we have because they have preoccupied scholars in the past and continue to attract sustained attention of International Relations scholars today. The degree to which we discuss certain themes in individual chapters varies. However, even though we have a relatively short discussion of peace and security in our chapter on structuralism, we are certainly not suggesting that a structuralist has nothing to say about this area. Rather, we are offering you an aid to study which identifies the dominant concerns of, in this instance, structuralist work in the field, which have shaped the way in which this particular perspective has emerged and developed within the context of International Relations specifically. Inevitably, you are going to find that there are some 'grey areas' both in terms of intellectual orientation and key concerns.

The structure of the chapters themselves follows a pattern to enable easy comparisons and cross referencing. In these sections of the text, you will periodically be invited to consider similarities between different ways of thinking about the nature of security, or the problems of inequality and justice. Alternatively you might be asked to consider the differing understanding of the relationship between the 'national' and 'international' realms, offered by liberal or realist thinkers. A reflection box looks like this:

REFLECTION BOX

Transnationalism and Interdependence

- What are the implications of transnationalism for how we understand the nature of international relations?

- How did Morse's work challenge the realist view of the state?

Obviously, the various themes have been addressed at length by different thinkers at different times in the history of International Relations theory. From time to time, we will offer you short discussions of what we consider to be interesting and relevant discussions of human rights or peace which are drawn from some influential International Relations texts. Any discipline will have its classic or founding texts; these are works that any student or scholar would be expected to have a certain level of familiarity with. In occasionally presenting the key ideas of a particular text we are intimating that this text is regarded as one of those books and that you should look more into the ideas of a particular author. An author box looks like this:

AUTHOR BOX

David Ricardo

Ricardo argued that individual countries had a comparative advantage in the production of certain kinds of goods and services. For reasons to do with their natural resource base or climate, perhaps, or because of the particular composition and skills of the workforce, some countries would always be able to produce certain types of goods more cheaply and efficiently than others. Ricardo argued that for this reason it made sense for countries to specialise in the production of certain goods and services and engage in trade with each other. Trade was to be positively encouraged because even though not all individuals, groups and countries benefited equally, it was beneficial to everybody's overall welfare.

In addition, we will also illlustrate some of our examples with discussions of key debates which claim to be based on statistical data, evidence or represent some 'agreed' version of events. We refer to these as information or historical boxes. A box of this type looks like this:

INFORMATION BOX

Environmental Disasters and Accidents – A very selective chronology

1960s – Pesticide DDT discovered to have polluted entire planet

1979 – Three Mile Island (nuclear accident in USA)

Late 1970s – Hole discovered in ozone layer. 'Miracle' refrigerant CFCs held to blame

1984 – Bhopal (explosion and chemical leak at factory in India kills around 2000)

1986 – Chernobyl nuclear accident (dwarves the effects of Three Mile Island)

Before and since this list there have been many accidents – explosions, leaks, oil tankers running aground, food safety scares – but these things particularly got environmental issues into the public limelight by the late 1980s. Remember they are just the tip of the iceberg (though of course global warming is melting the iceberg!).

Finally, of course, 'themes' have emerged from perceived processes, tendencies or problems in the 'real world'. As we have alluded to above, the discipline of International Relations emerged in the wake of the First World War, when the need to understand the tragedy of human conflict, as a first step in creating a more stable and just world order, seemed urgent. Some scholars have been concerned with solving the immediate problem posed by nuclear weapons, or have been interested to discover patterns or cycles in world events. All assume, of course, that there is a real world 'out there' which forms the object of their study. Whether there is a real world out there, or only differing representations and 'stories' about the world is an interesting and important question which will be discussed at greater length in later chapters (especially chapter 5). At this stage, we simply offer some examples of events which have been interpreted as significant and suggestive of particular trends or processes in international relations, or which have been offered up as illustrative of profound and certain 'truths' about the human condition. In so doing, we are trying to convey a sense of how theoretical discussions are inevitably shaped by context and historical circumstance. A world example box looks like this:

WORLD EXAMPLE

The Oil Crisis

In 1973 the major oil producing countries decided that if they worked together they could control the supply and price of oil, by forming a cartel called OPEC. In this way, OPEC was able to charge oil consumers four times as much almost overnight. The effects were fuel shortages and panic. The oil crisis was significant for two reasons. First, it signalled the increasing importance of economics in IR. Second, both the immediate impact and aftermath of the oil crisis provided a powerful demonstration of just how vulnerable states could be even while their borders were policed, defended and secured. Clearly states existed in a world where the economy was becoming increasingly internationalised. In a situation of

---

WORLD EXAMPLE (continued)

---

such interdependence states increasingly lacked control. The oil price rises of 1973 (and again in 1979) are just one reason why it became clear to some scholars that a concentration on military capabilities simply did not capture the full complexity of IR. The rise of economics also gave more weight to the claim that states were not the only actors of significance in international relations. So, whereas at the height of the Cold War in the 1950s and 1960s, liberal approaches failed to make any serious inroads into the dominance of realism in the discipline, during the 1970s and 1980s the 'liberal' perspective, and more specifically liberal-pluralism, became integrated into the IR mainstream.

Summary, Criticisms, Common Misunderstandings and Further Reading

Each chapter will include a summary listing the main points made about each perspective. After such clarification, since International Relations is characterised by disagreement among scholars, each chapter looks at criticisms which might be offered of each perspective. To aid understanding each chapter also includes a page box on common misunderstandings and also appropriate guidance on further reading; it is important to read the original works once you fully understand the basic ideas and assumptions which inform each distinctive approach.

At the end of the book you will find a glossary of key and problem terms which will include most of the words which are not readily apparent to a beginner in IR or the social sciences more generally.

Finally, it is important to realise that the meanings generated by IR theories are conditioned by the specific context in which theoretical debates take shape. It is only by gaining a sense of how and why IR theories have evolved, that we can fully appreciate the insights which they offer us.

Referencing

Finally, just a word about referencing. We hope that many people will use this book but it is aimed particularly at students of the discipline. If this provides some students with their first introduction then it is important to emphasise some golden rules of referencing and to explain the approach we have taken here, since it may not meet with the approval of all scholars/tutors.

First, *your* work should be properly referenced using one of a number of accepted systems which you can learn by asking a tutor, consulting books or, perhaps, from your library and information service. Second, your work should always have a bibliography of all sources used (not just quoted) at the end.

Why then, you may ask, have we kept referencing to a minimum whilst providing a bibliography in the form of further reading? Our rationale, which some accept and others query, is that in our experience, too few students consult original texts. Where introductory work is heavily referenced it is too often used in instrumental fashion to 'mine' key ideas and pad bibliographies.

We want you to understand the *ideas*, but to use our work to enable you to *understand* some of the 'classics' of IR rather than as a way of avoiding them. This is not an uncontroversial approach but one based on extensive teaching experience, and one which seeks to address a perceived willingness to accept 'second hand' theory on the part of many of our students. Where we have quoted from texts directly or closely followed a line of argument, our sources are acknowledged. Otherwise key authors and works are listed in the further reading.

Having explained the basic pedagogic and intellectual underpinnings of this text and described the structure, we will now turn to our first major IR perspective, which is realism.

Common Misunderstandings

International Relations is International Politics. International Politics is one aspect of International Relations. We might also talk of International Economics, World Sociology, International Cultural Studies and so on. IR has come to involve elements of all of these but has also evolved in its own particular way.

International Relations is current affairs. Much of what we watch on the news has an international dimension; much of it makes judgements about what is 'good' or 'bad'. However, International Relations is more than simply what happens – it is about how we understand what happens and even how we (and that includes news programmes) come to define some international events as more worthy of coverage than others.

International Relations has a clear definition. It should be clear from the above that IR can be many different things to different people. Apart from the different emphases of the perspectives, however, it is often convention to divide IR into 'International Relations' (the theory and the discipline itself) and 'international relations' (the events of world politics, transnational economics and so on).

Theory is a waste of time. IR theory is difficult at times and may sometimes seem purely academic. But examiners are looking for the level of sophistication of theoretical arguments and in terms of marks a little well-used theory can go a lot farther than a thousand parroted 'facts'.

Further Reading

Baylis, J. and Rengger, N.J. (1992), *Dilemmas of World Politics*, Oxford: Clarendon Press.

Baylis, J. and Smith, S. (eds) (1997), *Globalization and World Politics*, Oxford: Oxford University Press.

Berridge, G. (1992), *International Politics* (2nd edition), Harlow, Prentice Hall.

Bretherton, C. and Ponton, G. (eds) (1996), *Global Politics: An Introduction*, Oxford: Blackwell.

Brown, C. (1997), *Understanding International Relations*, London: Macmillan.

Burchill, S. and Linklater, A. (1996), *Theories of International Relations*, Basingstoke: Macmillan.

Calvocoressi, P. (1991), *World Politics Since 1945*, Harlow: Longman.

Evans, G. and Newnham, J. (1991), *The Dictionary of World Politics*, Harlow, Prentice Hall.

Frankel, J. (1988), *International Relations in a Changing World*, Oxford: Oxford University Press.

George, J. (1994), *Discourses of Global Politics: A Critical Re(Introduction) to International Relations*, Boulder, CO: Lynne Rienner.

Goldstein, J. (1996), *International Politics* (2nd edition), New York: Harper Collins.

Hocking, B. and Smith, M. (1995), *World Politics: An Introduction to International Relations* (2nd edition), Harlow, Prentice Hall.

Hollis, M. and Smith, S. (1990), *Explaining and Understanding International Relations*, Oxford: Clarendon Press.

Jackson, R. and Sorensen, G. (1999), *Introduction to International Relations*, Oxford: Oxford University Press.

Kegley, C. and Wittkopf, E. (1997), *World Politics: Trends and Transformation* (6th edition), New York: St Martin's Press.

Kennedy, P. (1994), *Preparing for the 21st Century*, London: Fontana.

Little, R. and Smith, M. (1991), *Perspectives on World Politics*, London: Routledge.

Nicholson, M. (1998), *International Relations: A Concise Introduction*, Basingstoke: Macmillan.

Russett, B. and Starr, H. (1996), *World Politics: The Menu for Choice* (5th edition), New York: WH Freeman.

Smith, S., Booth, K. and Zalewski, M. (1996), *International Theory: Positivism and Beyond*, Cambridge: Cambridge University Press.

Woods, N. (1995), *Explaining International Relations Since 1945*, Oxford: Oxford University Press.

CHAPTER 1

Realism

Introduction

Realism is the most established theoretical perspective in International Relations. Indeed, it has been argued that realism has dominated International Relations to such a degree that students, and indeed, scholars, have often lost sight of the fact that it is simply a perspective, and present realism as if it were a 'common sense' view of the world against which all other perspectives should be judged. We will return to this notion of realism as 'common sense' later in the book. At this juncture, it is enough to highlight that realism is one perspective, not *the* perspective.

Realism is a complex and rich tradition of thought and you need to be aware of its nuances. Hans Bartelsen, for instance, has argued that realism is an area of debate rather than a single specific position. So, just as in a different context, 'Christian' implies a certain set of beliefs but there are variations within this belief, so within realism we can identify classical and scientific versions, some realists who call themselves neo-realists or structural realists and so on.

Differences and nuances aside, a number of texts and authors in International Relations have been collectively labelled 'realist', because they share common assumptions and key ideas. In line with our desire to simplify somewhat as a first stage in understanding, in this chapter we will present realism as a coherent position or perspective in International Relations. For the sake of simplicity and clarity we concentrate on two versions of realism, classical realism and neo-realism.

As we noted in the introduction, International Relations originated in the aftermath of the First World War. While this conflict was horrific, International Relations scholars were initially quite optimistic about the possibilities of ending the misery of war.

LITERATURE BOX

Siegfried Sassoon

Poems like this one by Sassoon conveyed powerfully the horror, tragedy and senseless sacrifice of human life during the First World War and contributed, in no small way, to the growth of pacifist sympathies in the post-war period.

ATTACK

At dawn the ridge emerges massed and dun
In the wild purple of the glowering sun
Smouldering through spouts of drifting smoke that shroud
The menacing scarred slope; and, one by one,
Tanks creep and topple forward to the wire.
The barrage roars and lifts.
Then, clumsy bowed
With bombs and guns and shovels and battle-gear,
Men jostle and climb to meet the bristling fire.
Lines of grey, muttering faces, masked with fear,
They leave their trenches, going over the top,
While time ticks blank and busy on their wrists
And hope, with furtive eyes and grappling fists,
Flounders in mud.
O Jesu, make it stop!

Sassoon 1918

The idealist enterprise, which will be discussed in greater detail in the following chapter, rested on the belief that since people in general had no interest in prosecuting wars, and suffered greatly in consequence, all that was needed to end war, was respect for the rule of law and stable institutions which could provide a semblance of international order conducive to peace and security. It was thought that this could be achieved through a League of Nations (see box).

WORLD EXAMPLE

The League of Nations

Prior to the First World War every country adhered to the view that governments were the legitimate representatives of sovereign states and that all sovereign states had the right to judge without question their own best interests and pursue these interests through an independently formulated foreign policy, through negotiation – diplomacy – and, when necessary, through military action. Moreover, among élites, the view prevailed that the 'national interest' and security concerns demanded that diplomatic relations be conducted in secret and foreign policy be guarded from public scrutiny and criticism. The horrors of the First World War brought about a far-reaching change in the attitudes among both political élites and influential sections of the public across the European continent. Even before the end of the war, the principle of sovereignty was being subjected to critical challenges. A League of

Failed Eg of a sovereign authority

after WWI

Nations Society was formed in London in 1915 and similar bodies sprang up in a number of European countries including France, and even briefly, Germany. In Britain the idea of forming a League of Nations won backing from across the political spectrum, as leaders joined together to argue for the formation of a new international system which would secure the peace, if necessary by the collective efforts of the 'peace loving' powers.

The League of Nations was formed at the end of the First World War. The aims of the League were to provide a system of collective security and to deter aggressor states from pursuing their 'national interests' at the expense of their smaller, weaker, neighbours. The basic idea which underpinned collective security was that if any one member state fell victim to the aggression of a powerful neighbour, all members of the Organisation would collectively join together in a determined attempt to deter or repel the aggressor. The idea was to make violence illegitimate as an option for states and for other states to combine and oppose any state which used violence as a means for resolving its disputes in international relations. While it was recognised that this might ultimately require armed force, it was widely believed that 'world public opinion' would, in itself, prove to be a powerful deterrent to any would-be belligerent power. It was recognised that if the League was to be a success, the United States of America would need to end its period of 'isolation' and play a leading role in world affairs. Unfortunately, this was not to be. Although the US President Woodrow Wilson played a prominent role in the original conception and planning of the League, the US Senate refused to ratify the Covenant of the League of Nations, thus preventing US membership. Thus the League suffered a major moral and political blow almost before it got off the ground. Nevertheless, the League continued to function during the inter-war period, acting as an important forum for diplomacy by facilitating regular meetings between Heads of State. The League also gradually expanded its role in world affairs, setting up, among other things, a Permanent Court of International Justice to arbitrate international disputes.

However, although the existence of the League was, in itself, a powerful challenge to the view that states were exempt from public debate and criticism in their relations with other states, major powers were reluctant to refer their own disputes to the League. Similarly, action to achieve general disarmament was not successful. Indeed, by the late 1930s events in world politics had served to undermine the wave of optimism on which the League was born, as the behaviour of some states failed to live up to idealist expectations. In 1931 Japan attacked China, and the latter appealed to the League under article 11. The League sent commissions and issued condemnations, but Japanese aggression was not punished. Italy invaded Abyssinia (Ethiopia) in an attempt to establish Italy as one of the great European imperial powers. This led to economic sanctions and protest by the League, but without the backing of military sanctions these were ineffective. In Germany, Hitler sent troops into the demilitarised zone of the Rhineland in 1936 but referrals to the League, rather than resulting in resolute action, allowed Hitler to get away with a huge military and political gamble. Power politics appeared to be very much the order of the day and by the end of the decade, the world was at war once again.

In the light of the failure of the League of Nations and the outbreak of another devastating war, it is not entirely surprising that a much more pessimistic view of world politics prevailed in the post-Second World War period. Realism claims to be realistic in comparison with the hopeless utopianism of idealism. Some of its major exponents have argued that their personal moral concerns or despair at the way the world is, do not mean that we can change it. Some aspects of human behaviour are eternal through time and space. As we shall elaborate below, some realists argue that there are unchanging laws which regulate individual and state behaviour; states, like *men*, are by 'nature', self-interested and aggressive and will pursue their interests to the detriment of others and without regard to the constraints of law or morality. Realists held that the major problem of international relations was one of anarchy. Anarchy prevailed because in international relations, there was no sovereign authority that could enforce the rule of law and ensure that 'wrongdoers' were punished. The League of Nations was a poor substitute for a truly sovereign power which possessed a system of law and a military under the control of a single, sovereign government. However, realists went on to argue that it was impossible to set up a genuine world government because states would not give up their sovereignty to an international body. Accordingly, realists argued that war could not be avoided completely. It is necessary, therefore, to accept the necessity of preparation for war. Only in this way can war be properly deterred, or at least controlled.

 CONCEPT BOX

A 'Society' of States?

International relations is sometimes conceptualised as a 'system' or 'society' of states. The term states-system simply denotes the emergence of states as the dominant form of political organisation in seventeenth century Europe, in the wake of the decline of feudalism. The modern states-system emerged as a consequence of the Treaty of Westphalia, in 1648. The emergence of the states-system encouraged the growth of diplomatic relations with the exchange of ambassadors, the negotiation of treaties and the emergence of alliances. All of these features continue to be important characteristics of international relations today. The notion of a 'society' of states implies something more than merely the existence of independent states who engage in relations at various levels. The notion of a society implies something akin to rule governed behaviour, or the conscious recognition of norms which regulate behaviour.

The conception of a society of states, or international society, is associated particularly with the so-called English School of International Relations. Superficially the English School resembles realism in so far as it continues to emphasise the centrality of states. However, this conception of international society is qualitatively different from the rather mechanistic view of states as autonomous and self-interested entities pursuing their interests under conditions of anarchy. Indeed, one of the most noted proponents of the English School, Hedley Bull, coined the term 'anarchical society' to convey the degree to which a semblance of order was possible on the basis of shared understanding and compliance with norms and procedures, even in the absence of a central government.

After the Second World War realism emerged as accepted wisdom in International Relations. Realists argued that the long history of world politics demonstrated that it was not an exercise in writing laws and treaties or in creating international organisations. Instead it was a struggle for power carried out under conditions of 'every country for itself'. By way of reference, they called themselves realists and labelled the previous approach idealism. Realists argued that the focus of research in world politics should be on discovering the important forces that drive the relations between states. Realists believed that the pursuit of power and national interest were the major forces driving world politics. Focusing on these important forces, they argued, revealed that leaders had far less freedom to organise the world, and solve its problems, than proponents of idealism had originally suggested. Although realists accepted that laws and morality were a part of the workings of world politics, respect for law would only be achieved if it was backed by the threat of force. Realists also insisted that a state's primary obligation was to itself, not to a rather abstract 'international community'.

AUTHOR BOX

E.H. Carr

The reaction against idealism produced a number of very influential works in International Relations which mark the emergence of realism as the dominant world view in the post-war period. One such work was E.H. Carr's *The Twenty Years' Crisis*, published in 1939. Carr produced a powerful critique of the core assumptions of idealism, arguing that the tragic events of the 1930s bore witness to the fragility of international institutions, the realities of the underlying struggle for power among states and the fallacy of a world public opinion supporting pacifism. Carr also rejected the normative underpinnings of idealism (a concern with questions of law, morality and justice) arguing for a 'science of international politics'.

Realists argued that rather than concentrate on disarmament as a root to peace and security, states must prepare for war. Realists believed that conflict was inevitable and so the best chance of avoiding war was to be strong in the face of aggression. Realists claimed that relying on reason to resolve the problem of war was utopian and ignored certain objective truths about world politics.

AUTHOR BOX

Hans Morgenthau

Hans Morgenthau's *Politics Among Nations*, published in the United States in 1948, took the call for a science of international relations one stage further. *Politics Among Nations* has been widely regarded as the first attempt to develop a 'scientific study' of relations between states based on a recognition of the realities of power. Morgenthau attempted the first systematic and comprehensive account of state behaviour, insisting that the study of International Relations should be empirical and theoretical rather than centred on a normative concern with justice.

Although still in its infancy, even at this stage International Relations theory was showing signs of what was to become a central characteristic; it 'evolved' through a series of debates. The Second World War effectively settled the first great debate of International Relations in favour of the realists. The Cold War simply reinforced this pessimistic view and allowed realism to continue to dominate International Relations scholarship throughout the 1950s and 1960s.

HISTORICAL BOX

The Cold War

This phrase describes the period of history from the late 1940s to late 1980s in which the superpowers (USA and USSR) and their respective allies formed opposing blocs or camps in world politics. The causes of the Cold War continue to be hotly disputed. However, the initial cause of tensions was a series of bitter disagreements about the status of Germany after the Second World War. At the end of the war, the Soviet Union (USSR), the United States (USA), France and Britain administered separate sections of occupied German territory. The Soviet Union and the Allies then began a series of meetings to negotiate over what would happen to Germany now that the war was over. To simplify somewhat, the Soviet Union believed it was important to ensure that Germany did not pose a threat to the Soviet Union in the future. They demanded that Germany be prevented from becoming a significant, economic and military power again. Furthermore, they believed that the Soviet Union was entitled to massive compensation for the war damage inflicted on them by Germany. On the other hand, the Allied Powers believed that the economic recovery of Germany was vital to the future prosperity of the European continent. Moreover, there is no doubt that the Allies also believed that a resurgent Germany would prevent the Soviet Union from becoming the dominant European power in the post-war period. Clearly, the peace time aims of the two sides were incompatible.

The Cold War is sometimes described as, fundamentally, a struggle about ideologies. While the origins of the Cold War were rooted in tangible conflicts of interest, undoubtedly the competing value systems and world views of the Soviet Union and United States exacerbated tensions, generated suspicions on both sides and made it more difficult to reach agreement. Indeed, Germany and much of the European continent was to remain divided between East and West for over 40 years. This conflict was a 'Cold' War because troops of the USA and USSR did not come into direct combat contact for fear that such contact might escalate into nuclear conflict. The Cold War quickly became a struggle for influence throughout the world, with relations oscillating between stages of relative friendliness, such as the *détente* period of the 1970s, and unfriendliness, including a so called 'second Cold War' in the early 1980s. The Cold War ended with the collapse of East European communism in 1989, symbolised by the fall of the Berlin Wall.

In summary, the key points of the realist perspective are: (1) sovereign states are the key actors in international relations; (2) states are motivated by a drive for power and pursuit of the 'national interest'; (3) the central problem in international relations is the condition of anarchy, which means the lack of a central sovereign authority to regulate relations between states; (4) the aggressive intent of states, combined with the lack of world government means that conflict is an ever-present reality of international relations; (5) a semblance of order and security can be maintained by shifting alliances among states which prevent any one state from becoming overwhelmingly powerful and, thus, constituting a threat to the peace and security of others; (6) international institutions and law play a role in international relations, but are only effective if backed by force or effective sanction.

Origins

Although realism came to dominate the relatively young academic discipline of International Relations after the Second World War it claims that what it is saying is not new and attributes its insights to a variety of sources. This section sketches the ideas of these writers, who have either written on International Relations or had their ideas applied to it. The texts chosen here are not exhaustive but seek to make the basic point that realism makes a claim not just to validity across the globe but throughout time as well. To emphasise this point, realists are inclined to trace back their intellectual origins to over 2500 years ago and the writings of Thucydides.

AUTHOR BOX

Thucydides

The guiding ideas and the basic assumptions of realism are rooted in a tradition of thought dating back at least to the writings of Thucydides on the Peloponnesian wars, between the Greek city states of Athens and Sparta. Thucydides used the war to demonstrate how the logic of power politics (the pursuit of power and national interest) characterised inter-state relations and conflict, rather than cooperation or action guided by higher moral principles.

It is sometimes argued that today's students do not know any more about state behaviour than did Thucydides. His studies showed that the powerful did what they were able and the less powerful just had to accept. Appeals to higher principles such as those by the people of Melos to the Athenians met with the same iron fist which has been the fate of so many powerless peoples throughout the twentieth century.

The thoughts of Niccolo Machiavelli, a sixteenth-century Italian political thinker, and the seventeenth-century English philosopher Thomas Hobbes, are also invoked to demonstrate how realism is supposedly founded on age old wisdom. Niccolo Machiavelli is famous, or perhaps notorious, for offering practical advice to the statesman which would ensure that they remained in power and achieved their objectives. Machiavelli proposed a series of guides by which states' leaders might maximise their power. His advice included the instruction that promises must be broken when there is an interest to do so. This is one of many reasons why Machiavelli is often accused of being an immoral thinker. The term 'Machiavellian' is used in common parlance to denote cynical and unprincipled behaviour, or used to describe people who act in a cunning and subtle manner, unscrupulously manipulating situations to their own advantage.

Perhaps, it is more accurate to describe Machiavelli's thought as amoral, rather than immoral, since he believed that moral or ethical behaviour was only possible under certain conditions of human existence and the statesman had no real choice other than to act prudently and with due regard to the fragility of the political and social order. Although Machiavelli was not explicitly concerned with ethics or justice, it is clear that he regarded moral principles or justice as simply the stated preferences of the already powerful. There is no doubt that Machiavelli held an extremely dim view of human nature. Realists continue to argue there is no place for trust or sentiment in politics and point to Machiavelli's wisdom in elucidating this point.

The work of Thomas Hobbes has also been a key influence on realist thinkers. Hobbes is influential because he was among the first political thinkers to undertake a sustained discussion of the nature of secular (non-religious) power and authority.

AUTHOR BOX

An International 'State of Nature'?

Hobbes lived at a time of great social change and political instability. Perhaps, not surprisingly, therefore, one of his major preoccupations was the nature of political power, the basis of political order and, particularly, the origins of the state as the central, sovereign power. In order to explain the reasons and justification for the state and government, Hobbes posited the existence of a 'state of nature' in which all enjoyed freedom from restraint but in which, in consequence, life was 'nasty, brutish and short'. The conditions of life were unpleasant because it was man's nature to try and dominate and oppress others. Only mutual vulnerability (all men were vulnerable because they must of necessity sleep) and the desire for self-preservation allowed the setting up of a sovereign body that would secure the conditions necessary for civilised life. However, while men might be persuaded to give up their natural liberty for the protection of the sovereign, the international realm would remain a war of all against all, since the conditions which forced men to give up their natural liberty for security in the 'state of nature' could never be realised in an international context. Put simply, states did not need to sleep and so were not equally vulnerable to attack. Hobbes' classic work *Leviathan* remains one of the most influential writings on the nature of sovereignty and international anarchy. Indeed, international relations is sometimes likened to a 'state of nature'.

At times, Hobbes appears to evoke images which suggest religious influence and sympathies – inherent evil or wickedness for example. However, his beliefs about the essentially selfish impulses of human beings, were actually rooted in what he understood to be the insights of modern science. The extent to which we can discern scientific laws which help us to explain individual or social behaviour, or the extent to which the analogy of the individual in the state of nature can be made with the state in the international realm is debatable. However, together, these two central assumptions provide realists with support for their argument about the need for states to behave selfishly in international relations. Such a view suggests that states are unified, purposive and a rational actor in international relations in the way that individuals are in society. We might ask if this is an appropriate view. In order to help us decide whether these analogies are indeed appropriate and useful, we need to unpack the key assumptions of realism further.

Assumptions

why Realism think int's is stable

Whilst there are different variants of realism and indeed some subtle and intriguing differences between them, the perspective has some central assumptions which provide a common link. What is so important about these assumptions (or indeed any assumptions), is that whilst realists argue that they are based on observations about the 'real world', it is interesting to note that our basic assumptions about the world, colour our picture of reality. It follows, therefore, that different assumptions are likely to lead to a very different world view. The extent to which realism helps to shape the very world it seeks to describe forms part of some more sophisticated critiques of realism which we will return to in later chapters.

So what are the key ideas and assumptions which underpin realist thought? In summary the assumptions of realism are that:

1. Human nature is selfish. States, like men, behave in a self-interested manner.

2. States are the central actors. The study of International Relations is, therefore, the study of states and how they interact. Two important things to say about states are that:

    (a) States are sovereign. Sovereignty is, therefore, a key concept in International Relations.
    (b) States are said to be motivated by national interest. They conduct foreign policy to achieve this.

3. Power is the key to understanding international behaviour and state motivation.

4. International relations are inherently conflictual. This claim is based on one of three distinctive grounds:

    (a) Human beings are selfish and act to further their own interests even though this might be to the detriment of others and so cause conflict. Human nature is unchanging and there is no prospect that this kind of behaviour will change.
        OR
    (b) At the state level, relations are constructed in such a way that pursuit of national interest inevitably leads to nationalistic clashes (sometimes war) with other states.

OR

(c) The problem is not one of 'human nature' *per se*, but the lack of any central authority in the international realm. This gives rise to anarchy and insecurity and states are forced to act prudently and in a manner which puts the national interest first. Rather than emphasising the wickedness or belligerence of states, this view conveys a sense of tragedy.

 REFLECTION BOX

You will note the use of gendered language in this chapter.
This is typical of realism, though not encouraged in your essays.
Do you think realism is able to explain the behaviour of all *people* at all times?

Themes

The State and Power

Perhaps the core theme in realism is the centrality of the state. Indeed, states and inter-state relations constitute the very definition of the subject. The central characteristic of the modern state is that it has a defined territory, and a government which is invested with sovereign authority and exercises power over a people. Some commentators add a fourth characteristic – recognition. Recognition means that the state's claims over that defined territory and its right to exercise sovereignty over its people are recognised by other states. Recognition can take many forms, but typically it involves opening up diplomatic relations or entering into treaty obligations with another state.

It follows from this that a central characteristic of the state is sovereignty. There are two types of sovereignty relating to states: internal sovereignty signifies the holding of authority within a given territory and over a given people; external sovereignty, meanwhile, involves being recognised by other states as legitimate in the sense of having the right to act independently in international affairs, that is, to make alliances, declare wars and so on.

A second major theme in International Relations is that of power. Power can be regarded as an essentially contested concept, that is, one over which there are fundamental disagreements. Furthermore it is a word which seems to be very similar to other words; words such as authority, influence and coercion. Realism has much to say on the concept of power in international relations.

CONCEPT BOX *Example . Israel*

What is a 'State'?

Despite the centrality of the concept of the state in International Relations there are pro-found disagreements about, first, its nature and, second, its importance relative to other 'actors'. These differences will become apparent as we work our way through the text. There are other problems with the notion of the state as actor, or in conceiving of inter-national relations as a system or society of independent, or autonomous, nation-states. It is not at all clear that a state does have to have a clearly defined territory in order to be a state. For example, the borders of the state of Israel are contested by almost all its Arab neighbours. Furthermore, members of the Israeli government might have a difficult time in identifying precisely where the boundaries of their state begin and end! At the same time, world leaders frequently meet with representatives of the Palestinian 'people', while some governments actually recognise the existence of a Palestinian state, although there is no clearly defined territory on the map which one could point to as 'the State of Palestine'.

For a very long period of time, the US and some other Western states refused to deal with the communist government of China and continued to recognise the exiled nationalist 'government' in Taiwan as the legitimate representatives of the Chinese people. Moreover, there are numerous examples of states around the world where significant sections of the population clearly do not recognise the sovereign government as legitimate. The national-ist community in Northern Ireland is one such example. At first sight, these may appear to be isolated or exceptional cases, but in fact, there are large areas of the globe where boundaries are contested and dominant articulations of 'national interest' challenged. Does this rather messier 'reality' render the realist concept of a system or society of bounded, unified and coherent state 'actors' somewhat problematic?

Realism does not claim to deal with all types of power, nor all types of power relationships, but it does claim to identify the fundamental essence of what constitutes power in international relations. Realists have been fairly careful to provide a clear definition of power, and show how it can be quantified and, crucially, who has it. For realism, the essence of power is the ability to change behaviour/dominate. Some realists see power in stark, zero-sum terms. Indi-viduals, like states, have power at the expense of others. Traditionally real-ists have seen military capability as the essence of power for fairly obvious reasons. The capacity to act militarily gives states the ability to repel attacks against them, and therefore to ensure their security. Or it enables them to launch attacks against others for specific ends. Realists have assumed that it is military capability that counts. It represents the 'bottom line', the ultimate arbiter of international disputes. Power is both an end in itself and the means to an end in that it will deter outside attack or allow the acquisition of territory abroad.

In a world made up of independent states, force has been regarded as the ultimate arbiter in the settlement of differences. It follows from this that the potential for military capability, and hence power, depends on a number of fac-tors such as size of population, abundance of natural resources, geographical factors and type of government.

CONCEPT BOX

The Balance of Power

Realists have developed an analysis of how power is distributed in the international system. This idea is referred to as the 'balance of power'. A simple definition of the balance of power is that it is a mechanism which operates to prevent the dominance of any one state in the international system. The balance of power is sometimes viewed as a naturally occurring phenomenon, or a situation that comes about fortuitously. At other times it is suggested that it is a strategy consciously pursued by states. States engineer such balances to counter threats from powerful states and so ensure their own survival. As we would expect, the balance of power is frequently measured in terms of military strength. For realists, the primary aim of the 'balance of power' is not to preserve peace but to preserve the security of (major) states, if necessary by means of war. The balance of power is about the closest realists ever come to outlining the conditions for a peaceful international order, in so far as peace is defined negatively as an absence of war.

In nineteenth-century Europe the situation was characterised by five or six roughly equal powers. These countries were quite successful at avoiding war, either by making alliances or because the most powerful state, Great Britain, would side one way or the other to act as a 'balancer' of power. Unfortunately, the system of alliances which became 'set' in the early twentieth century saw Europe ultimately embroiled in the First World War.

Though such ideas are easy to challenge by reference to many states in the modern world, a state is said to have power if it has a large population, abundant natural resources and a large area, mountainous terrain or other features making it hard to attack. There is, at times, an almost mathematical idea that adding and subtracting the strengths and weaknesses in these areas will lead to an accurate calculation of a state's power potential. In fact it is not quite so simple since population is not always a power blessing if such mouths cannot be fed. Moreover, control of natural resources rather than possession is undoubtedly crucial in today's world. The situation is further complicated by other factors such as morale, quality of leadership, readiness and size of armed forces, and ability to convert civilian to military production including the mobilisation of people.

WORLD EXAMPLE

Population

The realist conception of power is challengeable in a very simple way if we look at population. Realists have assumed that large populations provide soldiers and are therefore elements of national power. If we look at China and the huge sacrifices it was able to absorb in say the Korean War (1950–53), then there is some evidence for such a case. However, for many countries today population size and growth is creating a range of problems. People are mouths to feed and brains to educate and place a great strain on resources. If we argue that power, even military power, must have an economic base then a large population is a big source of weakness for a country like Bangladesh. Even for China, the size of the population is very much a double-edged sword.

In fact, as realists readily admit, in practice only putting power to the test in war can adequately resolve questions about the relative power of states, and even then, military power will not be decisive if there are reasons why it cannot or will not be used. For example, few doubt that the United States is a more formidable military power than Vietnam although the former was unable to defeat the latter in the particular conflict in which they were engaged in the 1960s and 1970s due to various factors such as the weight of US public opinion and differences in the leadership, tactics and morale of either side. In addition, the amount of power that a state can exert in any particular encounter may be specific to the issue or area under consideration. For example, collectively the states that make up the Organisation of Petroleum Exporting Countries (OPEC) have less 'military muscle' than the United States and some European countries, but they were able, collectively, to exert their will against the West and raise the price of oil dramatically in the early 1970s. As we will see in later chapters, there are many and varied ways of understanding power relations.

As well as developing a view of power as a capacity and a resource which can be drawn upon or utilised by states, as we will see below, neo-realists have developed a conception of power which emphasises economic factors to a much greater degree than traditional realism. We will return to the differences between realist and neo-realist conceptions of power later.

 REFLECTION BOX

If you think for just a few seconds about those countries of the world which you regard as powerful, your list will probably include some, like Japan and Germany which are not particularly strong militarily. Other countries such as China and Russia, which are very strong militarily are increasingly realising that their stability could be jeopardised without improved economic performance. In today's world not just raw power but also influence are increasingly complex phenomena.

Conflict and Violence

Conflict may be simply defined as disagreements which the parties involved seek to resolve to their own satisfaction. According to such a definition, conflict need not be violent and seems an inevitable part of human interaction including arguments over whether to visit the cinema or a football match, jealousy in relationships, pub brawls and so on. Human interaction it seems leads to disagreements. To realists, the conflict in which they are interested is the specific variety of interstate conflict of a violent nature; most usually, but not always, wars.

With this focus in mind, realists limit their interest for the most part to the causes and nature of wars. There are differences of opinion as to where the focus should lie if we are talking about general rather than specific causes. Various scholars have argued for a concentration on the nature of human beings; others have suggested a focus on states themselves; and still others have preferred to pin the blame for conflict on the workings of the international system as a whole. It is possible to argue for consideration to be given to all three.

AUTHOR BOX

Kenneth Waltz *— Refute — why he may fight*

The notion of 'three images' is associated particularly with the work of Kenneth Waltz, especially his influential book *Man, the State and War*, first published in 1959. To simplify somewhat, Waltz's first image focuses on human nature as the root cause of war. This view suggests that as a species we are inherently greedy, aggressive, selfish and generally nasty. There is a good deal of evidence with which to support this claim but equally much to dispute it. The second image focuses on the state level, arguing that these are constructed in such a way that pursuit of national interest inevitably leads to nationalistic clashes with other states. The third image is that the structure of the international system itself leads to conflict by forcing states to act in a certain way.

Waltz is sometimes referred to as a 'structural realist' because he emphasises the 'third image'. Though the use of the word 'structural' can cause problems for some students, the argument is that the anarchical *structure* of international relations literally forces states to behave as they do (this is not to be confused with structuralism which we discuss in detail in chapter 3). Rather than emphasising the wickedness or belligerence of states, this view conveys a sense of tragedy. The 'belligerent' view of realism sees conflict as fundamentally stemming from the pursuit of national interest involving the use of, or backed by the threat of, military force. In contrast, this 'tragic' strand of realist thinking sees conflict as occurring as a consequence of anarchy.

More often realists look for concrete and specific causes of conflict, for instance, 'economic' arguments like trade wars, ideological differences (that is, different values), ethnic differences or religious differences, even because of the aggression of particular leaders. Some of the most bloody conflicts of recent history have been over access to resources. We will expand upon how access to resources and environmental degradation might increase conflicts in chapter 7.

WORLD EXAMPLE

The Middle East

The Middle East is a region which has experienced considerable conflict in the twentieth century. Though water is not usually the specifically cited cause of conflict, in very many cases analysts believe it underlies it. Israeli needs for water, for instance, may be the most intractible reason for the lack of a lasting peace with the Palestinians. Water is a precious resource and becoming more scarce as populations continue to expand. With rivers forming borders throughout the region and usually flowing through more than one state, efforts to control water in one state (say through dam projects) may well lead to reduced supply in another. Such problems complicate the Arab–Israeli relationship but also reveal cracks in the notion of Arab brotherhood itself.

Peace and Security

In realist thought, peace is viewed in negative terms. That is to say that peace is a condition characterised by an *absence* of war rather than the existence of something. Realists concentrate on the conditions necessary to prevent wars; the relationship between power, security and conflict is an intimate one. Security is a word used in a variety of contexts in everyday life with a variety of meanings including issues of personal emotions, to whether something is done up or tightened properly, to ideas of safety and invulnerability. For realists in IR, security pertains to the state and a state is more or less secure to the extent that it can ensure its survival in the international system. The relationship between peace and security is not then straightforward.

For realists, security is about (state) survival. For those states, the majority, unable to guarantee their own safety through their own military forces, the balance of power represents a reasonable hope of being able to feel secure in international relations. Realists argue that unlike domestic politics (where governments are responsible for enforcing laws), in world politics there is no government to enforce laws and, as a result, each state has to provide for its own security. Self-preservation under such conditions demands that a state be able to protect itself, because it cannot rely upon help coming from other states. Policy makers, conclude realists, must therefore seek power for their country. To do otherwise, it is argued, would invite war and defeat, as another state or states would take advantage of this misjudgement by attacking you. Realists argue that creating institutions, such as the League of Nations, that presupposes states have an interest in cooperation, was foolish and therefore bound to fail.

ANALOGY BOX

The Stag/Hare Analogy

This analogy is sometimes used to illustrate the 'security dilemma' and problems of co-operation in international relations. A group of primitive hunters are isolated on an island. They agree that if they can kill a stag they will have enough to feed all of them, but that to do this they must cooperate as it will require all their efforts to entrap and kill the animal. They set off to hunt the stag. Shortly afterwards one of the hunters sees a hare, which would certainly be enough to satisfy the hunger of an individual. In breaking off from the stag-hunt to capture the hare the hunter ensures that he will satisfy his need for food. However, in so doing he effectively allows the stag to escape and the rest of the group are condemned to hunger. Cooperation among all the hunters could have led to an optimal solution where all were fed. However, the hunter faced a dilemma because he could not be sure that the group would catch the stag. Furthermore, he could not be sure that another member of the group would not break ranks in pursuit of the hare, in which case he would have gone hungry. In the context of uncertainty, it was, therefore, rational to behave in a self-interested manner. The point of the stag/hare analogy is to illustrate that under conditions of uncertainty (anarchy) it is rational to act in a self-interested way. The tragedy of international relations is that under conditions of anarchy even mutual interest does not guarantee cooperation.

Institutions and World Order

Given the emphasis on the state, power, conflict and security, it is not entirely surprising that throughout much of its history, cooperation has been a secondary concern for realists. Broadly speaking, realism has tended to marginalise areas which are not the 'real stuff' of international relations, and therefore contends that international cooperation is significant only to the extent that it is engaged in by states for the benefit of states. Realism's basic assumptions involve the belief that whilst much can interest us about the world, these should not sidetrack us from its essential features. In suggesting that certain facets of international relations are timeless, the traditional realist distinction has always been between the 'high politics' of foreign policy, diplomacy and war and the 'low politics' of economics. This means that the former has been regarded as much more important than the latter.

At first sight then, a perspective based on assumptions concerning the sovereignty of states, the primacy of national interest and the violent nature of conflict cannot have very much to say about international institutions. To some extent, institutions have been something of a subsidiary theme in realist writings, but this does not mean that realists have no view on the character and role of institutions in international affairs. As we will see below, neo-realism has developed a detailed exposition on the nature of institutions like the International Monetary Fund or World Bank. Realists do not ignore the United Nations or the European Union, just as they do not deny that limited forms of cooperation occur and that international institutions might facilitate this to some degree.

AUTHOR BOX

Hedley Bull

Hedley Bull argued that supranational organisations such as the EU can be regarded as 'states in waiting'. In other words, they may acquire an identity of their own such that they become the citizen's highest source of loyalty. At such a point though, current states, such as Germany or France become simply regions of a European state and the fundamental rules or logic of IR remain unchanged.

However, realists never lose sight of the central importance of states as the predominant actors of world politics. They believe that states only join international institutions and enter into cooperative arrangements when it suits them. Accordingly, such arrangements, alliances or cooperative agreements can be backed out of or broken, if and when they cease to be in the national interest, as easily as the hunter, in the stag/hare analogy above, left pursuit of the stag in order to catch a hare. The bottom line, to realists, is that international institutions are significant only to the extent that they allow states to pursue their interests.

That said, one of the most important differences between classical realism and neo-realism is that neo-realism has developed a much more sophisticated analysis of cooperation and the role of institutions in international relations, particularly in relation to the governance of the global economy. If it was indeed the case that economic interdependence between states was becoming more widespread and complex, how could economic activity which was taking place across state boundaries be coordinated effectively? Moreover, how could the international and economic order be 'governed' in the absence of government? As was suggested above, the point of departure for realists in answering these questions was a fairly orthodox one: the problems generated by an essentially anarchic international system. However, neo-realists also draw upon classical liberal economic theories which suggest that a degree of governance is necessary to allow free trade and dynamic growth to take place. Classical economic theorists recognised that the state has an important and necessary role to play, but one which should be kept to a minimum. Attempts to fuse an analysis of the growth and expansion of a liberal international economy with an analysis of where power lies in the international state system, gave rise to a revised version of realism – neo-realism.

This increasing preoccupation with all things economic eventually gave rise to International Political Economy (IPE) emerging as a distinctive sub-discipline within the broader domain of International Relations, as scholars attempted to get to grips with the increasingly complex forms of interdependence and the proliferation of institutions and regimes to regulate international economic exchanges. The central concept in neo-realist IPE is hegemony, a word derived from the Greek for 'dominance' or 'leadership'. Realists have viewed major wars as attempts by states to establish hegemonic domination. Neo-realists frequently cite two major phases of hegemonic domination (pax-Britannica and pax-Americana) which describe the periods of British dominance over the global economy in the nineteenth and early twentieth centuries and US domination in the post Second World War period.

Neo-realism combines some fairly traditional realist ideas about power and the centrality of states in international relations, with certain liberal ideas about rationality and economic cooperation. A more detailed discussion of similarities and differences between neo-realist and neo-liberal accounts of governance will be undertaken in the next chapter. We will not dwell on this here, but rather concentrate on how neo-realists have developed a view of governance based on an analysis of the role played by dominant states in maintaining international economic order.

Neo-realists have found the concept of hegemony useful in explaining how an international economy based on fundamentally liberal principles and liberal economic practices could be carried out effectively in a world in which political authority was vested in nation-states. In the absence of an international 'public good' which would allow the international economy to run smoothly, the concept of hegemony is used to explain how a degree of regulation, or governance is possible.

Neo-realists believe that states aim to maximise wealth and that this is best achieved by securing a broadly liberal, free-market international economy. While ostensibly concerned with understanding the inter-connections between economics and politics, neo-realist scholars have continued to stay close to the 'self-interest' emphasis of realism. This has particular consequences. For example, it means that although scholars became more interested in the activities of, say, multinational corporations (MNCs), these were not regarded as independent or autonomous actors in the international economy, but rather were seen as an extension of state power or instruments of foreign policy. MNCs were not, then, held to be a significant economic and political force in their own right, but a measure and reflection of the power and might of particular states.

REFLECTION BOX

Much realist IPE analysis has been framed in terms of the US state and US domination of the international system. Do you think that it is appropriate to view MNCs as an extension of state power? What are the implications of looking at the world from the perspective of dominant states?

Arguably the major contribution of neo-realism to the study of international political economy is hegemonic stability theory, an idea originally advanced by Charles Kindleberger in 1973 to explain the collapse of the international monetary order. Hegemonic stability theory holds that there is always a proclivity towards instability in the international system, but this can be avoided if the dominant state assumes a leadership or hegemonic role. This role involves creating and upholding a system of rules which provide a secure basis for international order and cooperation under conditions of anarchy. In this way liberal values and norms could be fostered and upheld. Hegemons are able to control finance, trade, and so on. The Bretton Woods System which comprised the General Agreement on Tariffs and Trade, the International Bank for Reconstruction and Development and the International Monetary Fund provided a system of rules, values and norms, based broadly on liberal economic principles (see chapter 2).

AUTHOR BOX

Robert Gilpin

Robert Gilpin, who is arguably the pre-eminent contemporary neo-realist IPE scholar, developed an analysis of US hegemony which rested on the premise that there was a direct relationship between US power and the stability of the international economic order. The Bretton Woods System eventually broke down because of a decline in the power and influence of the US, a decline reflected in the switch to a regime of floating exchange rates from 1971. The US could no longer maintain its currency at a high rate relative to its economic competitors. Gilpin argued that economic realities would eventually bring about an adjustment in the system and so the US would eventually retreat from its commitment to the multilateralism of the Bretton Woods System as US foreign policy adjusted to harsh economic realities. This had obvious implications for the stability of the international economic and political order.

Identity and Community

Realists argue that people identify first and foremost with the nation-state. That is to say, that most people see themselves as British, or French or Canadian, rather than as members of the 'human race' or of an abstract 'international community'. For realists the only community of any significance in international relations is the nation-state. The state is also held to be of moral worth, because it is the best form of political community that the human race has yet devised. There is a strong sense in realist writings that national security issues, particularly in times of war, offer a sense of shared political purpose. Therefore, it is meaningful to speak of an underlying national interest which governs state behaviour particularly in relations with 'foreigners'. The state must, of necessity, be concerned, first and foremost, with national security, hence the preoccupation most states have with military power.

Inequality and Justice

Realist arguments frequently make much of the dangers inherent in not accepting what we cannot change. Thus for instance, they see great dangers for the international system in emphasising social justice or human rights. Realists emphasise the principle of sovereignty as the cornerstone of the international system. We outlined the realist critique of international law and problems of conducting relations between states on the basis of moral principles earlier and will not labour this point again. As is apparent from our earlier discussion, sovereignty bestows exclusive jurisdiction over a territory and people. To intervene in the affairs of other states, is then, to risk undermining the sovereign independence and autonomy of states. For this reason, realists also argue that states have no grounds to comment on or criticise the domestic political, social or economic order of other states. States are relatively silent on the rights of other states' citizens and indeed should be. If all such issues were taken up by all states, that is if internal sovereignty were not accepted, great instability might well result as states meddled in each others' affairs. Put another way, turning a blind-eye is the lesser of evils. Thus we might object to authoritarianism in Burma, communism in China or the death penalty in the United States but, ultimately, we have no 'right', either political or moral, to judge the actions of other states in regard to their own peoples. Indeed, ultimately this could lead to international conflict.

If at first sight realists appear to be giving a green light to dictatorship and oppression, they might argue in their defence that the principle of sovereignty protects the 'weak' to some extent. Whatever the realities of power and influence in the international system, sovereignty at least guarantees a certain formal equality among states. In contrast, English School scholars subscribe to the notion of an international society or society of states, pointing out that increasing respect for human rights is becoming an accepted norm of international society and might, in exceptional cases, form the basis for 'intervention'.

Generally speaking it is fair to say that most realists adhere to a view of sovereignty as the foundation of the international system and so emphasise the principle of domestic jurisdiction and, relatedly, non-intervention into the domestic affairs of another state.

Realists are not unaware of issues of social and economic inequality and injustice. However, as we have suggested before, realists accept the world as it is rather than trying to change it. Realists believe that certain proposals for the eradication of poverty by means of world government, for instance, hold within them the seeds of disaster or are simply impossible.

Summary

1. Realism is one perspective within IR.

2. Realism is a label attached to certain ways of thinking. There are, however, a number of distinctive strands in realist thought.

3. Realism is sometimes referred to as Power Politics, the Hobbesian approach to International Relations or the 'billiard ball model'.

4. Realism developed in International Relations as a rejection of idealism in the post Second World War period.

5. The intellectual roots of realism go back much further. Realism supports its view by reference to a whole series of authors and events going back millennia.

6. Realism is a label given to a particular set of assumptions about international relations which emphasise the importance of states, motivated by national interest and driven by power.

7. Realism does not make a claim to explain every aspect of international relations. It aims to capture the essence of one specific aspect of the world – i.e. power politics.

8. Realism claims to describe a world it is not possible to change and gives us a guide on how to survive in that world.

9. By extension, realism claims to be based on certain essential 'truths' about the human condition.

10. Realists make clear distinctions between the 'domestic' and the 'international' realms.

11. Neo-realism emerged in response to the need to explain the increasingly interdependent nature of international relations; an interdependence which was in large part driven by the expansion of the international economy.

12. The dominant themes in realism are states and power, conflict, and security. In more recent years, neo-realists have made some contribution to our understanding of the nature and purpose of international institutions and processes of governance.

Criticisms

Historically, realism has been the dominant tradition in IR and perhaps it is for this reason that it has been subjected to so much criticism. Liberalism and structuralism can both be used to develop a critique of realism. In more recent years, realism has been subjected to complicated critiques from critical theorists, postmodernists, feminists and greens. These are covered in chapters 4–7 of this book and this chapter on realism might be usefully re-read once an appreciation of the insights of these 'critical' theories has been fully understood and assimilated. Some of the most devastating criticisms of realism and neo-realism concern its epistemological and ontological underpinnings. This is the difficult language of theory and it is, therefore, appropriate to visit this debate in the concluding chapter of the book. At this stage, however, we can consider some of the possible shortcomings or weaknesses of this approach.

First, the fact that realism is simple and understandable is presented as a strength of the perspective. However, an opposing argument would suggest that realism is too simple, reducing the complex reality of world politics to a few general laws which are said to be applicable over time and space and which therefore omit much of interest and importance from our analyses.

Second, realism, in emphasising the principle of power politics and the enduring features of the international system, fails to allow for the possibility of real change. Realists accept that great powers rise and fall, and wars come and go, but the basic rules of the game cannot be changed. In failing to embrace the idea of substantive changes, realism is inherently conservative and anti-innovative, meaning that it is highly attractive to, and politically malleable by, those who would have things continue as they are. Whether it is intentional or not, realism also serves to justify injustice on the grounds that nothing can be done to change things.

Third, whilst realism has a cyclical view of history (a repetition of patterns of behaviour) it has failed to make any specific predictions. Most startlingly, realists failed to predict the end of the Cold War; given its pretensions to be, if not scientific, then at least useful, this is a very serious weakness. Realism does not help us explain which decisions will be made by states' representatives, but only why they will be made. Thus states-people will make decisions rationally and on the basis of national interest. However, how do we know if it is the national interest of State A to attack State B? Perhaps it would serve the national interest better to delay an attack or to seek an alliance against State C.

Is national interest a self-evident thing? After the event, when State A has attacked State B the realist could say it was due to a rational calculation based on assessment of national interest (even if it was subsequently destroyed by State B's secret nuclear arsenal!) but the realist offers no way of deciding which option is actually in the national interest and simply tells us that this is the motivation.

Fourth, if we accept the possibility that the assumptions of realism are relevant only in a particular context then there is possibly great danger in treating them as if they were universal truths, that is, applicable everywhere and at all times. Far from providing universal truths, realism may simply have seemed the most appropriate way of viewing a short historical phase; the idea of universal truth may have held back scholarship which would have been better directed at freeing us from realist despair.

Fifth, in emphasising the centrality of the state and the national interest, realism encourages people to view the world from a very narrow, ethnocentric perspective.

Sixth, realism ignores or significantly downplays the degree to which states might have collective or mutual interests, and so underestimates the scope for cooperation and purposive change in international relations.

Seventh, we should ask if foreign policy really is conducted rationally and indeed what is implied in the idea of rationality. Rationality seems unlikely to be the same for the leaders of states with strong ideological or religious bases as it is for leaders of liberal democracies. Furthermore, even within, for instance, liberal democracies, can we be sure that in the hurly-burly world of foreign policy, decisions will always be made rationally? The decision maker is likely to be bombarded with information, denied sleep and asked to make several choices at once; it seems plausible at least, that rationality will be compromised, affected by mood, modified by spur of the moment decisions and so on.

Eighth, the antecedents of modern realism have perhaps been selectively read or interpreted in a biased fashion. As people are fond of saying in relation to statistics, if you select your evidence carefully enough it is possible to prove almost anything. We can simply note at this stage a certain selectivity in the historical memory of realism.

While in its simplified form realism can present an easy target for criticism, realism's detractors, bent on exposing its shortcomings, have often found it a formidable task! Modifications of realism have been proposed by various authors and many differences exist within the broad category of realist. Moreover, realists acknowledge a changing world and are aware of ecological threats, gender issues and so on. However, and crucially, realists believe that their basic assumptions capture the real essence of international relations, so they argue that they are perfectly entitled to privilege some areas and issues in international relations, and, indeed, marginalise or ignore others. Although it is sometimes debated as to whether books and courses should begin with realism, or even cover realism at all on the basis that it is outdated, amoral and so on, it would be difficult to overcome the decades of dominance that it has had in the discipline and therefore the tendency to regard it as an almost natural starting point, even for those eager to criticise it or offer a more adequate framework for analysis. Furthermore, whilst realism may be under attack from all sides in academic circles it continues to find favour amongst policy makers and states-people and accordingly is implicit in rationalisations of policy offered by foreign policy decision makers. We have chosen realism as our starting point for the simple reason that it has indeed provided a backdrop for much discussion in International Relations theory. To an extent this bears out our opening comments about the prevalence of realism and the degree to which it has become the basic point of departure for much 'critical' international theory.

Common Misunderstandings

It's called Realism because it's realistic. Some of you may come to regard what International Relations calls 'realism' as being highly *un*realistic. Clearly the adherents of realism regard it as a realistic explanation of the dynamics of the world in which we live and the name represents almost an unfair advantage in terms of students' initial reaction to it. However, 'realism' should be regarded as simply a name for a particular way of thinking about the world; a label which is understood to imply certain basic assumptions. It is for you to decide if realism is realistic or not.

Realists ignore so much. Once you understand the basic assumptions of realism and what it regards as important in international relations, you may decide that it fails to address some crucial issues. Environmental degradation, torture, rape and many other issues are ignored by realists in favour of concentrating on states, state interest and military power. Realists are not ignorant in this sense; they do not deny the existence of other actors, interests and issues. However, they suggest that IR should be about the really crucial aspects of international interactions and thus deliberately limit the scope of their analysis in an attempt to better understand what is vital.

Realists are nasty people. From the above it might follow that realists are necessarily heartless people who do not care about starvation, repression and rainforests as long as the international system persists and wars are understood and perhaps limited or controlled as much as is possible. Whilst we are sure that nasty realists exist this is not necessarily the case. Some realists are simply pessimistic about human nature or the international states system to the extent that any other view is utopian nonsense. In effect they argue that what we would like and what we get may be very different.

Structural realism is the same as structuralism. No. Structural realism bears little relation to the 'structuralism' mentioned in the introduction and expanded upon in chapter 3, except in so far as they do both concentrate on the idea of 'structure' as being crucial in explaining international relations. However, for structural realists it is the structure of the inter-state system which interests them and which constrains state behaviour, forcing states to act in particular ways.

Anarchy means chaos. For the mature student schooled in the punk era of the mid to late 1970s this is an understandable way of thinking. However, anarchy actually means absence of government, a situation which characterises international relations where there is no world government. Thus states exist in a state of anarchy. However, given the existence of international law this does not mean that order is entirely absent; this is one important reason why some authors talk of an 'anarchical society'.

Further Reading

You will probably first want and need to read relevant sections of other texts as recommended by tutors and available in academic bookshops. However, it is important that you also read the classic foundational texts (that is, those which provide a base) of realism. Some of the most important are suggested here.

Aron, R. (1966), *Peace and War: A Theory of International Relations*, London: Weidenfeld and Nicolson.

Beard, C. (1966), *The Idea of National Interest: An Analytical Study in American Foreign Policy*, Chicago: Quadrangle.
Bull, H. (1977), *The Anarchical Society: A Study of World Order in Politics*, Basingstoke: Macmillan.

Carr, E.H. (1946), *The Twenty Years' Crisis 1919–1939: An Introduction to the Study of International Relations*, London: Macmillan.
Clausewitz, C. Von (1943), *On War*, Modern Library Education.

Herz, J. (1951), *Political Realism and Political Idealism*, Chicago: University of Chicago Press.
Hobbes, T. (1904), *Leviathan* (edited by A.R. Waller), Cambridge: Cambridge University Press.

Keohane, R. (1986), *Neorealism and its Critics*, New York: Columbia University Press.

Lippman, W. (1943), *US Foreign Policy*, Boston: Little, Brown and Company.

Machiavelli, N. (1988), *The Prince* (edited by Q. Skinner), Cambridge: Cambridge University Press.
Morgenthau, H. (1978), *Politics Among Nations: The Struggle for Power and Peace*, New York: Knopf.

Niebuhr, R. (1932), *Moral Man and Immoral Society*, New York: Charles Scribner's Sons.
Niebuhr, R. (1953), *Christian Realism and Political Problems*, New York: Charles Scribner's Sons.

Sassoon, S. (1918), 'Attack' from *Collected Poems of Siegfried Sassoon*, London/New York: Viking Penguin.

Schelling, T. (1960), *The Strategy of Conflict*, Cambridge, MA: Harvard University Press.

Spykman, N. (1942), *America's Strategy in World Politics: The United States and the Balance of Power*, New York: Harcourt, Brace and Company.

Thucydides (1998), *The Peloponnesian War* (a new translation by W. Blanco, edited by W. Blanco and J. Tolbert Roberts), New York: Norton.

Waltz, K. (1959), *Man, the State and War: A Theoretical Analysis*, London: Colombia University Press.

Waltz, K. (1979), *Theory of International Politics*, Reading, MA: Addison-Wesley.

Wight, M. (1979), *Power Politics*, Harmondsworth: Pelican.

Wolfers, A. (1962), *Discord and Collaboration: Essays on International Politics*, Baltimore: Johns Hopkins Press.

CHAPTER 2

Liberalism

Introduction

There is a long tradition of liberal thought about the nature of international relations. In the eighteenth and nineteenth centuries, philosophers and political thinkers debated the problems in establishing just, orderly and peaceful relations between peoples. One of the most systematic and thoughtful accounts of the problems of world peace was produced by the German philosopher Immanuel Kant in 1795 in an essay entitled Perpetual Peace. Kantian thought has been profoundly influential in the development of what we now refer to as liberal theory (see box).

AUTHOR BOX

Immanuel Kant

Starting from the premise that the international system was, indeed, something akin to an international 'state of nature', Kant argued that the only way that this state of affairs could be overcome would be for states to found a 'state of peace'. Kant did not envisage the founding of world government, or even the pooling of sovereignty, but, rather, a looser federation of free states governed by the rule of law. He did not see this state of affairs coming about fortuitously, or quickly. While the application of Kantian thought to international relations has been dismissed as 'utopian', it is important to note that Kant recognised that in order to achieve a just world order, certain conditions were necessary, including the establishment of republics, as opposed to monarchies or dictatorships and, perhaps, a near-universal commitment to liberal democracy. Indeed, Kant held that only civilised countries, those countries which were already governed by a system of law and in which people were free citizens rather than subjects, would feel impelled to leave the state of lawlessness that characterised the international state of nature. There has been some debate about how Kant saw the relationship between republics and other forms of polity. However, Kant is frequently interpreted as suggesting that countries where people were not free citizens, but rather subjected to the rule of a monarch, perhaps, or a dictator, were much more likely to be belligerent and warlike. If this was the case, logically it followed that a world federation would only be achieved when all states were republics.

Solutions to the problem of war have evaded even the most eminent of thinkers. In the nineteenth century, scholars contented themselves with merely describing historical events, and the study of international affairs was largely confined to the field of diplomatic history. In the wake of the First World War, the need to discover the means of preventing conflict seemed more urgent than ever. The senseless waste of life which characterised this conflict brought about a new determination that reason must prevail. The new generation of International Relations scholars were deeply interested in schemes which would promote cooperative relations among states and allow the realisation of a just order, such as the fledgling League of Nations. The widespread anti-war sentiment which existed at the time, seemed to provide the necessary widespread public support for such an enterprise to succeed.

Idealism was then to dominate the academic study of International Relations between the First and Second World Wars. However, the basic faith of idealism in the potential for good in human beings, a positive view of human nature, was dealt a cruel blow by the aggressive actions of Germany, Italy and Japan in the 1930s who flouted the authority of the League of Nations, seemingly without a second thought, and without regard to questions of legal or moral 'right'.

After the Second World War, idealism fell out of favour for a long period of time. However, by the 1970s, a new generation of liberal scholars, called liberal pluralists for reasons which will be elaborated below, were beginning to make inroads into the dominance of realism in IR. Rapid advances in technologies, the growth of organisations like the European Community, and the impact of events like the 1973 oil crisis were all pointed to as evidence of growing interdependence in international relations. The 1970s also saw the emergence of a liberal literature on transnational relations and world society. In distinctive ways, these literatures made significant inroads into the rigid inside/outside, domestic/international distinctions characteristic of realism. Moreover, liberal pluralists pointed to the growing importance of multinational corporations (MNCs), non-governmental organisations (NGOs) and pressure groups, as evidence that states were no longer the only significant actors in international relations. Liberal pluralists believed that power and influence in world politics were now exercised by a range of actors. Furthermore, conflict was not the major process in international relations as, increasingly, cooperation in pursuit of mutual interests was a prominent feature of world politics. In more recent years, liberals have made important contributions to the study of international relations in the areas of international order, institutions, human rights, justice and peace studies.

In this chapter, we aim to highlight the many and varied ways in which liberal thought has contributed to International Relations, but first a few qualifications and clarifications are needed. First, as we hinted above, liberalism should not be conflated automatically with idealism. In everyday usage, the term idealist is sometimes used in a negative, or pejorative sense, to describe a person who is considered unrealistic – a dreamer. However, it has a specific

AUTHOR BOX

Francis Fukuyama

It is somewhat ironic, perhaps, that one of the most celebrated works on the end of the Cold War, Francis Fukuyama's *The End of History and the Last Man* (published in various forms in the early 1990s) contained much which would have been familiar to Kant. Fukuyama's dramatic phrase 'end of history' is not intended to imply that we face some apocalyptic future. On the contrary, in simple terms, Fukuyama argues that human history has been driven by conflict and struggle over value systems and different ways to organise human societies. The driving force behind the Cold War was the ideological struggle between East and West, communism and capitalism. According to Fukuyama, the end of the Cold War had seen the ultimate triumph of Western capitalism and liberal democracy. Liberal values are then, now widely accepted – if not widely practised – across the world, and, since communism is seemingly discredited, there is no longer a credible alternative form of social, political and economic organisation. Fukuyama's thesis is an ironic twist on Marx's vision of communism as the highest form of human organisation and, thus, the ultimate end or destination of human history (see chapter 3).

meaning in philosophy where it denotes certain beliefs about the nature of the world and the nature of human understanding. Moreover, the term idealist also describes philosophers such as Hegel who was an important influence on Karl Marx (see next chapter). In addition, as we will see below, a great deal of liberal thought is rooted in a utilitarian or empiricist tradition which is quite distinct from idealism. That said, Kant's commitment to the pursuit of peace and the establishment of a just international order where states' actions are regulated by international law is widespread among liberals today. Clearly, just as Kant believed that a state of 'perpetual peace' would not be realised in the near future, contemporary liberals are under no illusions about the barriers to achieving justice and the rule of law under conditions of anarchy, but, like Kant, many insist that this is an ideal to be striven for.

Also, it is important not to lose sight of the fact that the term 'liberal' has been applied to the political beliefs of a wide variety of people. Liberals have views about the economic organisation of society for instance; here, we can detect a division in liberal thought between those on the political 'right' who believe that individual liberty must extend into the economic realm. That is, people must be free to buy and sell their labour and skills as well as goods and services in a free market which is subjected to minimal regulation. On the other hand, 'left' leaning liberals recognise that the principles of political liberty and equality can actually be threatened by the concentration of economic power and wealth. This school of liberalism supports a much more interventionist role for the state in the regulation of the economy, in the interests of providing for basic human needs and extending opportunities to the less privileged. As we shall see below, these two strands of liberal thinking live on in neo-classical and Keynesian approaches to international political economy.

LITERATURE BOX

The Brandt Report

The report *North–South: A Programme for Survival*, published by The Brandt Commission in 1980, is an example of liberal internationalist sentiment and Keynesian economic philosophy in practice. The 'Brandt Report' outlined the many and varied ways in which economic interdependence had made all of the world's peoples vulnerable to economic recession and a looming world economic crisis. Coming in the wake of the breakdown of the Bretton Woods economic system (see below) and, in some ways, anticipating the debt crisis and recession of the 1980s, it called for worldwide cooperation and active political intervention to protect the worst hit countries and to revive the world economy.

There have been an awful lot of innovations in liberal theory and these innovations are reflected in a number of distinctive strands of liberal thought within International Relations. For example, idealism, interdependence, transnationalism, liberal internationalism, liberal peace theory, neo-liberal institutionalism and 'world society' approaches. Furthermore, terms much in vogue in contemporary International Relations (and in the media), such as globalisation or multiculturalism, whilst not intrinsically liberal have liberal adherents or interpretations. In this chapter we will present liberalism as a coherent perspective or world view and, once again, our justification for doing so is that despite some differences, there is, nonetheless, a prevailing, all encompassing liberal ethos which runs through different strands of liberal thought. Liberalism as an 'ism', is a politics, an economics, a social theory and a philosophy. Liberalism is an all embracing ideology. It has something to say about all aspects of the human life. It is a philosophy based on a belief in the ultimate value of individual liberty and the possibility of human progress. Liberalism speaks the language of rationality, moral autonomy, human rights, democracy, opportunity and choice and is founded upon a commitment to principles of liberty and equality, justified in the name of individuality and rationality. Politically this translates into support for limited government and political pluralism.

The main points of the liberal world view or perspective can then be summarised thus: (1) rationality is the defining, universal, characteristic of human kind; (2) people rationally pursue their own interests, but there is a potential harmony of interests between people; (3) cooperation is a central feature of all human relations, including international relations; (4) government is necessary, but the centralisation of power is inherently bad; (5) individual liberty is of supreme political importance. From these five basic propositions we can deduce or infer a number of other propositions which continue to inform liberal approaches to international relations. For example, if there is a harmony of interests between people, then we might deduce that left to their own devices, people have no interest in prosecuting wars. If the centralisation of power is bad, then political pluralism and democracy must be a superior form of political organisation. Similarly, we would expect liberals to emphasise the distribution of power and influence among a range of actors, rather than focus solely on the state. Finally, if reason is the defining characteristic of the human race, then all people must have inalienable human rights. We will revisit these propositions below. First, we need to consider further the historical and intellectual origins of liberal thought.

Origins

In this section we will outline the main influences on liberal IR, which we have identified as Immanuel Kant, Adam Smith, David Ricardo, Jeremy Bentham, John Stuart Mill and John Maynard Keynes. For the sake of simplicity and clarity we have divided the origins of liberal thought into 'political' and 'economic' strands. We will then use these two broad divisions to contextualise the subsequent discussions of key themes within what we broadly term the liberal perspective in International Relations. We hope that making this distinction between political and economic liberalism will help you find your way through a dense literature. However, you should be aware that inevitably there is some overlap between the economic and political strands of liberal thought.

Economic liberalism is rooted in an intellectual tradition stretching back to the works of Adam Smith and David Ricardo. At this point, you might like to refer back to our brief discussion of Ricardo's work in the box in the introductory chapter. The key assumptions of nineteenth-century classical liberalism were that it is, in the long run, beneficial to all if markets are allowed to operate freely without state intervention and if countries are able to trade openly and freely with each other. This is because the market is seen as the most efficient means of organising human production and exchange, operating almost as if 'an invisible hand' were guiding and coordinating economic activity.

Liberals also assume that human beings act rationally. In this usage, 'rationality' is evidenced by a person's ability to carefully weigh up the costs and benefits of any course of action. According to 'utilitarian' thinkers like Bentham, people who are behaving rationally will always act to maximise their 'utility' or interest. If at first sight this appears to be entirely selfish behaviour rooted in a pessimistic view of human nature, liberals offer a moral justification for allowing such a state of affairs to continue. While individuals are essentially self-interested, collectively this type of behaviour is held to produce beneficial outcomes. According to Bentham we should base our judgements on what is 'right' or 'wrong', or 'good' or 'bad' on how far any action works to ensure the happiness of the greatest number.

This does not mean that liberals see no role for the state in the economy. Liberals like Adam Smith accepted that the market would not necessarily produce much needed 'public goods' and that governments would need to provide such goods. States were also necessary, because they provided a regulatory framework – a legal system – to, among other things, enforce contracts and protect against corruption and unfair competition. However, classical liberalism held that it is in the best interests of all people, in the long term, if state intervention is kept to a minimum. According to liberals, the advantages of an unfettered free market are not only confined to the domestic economy. Free market economics generates a need for 'inputs', such as raw materials, into the production process and some of these have to be imported from abroad. Enterprises are also constantly seeking new markets for their goods and services. In this way, trade between states is encouraged. According to liberals, the advantages of trade are numerous. This is, of course, a very strong argument against protectionism, which, from a liberal perspective, is a consequence of states acting according to short-sighted and perverse conceptions of the 'national interest'. Left to itself, trade would prove to be mutually beneficial by, for example, bringing about interdependence among states and generating wealth, both of which would reduce the likelihood of conflict.

In more recent years, neo-classical or neo-liberal economic theory, has been highly influential in the theory and practice of development in countries in the so-called Third World. The belief that unfettered market economies are the most efficient allocaters of resources, the best distributors of rewards, and the most effective means to foster economic growth continues to be widely held among élites at the International Monetary Fund, the World Bank and in many government overseas development agencies.

 WORLD EXAMPLE

Structural Adjustment Programmes

In recent years, the ideas of classical liberalism have once again become popular and influential in international relations. So called neo-liberal or neo-classical economic theory has been used to justify structural adjustment programmes (SAPs) in the developing world, even though the social consequences may be very harsh indeed. Structural adjustment programmes have been widely 'recommended' to third world states by the IMF and the World Bank as an effective means of dealing with the related problems of poverty and indebtedness. The idea is that indebted states should try to export their way out of debt. As well as generating much needed foreign currency to service foreign debt, export-led growth strategies are held to encourage economic competitiveness, dynamism and growth which will eventually 'trickle down' to all sectors of society. At the same time, developing countries are encouraged to cut back on welfare spending by the state, effectively privatising the provision of health and education services. It is argued that ultimately this will make economies more efficient. In the short term however 'spend less' means sacking government employees, not buying medicines, not building schools and slashing welfare budgets. Meanwhile 'earn more' can lead to wage reduction, chopping down forests, selling off assets to foreign firms at cut price rates and so on.

It was noted above that nineteenth-century liberal economic theorists were against state intervention and regulation of the economy. However, for much of the twentieth century, liberals have been less hostile to state intervention. Indeed the economic order which emerged in the aftermath of the Second World War, in Western economies at least, saw the state playing a much greater role in directing economic activity of private individuals and firms and providing welfare support for citizens – the so called welfare state. For much of the second half of the twentieth century, Keynes was an important influence on both liberal thinking in IR and in the actual practice of international relations. Keynesian economic theory, which supported interventionist government policies to regulate what were basically free market economies, formed the basis of the ideas which underpinned the Bretton Woods System.

WORLD EXAMPLE

The Bretton Woods System

This refers to a series of regimes, institutions and agreements which came out of the multilateral discussion at Bretton Woods, in the USA in 1944. The aim of the Bretton Woods System was to facilitate economic growth, development and trade by providing a stable framework for international economic activity. After the Second World War the prevailing wisdom was that the cause of the war was the economic collapse and world recession of the 1930s which created an unstable climate in which extreme nationalism flourished. It was believed that when the economic climate was harsh, states immediately took action to protect their own economies. Typically, this involved measures to protect domestic markets, such as increasing tariffs. The knock on effects of such 'selfish' behaviour were a slow down in world trade and, eventually, international recession. The Bretton Woods System was designed to create a framework in which it would be difficult for states to act in a self-interested way when the going got tough, by, at once, discouraging protectionism and providing a helping hand to countries in temporary economic difficulties.

The Bretton Woods System consisted of an International Bank for Reconstruction and Development (IBRD), the International Monetary Fund (IMF) and the General Agreement on Tariffs and Trade (GATT), now the World Trade Organisation (WTO). In the first years of its existence, it was envisaged that the IBRD, more commonly known as the World Bank, would play an important role in distributing aid to the devastated economies of Western Europe. In more recent history, the World Bank has served as a source of investment, aid and loans to the developing world. The International Monetary Fund was designed to ensure liquidity in the international economy. This means that, in effect, countries experiencing short-term balance of trade difficulties could borrow money and so continue to trade effectively. In the longer term, if any individual country had an enduring – or structural – balance of payment deficit, the IMF could insist upon changes in domestic economic policy, including the devaluation of the currency, in return for fresh loans. The General Agreement in Tariffs and Trade was designed to bring about a gradual reduction in trade barriers around the world. These institutions all played an important role in regulating the world economy. However, the linchpin of the system was the US dollar. The US dollar served as the major world trading currency. The relative value of all of the other world currencies was fixed in relation to the US dollar. Since, in the post-war period, the US

> **WORLD EXAMPLE (continued)**
>
> economy was easily the largest and most powerful economy in the world, it was believed that pegging all currencies to the US dollar would ensure confidence in the international economic system.
>
> The Bretton Woods System has been described as an economic order in which the broad principles of liberalism were 'embedded'. The system of multilateral institutions, fixed exchange rates, capital controls and trade regulation, aimed to encourage the progressive liberalisation of trade among countries and to promote the principles of free market economics internationally. However, none of these institutions or rules were incompatible with state intervention and the management of the domestic economy. This meant that even while encouraging a large degree of free trade and open competition, states could pursue 'liberal welfare' or 'social democratic' goals, such as full employment and the provision of welfare goods.

Just as there are distinct strands in economic liberalism, political liberalism is not all of one kind. Some liberals have applied the basic ideas of liberal thought as outlined above to their thinking about political community and obligation and to the nature and role of government. The insistence that individuals are the best judge of what is in their interests, is a powerful argument against authoritarian (dictatorial) forms of government. Liberals generally argue for representative government based on democratic principles.

One of the most celebrated liberal thinkers of the nineteenth century, John Stuart Mill, argued that government was a necessary evil. That is to say that government was necessary in order to protect the liberty of individuals, but could become oppressive and tyrannical if its power was unchecked. For these reasons, liberals generally argue for a 'separation of powers' and 'checks and balances' which ensure that no one political leader or arm of government can become dominant. This basic idea is the origin of political pluralism, which means the distribution or diffusion of power across a range of institutions or among a number of 'actors'. As we will see, so called liberal pluralism has been very influential in International Relations, although the usage of the term 'pluralism' in this context is slightly different. We will return to this point later in the chapter.

In addition to the utilitarian conception of rationality, there is another strand of liberal thought which, while committed to the principle of liberty and wedded to notions of progress, has a rather different view of human autonomy and rationality. Rather than viewing rationality in means–ends or cost–benefit terms, the essence of 'reason' is seen to be the ability of human beings to understand moral principles. This strand of thought is associated particularly with Kant. For our purposes it is enough to say that liberals believe that the capacity to reason and to understand moral principles is universal, that is it is something which all human beings possess. Collectively, these beliefs in human rationality, the possibility of progress, individual liberty and the dangers of unchecked power, give rise to the liberal notion of universal human rights.

CONCEPT BOX

Human Rights

Though the idea of human rights may seem 'obvious' in some sense, it is surprising how many questions the idea raises. Though the principle that people have certain rights now meets with almost universal approval, arguments abound over the relative weights of different sorts of rights (economic or political for instance) and who they should apply to (individuals or specific groups). As we will suggest in the chapter on Green Thought, some even argue that *human* rights is too narrow a moral category and that the concept of rights should be applied to animals as well as human beings. (The related concept of 'duties' can also be considered more important in certain traditions.)

The UN has been particularly important in promoting human rights as a legal obligation of states, clearly recognising that such rights should not be confined within national borders and establishing a range of international standards. The original UN charter talks of 'the principle of equal rights and self-determination of peoples' and 'human rights and fundamental freedoms for all without distinction' (articles 1 and 55). By late 1948 a UN Universal Declaration on Human Rights had been signed after much wrangling by communist states such as the USSR, religious states such as Saudi Arabia and by other states such as South Africa, who feared that they would be accused of violating the human rights of some of their people. However, despite some initial resistance, the signing proved to be simply the beginning of a lengthy and ongoing process. In 1966, for instance, there were further declarations on civil and political rights and on economic, social and cultural rights. In more recent years, there have been significant conventions which cover the rights of minorities and indigenous peoples, the rights of the child, and the elimination of discrimination against women. Some commentators argue that the gradual expansion of human rights provisions has resulted in a situation where we now have a global consensus on human rights. However, it is important to note that many states have refused to ratify certain conventions and treaties. Moreover, the abuse of human rights is still widespread throughout the world despite the significant advances which have been made in international law.

The various strands of liberal thought have contributed to the study of International Relations in many and varied ways. Below we will look at how liberals have viewed our key themes. But first, it is helpful to set out explicitly the assumptions of liberalism.

Assumptions

1. Liberals believe that all human beings are rational beings. Rationality can be used in two distinctive ways:

    (a) In instrumental terms, as the ability to articulate and pursue one's 'interests'.

    (b) The ability to understand moral principles and live according to the rule of law.

2. Liberals value individual liberty above all else.

3. Liberalism has a positive or progressive view of human nature. Liberals believe that it is possible to achieve positive changes in international relations.

4. Liberals emphasise the possibilities for human agency to effect change.

5. In distinctive ways, liberalism challenges the distinction between the domestic and the international realm:

    (a) Liberalism is a universalist doctrine and so is committed to some notion of a universal community of humankind which transcends identification with and membership of the nation-state community.

    (b) The liberal concepts of interdependence and world society suggest that in the contemporary world the boundaries between states are becoming increasingly permeable.

REFLECTION BOX

Critics have accused liberals of ignoring significant differences which exist between peoples both within and between countries, such as class, gender, religion or culture. Liberals contend that while there exist differences between people this should not obscure the similarities – notably the capacity for rational thought and action, which is a *universal* characteristic. Do you believe that social and cultural difference invalidate the liberal claim that all human beings have basic, inalienable human rights?

Themes

Peace and Security

As we suggested earlier, liberalism is a doctrine which has a faith in the capacity of human beings to solve seemingly intractable problems through collective action. The notion that human beings understand moral principles, suggests that it is possible to transcend 'power politics' and govern relations between people (and indeed peoples) on the basis of legal norms, moral principles and according to what is 'right' and 'just'. However, liberalism should not be confused with pacifism. While some liberals might indeed be pacifists, it does not necessarily follow that a commitment to the peaceful resolution of disputes entails the rejection of the use of force whatever the circumstances. Clearly, even 'peace loving' peoples and states could not be expected to forgo the right to use force in order to defend themselves from hostile aggression, or, perhaps if there was no other way to right a wrong.

Peace and security are closely connected in liberal thought. The League of Nations was supposed to guarantee the security of states through a system which identified threats to 'peace and security' and allowed collective action to be taken against aggressive states, to deter or stop them. Clearly since insecurity was itself a possible cause of war, a system of collective security would strengthen the international order and make peace more likely. The League of Nations also had an International Court to arbitrate disputes and so provide a peaceful means to resolve conflicts. Although the League of Nations foundered, the idea that an international organisation was needed to provide some sort of system of collective defence, and a court of arbitration, lived on in the United Nations, which was set up after the Second World War.

HISTORICAL BOX

The United Nations

The United Nations was set up after the Dumbarton Oaks conference in 1944, in order to 'save successive generations from the scourge of war'. The conference was attended by only the United States and its war time allies, including Britain and France, the Soviet Union, and China, but despite this limited representation, nearly all of the basic features of the new organisation were agreed at that meeting. The United Nations remained close to the spirit of the League of Nations in its stated objective of maintaining peace and security through the peaceful settlement of disputes and the promotion of trade and economic and social cooperation. The UN also added economic and social development and the promotion of human rights to its stated aims. However, while similar to the League in many respects, it was recognised that the founders of the United Nations must pay due regard to the failures of the League in order to ensure that the organisation did not duplicate the shortcomings and weaknesses of its predecessor. Above all, the new organisation had to be as universal as possible, and must include the membership of both the Soviet Union and the United States. It also needed 'teeth' in order to ensure effective action, rather than rely upon the force of 'world opinion' alone.

The two organisations were very similar in structure. Like the League, the United Nations had an assembly, the General Assembly, which acted largely as a consultative body, a Court of Justice, located in The Hague, and a council (the Security Council) which formed the executive arm of the organisation. The United Nations also had a Secretariat headed by a Secretary General, who was charged with identifying and alerting the Security Council to 'threats to peace and security'.

Despite differences in ideology, the United States and Soviet Union were able to agree on most substantive issues to do with the structure and operation of the new organisation. However, they disagreed sharply over the structure and precise role of the Security Council. Eventually, these differences were resolved when it was agreed that the so called big five (the USA, the Soviet Union, China, France and Britain) would enjoy permanent representation on the Security Council and would have the right of veto over Security Council actions. Arguably, this concession to the realities of power politics was to effectively paralyse the Security Council, virtually preventing it from taking any effective action throughout the Cold War period.

Unlike realists who hold a negative view of peace (that is, peace is simply the absence of war), liberals have developed a distinctive 'peace theory' which holds that peace can only be secured if the sources of conflict are also addressed. Liberal peace theory returns to a familiar liberal theme that the people have no interest in war. It follows from this that wars are frequently the result of aggression on the part of belligerent leaders or states pursuing a particular interest. Many liberal peace theorists are of the view that it is only when there is an end of tyranny around the globe and universal liberal democracy and respect for human rights that international peace will prevail. In so far as democracy will also check the power of leaders and states, wars are likely to become less prevalent when, and if, democracy flourishes throughout the world. Therefore, a peaceful world order is also likely to be one in which human rights are respected and upheld. As Kant held, perpetual peace cannot be realised in an unjust world. However, as we noted above, this reading of Kant has been disputed and some liberals contend that it might be possible for different kinds of states to co-exist peacefully.

AUTHOR BOX

Michael Doyle

Do democracies fight one another? There has been a long standing debate within IR about whether democratic states are inherently more peaceful than other types of regimes. Michael Doyle has advanced the proposition that liberal democracies do not fight one another. This does not mean that democracies do not fight at all. The Second World War is widely viewed as a fight against fascism and therefore for democracy. More controversially, one justification for the Vietnam War of the 1960s and 1970s was that it was necessary in order to protect the values of the 'free' world. The argument is that liberal democracies are much more inclined to conduct their relations with others on a peaceful basis and according to international law. From this it follows that the best way to ensure a long lasting peace in international relations is through the spread of liberal-democratic governments on a global scale. This proposition is the subject of debate, rather than a matter of 'fact' and there are a number of objections. Overall, the empirical evidence or historical record seems to strongly support the case that democracies do not fight each other – so much so that the democratic peace has been described as the closest we have come to discovering a 'law' in international relations. However, there is still a debate about whether the absence of war is due to the existence of liberal democracy or some other factor, such as the balance of power, or the existence of a common 'enemy'.

In addition to the 'political' strand of liberal thought, 'economic liberalism' has similarly made a contribution to our understanding of peace. Along with the stress on moral reason and the capacity for good in human beings, after the First World War, liberals were also advancing a notion of a 'harmony of interests' which would have been familiar to Adam Smith and David Ricardo. Liberal internationalism is based on the idea of a harmony of interests between the states and peoples of the world, and, in good part, these mutual interests are rooted in the mutual benefits which arise from trade. However, just as Smith recognised the need for certain 'public goods', liberals acknowledge that in order to have peace it is necessary to establish international institutions which can overcome the problem of anarchy and facilitate cooperation. We will return to the theme of cooperation, and the role of institutions in providing sound governance of international relations shortly. First, we need to draw out rather more explicitly how liberals have conceptualised and understood the state.

The State and Power

Superficially, the liberal view of the nature of the state is similar to realism, in so far as liberals accept that the defining characteristic of the state is sovereignty. Liberals would also agree with realists that the basic characteristics of the state are that it has a territory, a people and a government. However, in important respects, the liberal view of the state differs significantly from the realist view. Liberals regard the state as, at best, a 'necessary evil'. As can be inferred from the earlier discussion, liberals also make distinctions between different kinds of states. Authoritarian or tyrannical regimes whose power is unchecked, are likely to be more belligerent, having little respect for human rights or regard for human suffering. In contrast, in liberal-democratic countries, the state is held to be essentially a 'neutral arbiter' between competing interests in an open and pluralistic society. The state provides a framework (legal and political) in which it is possible to go about one's everyday business in the knowledge that you will be secure from harm, that contracts of all kinds will be upheld and that people will be able to pursue their varied aims and interests without restriction, providing that they do not, in consequence, harm others.

This notion of the need to check the power of the state, gives rise to the liberal concept of pluralism. In its original usage, the term pluralism referred to the belief in the need to distribute political power through several institutions, none of which is sovereign. So for example, in a liberal democracy, the government has certain executive powers and legislative powers, and is superior to the armed forces, or police force, the so called coercive arms of state power. However, the powers of the government are divided up among different institutions. For example, in the USA, the President, the House and the Senate all have some powers and must compromise, bargain and cooperate if they are to govern effectively. Moreover, in liberal democracies the power of the Executive is checked by a constitution (written or unwritten rules) which sets limits on what the government can do. The Courts might also play a role in interpreting the constitution and so the judiciary has some control over the action of government. Similarly, government action is subject to critical scrutiny by opposition parties and the electorate. Some liberals believe that the state to some extent reflects the interests and concerns of interest groups. In political systems dominated by parties, this is to some extent inevitable. Moreover, there are also powerful élites within the government bureaucracy, the military and so on which might work to advance their own interests. However, liberals deny that the state reflects the interests of one, overwhelmingly dominant social class, or any one élite group. It is absolutely central to liberal thought that the state is seen as an autonomous body. In this context autonomy means that the state is fair and impartial, functioning as a neutral arbiter in disputes and policing the citizen body. This differs in fundamental ways from realist views, but also structuralist and some feminist views, which you will encounter in chapters 3 and 6.

Liberals are careful to distinguish between the state (which consists of the various arms of government, the police force, armed services and the law courts) and civil society. Civil society refers to those areas of human life where individuals engage in collective action and activity, but which are outside the realm of state action or not within the purview or control of the state. So for example, a vibrant civil society might be one in which people form associations like sports clubs or trade unions, or engage in social, cultural or 'independent' political activities, such as joining Greenpeace or Amnesty International.

Having said that state and (civil) society are clearly separated in liberal thought, liberals recognise that the state and civil society interact. The state provides a regulatory framework in which such activity takes place. For example, a 'social club' might be required to gain a licence to operate. The police might even monitor certain activities. Also, in a democracy at least, elements of civil society will try to actively influence the activities of the government – a central arm of the state.

AUTHOR BOX

Edward Morse

Morse has argued that the functions of the state changed somewhat as societies became more 'modern' and sophisticated. Morse contends that as the economy grows and society becomes more technologically and politically complex, the state has to extend its role into more and more areas of human life. So, for example, the state becomes involved in the provision of welfare, or plays a more central role in regulating telecommunications technology. The state has engaged increasingly in forms of 'low politics' such as welfare and technical regulation, as well as the traditional 'high politics' of diplomacy and foreign policy. For this reason, Morse argues that the distinction between 'high' and 'low' politics has actually been breaking down. The terms 'high' and 'low' politics imply a simple hierarchy according to the relative importance of each area; arms control is more 'vital' than trade negotiations. However, Morse argues that the legitimacy of the authority of the state no longer rests solely upon its ability to secure and defend its borders. The welfare orientation and interventionist nature of the modern state means that increasingly, the legitimacy of the state rests on its ability to meet the needs of its people for economic and social security. The security of a people is as much threatened by trade wars and worldwide economic recessions as by arms build-ups and the need to either accommodate or stand up to belligerent leaders. This is not to say that liberals like Morse think that 'high' politics is no longer important, only that it is becoming increasingly difficult to justify such a clear cut distinction and hierarchy. Moreover, the extension of the state's role into more and more areas of life, requires more sophisticated policy making and policy implementation networks. This in turn opens up more and more possibilities for both élites and pressure groups to exert influence over all areas of policy making.

This notion of pluralism has also been used to describe the distribution of power and influence among a range of 'actors' in international relations. Liberals argue that sovereign states are important, but they are not the only significant actors in international relations. Just as the separation of powers implies that the essence of sovereignty is difficult to pin down or locate, contemporary liberals argue that the state can cede some element of their sovereignty to other bodies, such as, for example, the United Nations or the European Union. Furthermore, actors such as multinational corporations, international and regional institutions, for example United Nations, FIFA, the Organisation of African Unity, international non-governmental organisations like Greenpeace or Amnesty International, new social movements and even terrorist groups can also be said to be influential or 'powerful'. Liberal pluralists were the first to significantly expand the purview of International Relations theory to 'actors' other than states and 'processes' other than foreign policy, war or diplomacy, which had dominated realist scholarship.

Pluralism implies or denotes a diffusion of power. In liberal democracies, power is held to reside with the people, in so far as the people are able to periodically vote to remove political leaders from office. However, the conception of 'people power' goes beyond the ability to periodically elect or remove governments from office. As we noted above, in a developed democracy with a strong civil society, we might also expect to see people more actively involved in politics through their membership of social movements or support for the work of NGOs. In Western societies it is common for people who feel strongly about an issue to engage in lobbying activities designed to influence the decision making process. Others prefer to work outside the formal structure of government, and take part in demonstrations. We noted above, that as the modern state has 'intervened' into more and more areas of human life, it has greatly facilitated this kind of politics.

Liberals take seriously the idea that people, sometimes individuals, but more usually acting collectively through pressure groups or institutions, can exert influence. In so far as power may be viewed as the capacity to act to advance an interest or to influence the outcome of an event or a decision, liberals believe that power is diffused across a range of institutions and among a variety of states and non-state actors. In International Relations, the notion of 'pluralism' is not used so much to suggest the way power 'ought' to be checked and balanced, but rather as an empirical observation – it describes the way power is actually distributed in the international 'system'.

Clearly, the realist emphasis on the state and power is challenged by liberal pluralism for a number of reasons. First, because liberal pluralists maintain that military power has become increasingly ineffective and so is no longer a reliable indicator of how powerful a state is in world politics. Second, because realism ignores the power of non-state actors. Third, because the realist emphasis on competitive power politics has blinded them to the amount of cooperation that exists between states and other actors in world politics. So, power need not be conceptualised in simple zero-sum terms. On the contrary power might be viewed in positive terms as the capacity to act collectively to

ANALOGY BOX

The Cobweb Model

The analogy of a cobweb is often used to describe the plural complexity of international relations. The image which the cobweb model conveys is an intricate matrix with an enormous number of nodes (that is, points of intersection) which represent the way that the vast number of actors in international relations are connected to one another. From a liberal pluralist point of view a multiplicity of actors interact in myriad ways. Liberals argue that these relationships are of different types and need not be characterised by conflict. Indeed, the spontaneous and voluntary nature of such linkages rather suggests that cooperation based on mutual interests is a major feature of international relations. Clearly, the cobweb model implies that power is widely diffused in international relations. However, one of the problems with this model and indeed, similar attempts by liberal pluralists to convey the complexity of actors and interactions in international relations is that it does not give us any sense of which 'threads' or nodes are most important or which 'actors' have the most power and influence.

CONCEPT BOX

Power

Liberal pluralists argue that it is impossible to quantify power simply in military terms. The economic wealth of countries such as Japan or many MNCs, such as Shell, IBM, Nissan and so on, is clearly a factor in understanding where power lies in international relations. Furthermore, 'actors' might also have more or less power depending on the issue area under consideration. For example, Norway is a relatively small country and does not play a particularly prominent role in organisations like the UN. However, Norway has tremendous influence in negotiations over the international ban on whaling as one of the major whaling states. Indeed, analysing the world according to different issue areas gives a very different, and perhaps comforting, impression of how power is distributed, compared to approaches such as realism. For example, in international negotiations over the dumping of toxic waste, developing countries – primarily the target for such waste – have been able to significantly affect negotiations and achieve global regulation of such activity.

realise a common 'good'. Fourth, the power which an 'actor' possesses may differ over time and according to the area under consideration (see box).

Institutions and World Order

As is evident from the earlier discussion, one of the ways in which liberalism has contributed to our understanding on international relations is through various works on the nature of institutions and world order. Obviously, the themes of cooperation and complex interdependence are strongly suggestive of how liberal pluralists see the regulatory and facilitating role played by institutions in international relations. In more recent years, neo-liberal institutionalists have developed a fairly sophisticated analysis of the nature of world order and the crucial role played by institutions and various regimes in regulating relations between states. In this section we will discuss both liberal pluralist and neo-liberal ideas in more depth. First, however, we need to consider briefly an earlier school of thought, which, while not strictly speaking 'liberal', anticipated many arguments about the nature of interdependence and the need for institutions which were later developed by liberal IR theorists.

Like many ideas in International Relations, functionalism has its origins in another branch of the social sciences – Sociology. However, as the idea 'crossed the boundary' so to speak, its meaning changed somewhat. Functionalists argued that interaction among states in various spheres created problems which required cooperation to resolve; the most obvious examples being areas like telecommunications and postal services. The positive benefits, and mutual confidence, which arose from cooperation in any one area would likely 'spill-over', encouraging cooperation in other more significant areas such as trade. Functionalists argued that integration was necessary because states were unable to cope with the effects of modernisation. International institutions were thought to be increasingly necessary as a complement to states, whose individual capabilities to deal with problems generated by new technologies were decreasing. Also, functionalists believed that as the level of cooperation and integration increased, it would be more and more difficult for states to withdraw from the commitments they had entered into since their people would be aware of the benefits achieved by cooperation. Such functional interaction would, in turn, have effects on international society, enhancing peace and making war so disruptive and costly that it would no longer be considered a 'rational' means for states to realise their aims and interests (see box).

 WORLD EXAMPLE

The European Union

Ideas such as functionalism were clearly supported and encouraged by developments in the 'real world', such as European integration, which has today reached the stage of a European Union. Indeed, the European Union provides an example of how functionalism can be seen as a prescription for how relations between states should be encouraged as well as an observation about perceived developments in the world of international politics and international economics. The EU is sometimes held up as an example of functionalist theory in practice. The European Communities (the European Atomic Energy Agency, the European Coal and Steel Community and the European Economic Community) were seen to be an effective way of achieving ongoing and extensive functional integration across a whole range of policy areas. Such integration would create a situation whereby national antagonism based on historical experience or competing interests, such as Franco-German border disputes, would no longer degenerate into outright conflict. War as a means to settle disputes would not only be disruptive and costly, but increasingly unfeasible since the economies of, in this case France and Germany, would be functionally integrated. From the earliest European agreements on tariff reductions and trade in certain areas, the European Community has developed through a combination of 'spill-over', functional integration and political will, to become a unified organisation – the European Union – with common rules and (almost) a common currency. Whereas war was once a regular feature of European international relations, few today expect EU member states to ever fight a war against each other again.

In the 1970s, liberal pluralist perspectives began to contribute to our understanding of institutions and world order in international relations. By the
1970s, it was clear that states were becoming more interdependent – more sensitive to, or even affected by the actions of other 'actors'. In any given issue area
in world politics the interaction of states and other actors was in need of, and
in many cases subjected to, regulation according to a system of rules and practices (norms). This notion of interdependence continues to have resonance
today. For example, many states and non-state actors have an input into the
global debate over deforestation through conferences and other regular meetings. In liberal pluralist interdependence theory, politics is presented as a
mutually beneficial process in which many actors seek to resolve problems in
international relations. Furthermore, we are now living in a world where there
are multiple linkages between, not just governments, but societies too. NGOs
and élite groups are increasingly involved in forging links with like minded
individuals and groups in other countries, which bypass, or perhaps even sub-
vert, state control. In addition, advances in technologies have made the boundaries of states increasingly permeable. For example, the development of nuclear
weapons had profound implications for the security of state boundaries; periodic
international recessions demonstrate the growing inter-connected nature of
economic activity across the globe, while, in more recent years, the growth of
satellite television and the internet have demonstrated forcibly how quickly
ideas and cultural 'artefacts' can travel around the world.

In contemporary IR, liberals continue to argue that interdependence com-
pels states to cooperate much more extensively than they had before. As we will
see below there is now an extensive neo-liberal institutionalist literature on the
nature and functions of regimes and institutions in international relations.
Neo-liberalism is also built upon the assumption that states need to develop
strategies and forums for cooperation over a whole set of new issues and
areas. Whether or not liberals of all types accurately describe the nature and
implications of interdependence is a moot point and one which we will return
to in later chapters. However, there is no doubt that the number and types of
regimes, treaties and institutions *has* multiplied rapidly in the past two decades.

As a starting point for understanding neo-liberal explanations for the growth
in regimes, treaties and institutions, we might usefully revisit our earlier discussion
of the state and the relative importance of high and low politics, using some
familiar liberal ideas to show how interdependence has particular implications
for how states behave. According to conventional wisdom, the fundamental
foreign policy problem for any policy maker is to construct a policy that allows
the state to gain the maximum benefit for its international exchanges while
minimising the negative costs. If states were able to retreat into isolation or self-
sufficiency whenever the costs of dealing with others became too great, then there
would be no reason to study the effect that interaction patterns have on world
politics and states' behaviour. However, states simply cannot avoid engaging in
relations with others. In the modern world autarky is not an option. Furthermore,
while some members of the international system will experience far greater

difficulties than others in either exploiting or coping with this interconnectedness, all will experience some sense of 'not being in control' of their own destiny. It is this combination of interconnectedness, plus loss of control, that is the hallmark of interdependence and leads states to seek cooperation with others.

The 'costs' and 'benefits' of cooperation are not necessarily distributed equally. The existence of asymmetries in costs and benefits allows some members to exercise relatively more power and influence than others in an interdependent world. The costs of interdependence can be grouped under two headings: sensitivity and vulnerability costs. Sensitivity costs refer to how quickly changes in one country bring about changes in another and the costs of those changes. Vulnerability costs refer to the disadvantages suffered by the state, even after it has changed its policies to try and cope with the actions of another state. In an interdependent world, then, states cannot simply rely on themselves and the principle of self-help decreases accordingly. Security considerations, defined as military defence, are consequently superseded by considerations of well-being, or welfare.

Moreover, modern states are incapable of meeting the complex and diverse needs of their citizens *without* cooperating with other states. International institutions and regimes become necessary to coordinate the ever more powerful forces of interdependence. Large and small states, developed and underdeveloped, are members of these institutions and all are said to benefit from cooperation. Although conflict is always present, institutions, or regimes, provide the fora for states to settle their differences without resorting to war.

In summary, for liberals, cooperation is possible because the nature of twentieth-century science, technology and economics has produced interdependence between states, and other actors, such as non-governmental organisations, multinational corporations or international institutions. In some cases, interdependence has forced states to give up some of their sovereignty and independence to international institutions, like the UN and EU. Increasingly, states are being required or compelled to engage in more intensive forms of cooperation which frequently give rise to regimes. The concept of interdependence implies a relatively symmetrical set of interrelationships amongst states and takes as its starting point the fact that the member states of the international system are interconnected. In other words, the actions of states, whether in imposing a tariff, signing a peace treaty, giving foreign aid, or building a new weapons system, create potential opportunities and challenges for the other members of the system.

REFLECTION BOX

What are the implications of 'transnational politics' and 'interdependence' for how we understand the relationship between the domestic and international realms? How might realists respond to the claim that the distinctions between 'national' and international politics are breaking down under the pressures of interdependence?

As is clear from the discussion above and in chapter 1, for realists the central problem, or tragedy, of international relations is anarchy. Realists have been at pains to show that even when states share common interests, the climate of mistrust and insecurity generated by the anarchical nature of the international system makes cooperation extremely difficult. Realists tend to think of international organisations and regimes as rather weak. They can be destroyed almost at whim by the more powerful states. The reformulation of realism to take account of the increasing importance of economics while still placing emphasis on the state and power struggles, led to the eclipse of liberal perspectives for a while in the late 1970s and early 1980s. During the Second Cold War tensions between the two Superpowers, the United States and the Soviet Union, were running high. In such a climate, neo-realism with its emphasis on the continuing importance of states and the underlying struggle for power and influence struck a chord. Certainly, the liberal pluralist contention that increasing economic interdependence would lead to less conflict and more cooperation seemed utopian at a time when massive debt, much of which was a direct consequence of massive spending on armaments and military technology, was causing major distortions in the world economy and generating attendant problems of inflation, high interest rates and recession.

However, liberals did rise to the challenge of neo-realism. In recent years liberal work on cooperation, regimes and institutions has been given a whole new lease of life with the development of neo-liberal institutionalism. Another important theme in the liberal pluralist interdependence literature was that since the early 1970s the United States had been in decline in both relative and absolute terms and could no longer be considered to be overwhelmingly dominant or hegemonic. Of course, this notion of US hegemonic decline was a central theme in neo-realist writings too. Despite the decline of US power, the international economic order established at Bretton Woods had not completely collapsed, as neo-realists like Gilpin predicted. For example, the World Bank, and the International Monetary Fund had endured. Moreover, a new trading organisation, the World Trade Organisation had superseded the GATT. At the same time, there had been a proliferation of other regimes. In the 1980s a new generation of liberal thinkers set about trying to answer the question: Why had institutions and regimes continued to function in the wake of US hegemonic decline?

Neo-liberal institutionalists argued that successful cooperation was not solely dependent upon the existence of a hegemon. There were mutual interests to be gained through cooperation. The success or failure of regimes did not just depend on hegemonic power, but rather on the number of players involved and the perceived long-term benefits. In this view, IR was still seen as fundamentally anarchic, with states as the dominant actors, but since cooperation was rational and mutually beneficial, international organisations and regimes would endure over time, surviving the changing shifts in power and influence among major states. The central idea in neo-liberal institutionalism is that international relations is fundamentally institutionalised – that is it consists of a persistent and connected sets of rules and practices that prescribe behavioural roles, constrain activity, and shape expectations. In this view, states are still the dominant actors, but institutional arrangements have a significant effect on outcomes in many areas. States are largely absolute gains maximisers, not relative gains maximisers. Cooperation now becomes rational, given absolute gains assumptions. Herein lies the explanation of the emergence and durability of international organisations, institutions and regimes.

Identity and Community

At first sight liberalism appears to have very little to say about issues of community and identity. After all liberalism places supreme emphasis on the individual rather than the group. Indeed, critics of liberalism frequently argue that it presents a very 'atomistic' view of human society, in that people are presented as isolated beings who engage in relationships with others only when mutual interests suggest a beneficial outcome. The notion of community based on contract in which the individual is seen to be protecting their independence or setting out their rights in opposition to their fellow citizens is central to classical liberal thought about the role of the state and the obligations owed to others.

However, contemporary liberalism does recognise the importance of issues of identity and community and their relevance to International Relations. In the first place, of course, liberals have offered a conception of community and identity which spans the entire planet and which defies the usual boundaries of state, nation, race, ethnicity, culture, class and gender. This is the community of humankind, who possess inalienable human rights by virtue of the universal capacity for reasoned thought. Liberal pluralists have long expressed commitment towards a global society as a means by which the sovereign state system is transcended and more inclusive forms of community are realised. 'Global society' can be viewed in terms of a normative consensus bonding people together. In this view, people owe obligations to the 'people of the world' rather than simply to their fellow citizens. Some commentators argue that forms of complex interdependence have resulted in the global spread of 'universal' values; for example, human rights (see box below) and democracy.

The growing significance of transnational politics and social movements in world politics also raises issues of identity and community. Transnationalism implies that people engage in numerous social interactions which tie people together across state boundaries. An alternative way of conceptualising global society is as a series of network type transnational relationships. In this view, technological innovations and increasing 'flows' such as media communications, technology and finance, bring in their wake the disintegration of previous forms of identity and attachment. In Morse's picture of 'modernised' states, a variety of interest groups were seen to be represented via the institutionalisation of non-governmental organisations (NGOs). The breakdown in the distinction between high and low politics, the increase in bureaucratisation

WORLD EXAMPLE

Liberalism and Multiculturalism

Given the emphasis on individual liberty and human rights, we would expect liberals to support the right of people not to identify with a dominant group, or to eschew membership of a particular community. Surely, a fundamental right is the right to assert one's individual identity? However, at the same time, liberals have been forced to concede that specific communities might also have rights which need to be recognised and protected. The rights of indigenous peoples to continue to enjoy a traditional way of life and the rights of certain ethnic or religious minorities in societies across the world, to celebrate their own unique expressions of identity and community, are now both enshrined in international law, even if they are not always respected in practice. The dilemma for liberals is not in accepting the concept of difference or the right to be different, but in what to do when certain cultural practices or religious beliefs conflict directly with the individual's right to choose. For example, we would expect liberals to support the right of a Muslim woman to defy customs and practices rooted in Islamic belief systems, in relation to say marriage or the family, if this was her choice. However, frequently, the position and role of women is absolutely crucial to the expression of group identity. In such circumstances, 'group' rights and the rights of the individual might be in tension. In such cases whose rights take precedence? It is not at all clear whether liberalism provides any clear guidance on how such tensions can be resolved.

and the politicisation of the broad mass of people, in distinctive ways, has encouraged an increase in NGOs and the growth of transnationalism. Furthermore, NGOs in themselves reflect the growing importance of transnational 'legitimised relationships'. Liberals like Mansbach argue that, increasingly, human beings identify themselves in a variety of politically relevant ways, are enmeshed in a multitude of authoritative networks and have loyalties to a variety of authorities. Indeed, some liberals see an open and participatory politics emerging from transnational linkages across societies, which transcend the state.

WORLD EXAMPLE

NGOs and the Environment

Probably the most common example today of transnational NGO activity is in the area of environmental politics. Certain groups already run effective global campaigns – such as Greenpeace against whaling and Friends of the Earth against aerosols – and other groups are looking to make their activities transnational in scope, such as Earth First!

Inequality and Justice

Traditionally liberals have concentrated on the importance of formal equality among people and equal rights. Idealists insisted that questions of justice and rights were absolutely central to international relations. We have also seen that liberals have been extremely active in promoting human rights regimes through the United Nations. However, in relation to concepts of justice and rights, the division between left-leaning and right-leaning liberals is of significance.

Liberals on the right of the political spectrum have tended to concentrate on the importance of formal equality and equal opportunities – the right of each individual to be treated equally in the eyes of the law and an equal opportunity to participate in society or compete in the market place – rather than equality in outcomes. From this perspective, a 'free' and 'just' world is one in which everyone has the *opportunity* to succeed. Right-leaning liberals remain committed to the idea that the free market is the most effective means of realising the greatest happiness of the greatest number. Left to their own devices people will pursue their own interests, but in so doing will generate a dynamic society and vibrant economy and, in the long run, the benefits of this will be felt by all. On the other hand, left-leaning liberals have been more willing to countenance state intervention in the interests of addressing social inequality and barriers to genuine equal opportunities. Left-liberals recognise that in order to create a 'level playing field' it might be necessary to ensure that all people are educated or have a basic degree of social and economic security. The creation of a society in which genuine equal opportunity is possible requires, therefore, a degree of state intervention to provide education, healthcare and a degree of social security. However, by and large, liberals believe that it is better to 'tinker' with a liberal, free market system to ameliorate its worse effects, than to risk individual liberty in the interests of social and economic equality.

Conflict and Violence

As demonstrated above, conflict and violence have been central concerns in liberal IR. We will not elaborate any further here, suffice to say that in distinctive ways, liberals have seen themselves as activists in advancing the cause of peace. This liberal desire to see an end to conflict and violence has manifested itself in liberal peace theory and liberal prescriptions for peace and security, of course. Liberals also see institutions as playing a central role in mediating and resolving conflict. Liberalism is sometimes dismissed as hopelessly utopian because of this strong desire to realise a less violent, less conflictual world. However, to reiterate, liberals do not see this occurring quickly or without political will and human effort.

Summary

1. Liberal thought has a long intellectual tradition. Early liberal thinking on international politics and peace was particularly influenced by eighteenth-century German philosopher Immanuel Kant.

2.   In terms of economics, liberal theories of the market are particularly asso-
     ciated with Adam Smith, David Ricardo and John Maynard Keynes.

3.   There have been a number of distinctive ways in which liberal thought
     has been applied to IR, for example, liberal pluralism, world society, inter-
     dependence and neo-liberal institutionalism, as well as the related schools
     of functionalism and idealism.

4.   Liberals are optimistic about human nature, because they believe that
     behaviour is largely the product of various interactions with our social
     environment.

5.   Because of the above, liberals have faith in the possibilities of education,
     human progress and the establishment of fair and just institutions.

6.   Liberals believe that the central characteristic of all human beings is ration-
     ality. This gives rise to notions of the intrinsic value of human life, the
     moral worth of the individual and the existence of inalienable human
     rights.

7.   Liberals believe that the role of government should be limited, although
     there is some disagreement about just how far and to what ends the state
     should intervene in civil society.

8.   In the international realm, liberals have faith in the possibility of cooperation,
     and suggest that all states can achieve their aims if they abandon the purely
     selfish notion of self-help.

9.   Liberals believe that not only states, but also NGOs, multinational corpora-
     tions and institutions are important 'actors' in IR.

Criticisms

One set of criticisms centres around there being a fundamental contradiction
between economic and political liberty. This criticism is centred on liberal support for the free market and the institutions of private property, both of which
appear to be central to the liberal conception of freedom and choice. Critics
argue that the operation of free markets and the private ownership of property
and resources leads to the progressive concentration of wealth in fewer and
fewer hands. This inevitably leads to a concentration of power among the
wealthy, which in turn impinges greatly upon the liberty and meaningful
choices available to poor groups. Left liberals have taken this criticism on
board, and support a limited form of state intervention and welfarism in the
interests of redistributing wealth. On the other hand, liberals on the right, often
referred to as neo-liberals or neo-classical liberals argue that state intervention
is always a threat to individual liberty and justify the continuing operation of

the free market on the grounds that it increases the overall level of wealth in society which then 'trickles down' to the poor. There is little empirical evidence to support this contention.

2. The liberal view can then, be reasonably criticised as simply providing a justification of the way things are; the way things are being of benefit to a very narrow section of humanity. For example, liberal pluralists generally provide a benevolent view of international institutions, MNCs and the whole liberal free-trade ethos which dominates today's international political economy.

3. In recent years, there have been numerous attacks on the notions of universalism found in liberal thought. We will return to these in the chapters on critical theory, feminism and postmodernism. Briefly though, it has been argued that the characteristics held to be essentially 'human' are actually specific to a particular group of people at a particular period in history. So called universalism actually expresses the particular experience of dominant groups in the West. Liberalism gives us a linear view of human progress and development. Again, this is because liberalism tends to universalise Western experience. In development theory, for example, liberals have suggested that poorer states are further 'behind' in the development process, but essentially on the same road and travelling in the same direction as richer, more developed countries. However, as we will see in the following chapter, it has been countered that much of the wealth of today's rich Western nations has been historically based on exploitation of the natural resources and cheap labour of the South. Green thinkers, who are discussed at greater length in chapter 7, also argue that liberal development strategies are resulting in environmental degradation, thus adding to the woes of already poor countries.

The pluralist view of international relations as a series of complex interactions between an enormous variety of actors is, at first sight, less contentious. However, it is disputed by realists, who, as we have seen, argue for the continued primacy or dominance of the state in IR, and Marxists, who argue that a pluralist view misses the fundamental issue which is inequality between various groups or classes at the international level.

Common Misunderstandings

Liberals believe that people are naturally good. This is a somewhat simplified and rather old fashioned view of liberalism. Certainly, liberals regard 'human nature' as malleable and are optimistic about the possibility of organising human life on a more just and harmonious basis. Thus human beings are *potentially* good.

States are insignificant. Liberal pluralists have not sought to deny the state's role in IR, but simply to highlight that other actors also have roles, big and small.

Cooperation means no conflict. Far from it. Cooperation actually *implies* conflict. The liberal commitment to limited government is based on the belief that left to themselves people will act to further their own interests, which can create conflict. This necessitates a legal framework, but general spontaneity and freedom is the best way to create wealth and growth. Similarly, at the international level, if states' interests coincided exactly (in other words if they were harmonious) they would have no need to cooperate. Cooperation takes place in order to try and resolve conflicts (of interest). Cooperation is one way of resolving conflict.

'Greenpeace should be involved in IR'. Many students have the impression that acceptance of a liberal pluralist perspective automatically implies *promoting* the involvement in IR of non-state actors (such as Greenpeace). Liberal pluralists may argue that non-state actors *are* increasingly important in IR and even that this is a good thing but theorists are concerned with how and why this is happening rather than (necessarily) directly sponsoring it.

Liberal means tolerant and wishy washy in a political sense. Sometimes in common usage the term liberal is used to mean progressive or left-leaning and is used in US politics particularly to contrast with conservative. Liberal tolerance is paradoxical given its inherent universalism, and certainly not all liberalism is politically progressive.

Further Reading

Claude, I. (1956), *Swords into Plowshares: The Problems and Progress of International Organisation*, New York: Random House.

Doyle, M. (1986), 'Liberalism and World Politics', *American Political Science Review*, Vol. 80, No. 4, pp. 1151–69.

Fukuyama, F. (1992), *The End of History and the Last Man*, New York: Free Press.

Hoffman, S. (1995), 'The Crisis of Liberal Internationalism', *Foreign Policy*, Vol. 98, Spring, pp. 159–79.

Kant, I. (1991), *Political Writings* (edited by Hans Reiss), Cambridge: Cambridge University Press.
Kegley, C. (ed.) (1995), *Controversies in International Relations*, New York: St Martin's Press.
Keohane, R. (1984), *After Hegemony: Cooperation and Discord in the World Political Economy*, Princeton: Princeton University Press.
Keohane, R. and Nye, J. (1977), *Power and Interdependence: World Politics in Transition*, Boston: Little Brown.

Luard, E. (ed.) (1992), *Basic Texts in International Relations*, London: Macmillan.

Morse, E. (1976), *Modernisation and the Transformation of International Relations*, New York: Free Press.

Mitrany, D. (1948), 'The Functional Approach to World Organization', *International Affairs*, Vol. 24, pp. 350–63.

Ricardo, D. (1971), *The Principles of Political Economy and Taxation*, Harmondsworth: Penguin.

Smith, A. (1910), *An Inquiry into the Nature and Causes of the Wealth of Nations* (with and introduction by Edwin Seligman), London: J.M. Dent.

CHAPTER 3

Structuralism

Introduction

Though structuralism has waned in popularity in recent years, it has been important in the history of International Relations theory, and continues to have relevance today. First, structuralist calls for justice continue to strike a chord with many people, particularly in the developing world. Structuralism can be seen as a 'bottom up' perspective on the world which prioritises the plight of the poor, the marginalised and the oppressed. (It is important to distinguish it from the 'top down' structural realism of Waltz – see chapter 1.) Structuralists argue that global economic relations are structured so as to benefit certain social classes, and that the resulting 'world-system' is fundamentally unjust.

Second, structuralism provides an important critique of liberalism and realism respectively. Superficially structuralism resembles realism because both emphasise conflict as a central process in international relations. Moreover, neo-realism and structuralism share the view that conflict is structural because of the framework in which inter-state economic relations take place. Structuralism also shares common ground with liberal pluralist approaches in emphasising the profoundly interconnected nature of international economic relations and the importance of non-state actors. However, structuralism stresses the conflictual nature of the global economy and structural relations of domination and dependence, rather than the anarchy of the state system, or complex-interdependence.

Finally, structuralism highlights the connection between politics and economics. Structuralists stress the importance of the overall structure of relations within which political and economic interactions take place and the processes and mechanisms which support this same structure. That is to say, that the individual parts of the world-system – states, MNCs, transnational élites and so on – must be understood in relation to their place in the overall structure of global capitalism. Structuralists believe that states and international institutions play a role in 'managing' the global capitalist order. However, they regard classes as the *key* actors in the global capitalist order. From a structuralist perspective, 'international relations', or 'inter-state' relations, are conditioned by the nature of global capitalism/economic relations. It makes more sense, therefore, to analyse international relations by reference to the big picture than by examining each and every individual actor, action and event. In this chapter, we are using the term structuralism to refer to the idea that individual parts can only be understood in relation to an overall system or to the structure of ordered relationships.

The first encounter with structuralism can be quite challenging. In the first place, structuralism goes by a number of names. It is heavily influenced by Marxist thought and is, therefore, sometimes referred to as structural Marxism, scientific Marxism or neo-Marxism. In 'Origins', below, we will concentrate on the central influence of Marx in structuralist thought, particularly the body of work Marx wrote later in his life, sometimes called 'the economics', economic determinism or scientific Marxism. This contrasts with earlier (humanist) writings of Marx which have provided the inspiration for critical theory.

Structuralism has other labels too such as dependency theory, world-systems theory, the core–periphery model and radicalism. Structuralism has its own 'language' which is not easy to penetrate, and which can be off-putting. Making sense of the subtle differences between these terms can often get in the way of a general understanding of structuralism as a perspective with particular insights.

As with other theoretical approaches, we offer a simplified account of what is a diverse body of work, without overly 'jargonising' the text. We simplify by outlining the guiding ideas and assumptions which are shared by different structuralist writers. We explain how structuralism provides a persuasive analysis of various themes. In summary, the main tenets of the structuralist perspective are as follows (though these will require further explanation as we work through the chapter): (1) the nature of international relations is profoundly shaped by the structure of the capitalist world economy, or capitalist world-system; (2) international politics is shaped by, or even determined by, economic factors; (3) the main 'actors' are states, multinational and transnational corporations and transnational social classes; (4) the state reflects the interests of dominant classes rather than there existing a genuine 'national interest'; (5) capitalism is a fundamentally unjust social and economic order which generates conflict and disharmony; (6) capitalism is characterised by internal contradictions and is subject to periodic crises.

Origins

The major influence in structuralism is Karl Marx. However, Marx's guiding ideas have been developed over the years by many other notable scholars. We only include here a limited number of structuralist scholars and influential works to give a general outline. For this reason, we concentrate particularly on dependency theory and world-systems theory. Although making reference to other influential neo-Marxist works where appropriate, these have been chosen because they constitute good examples of structuralist thought in ways which are relevant to international relations.

Marx lived a somewhat tragic life dedicated mostly to his writing, philosophy and activism. It has, furthermore, been a tragic death too, in that much of what has been carried out in the name of Marxism, and earned him such opprobrium in certain quarters, would certainly not have met with his approval. Marx was a prolific writer who produced a huge volume of work over his relatively short life. Much of Marx's early work is concerned with the historical and changing nature of material social and economic relations, human nature or subjectivity, and problems of alienation (see chapter 4). Structuralism owes more to the later works of Marx, produced after 1857, in close collaboration with Friedrich Engels.

By this stage in his life, Marx paid much closer attention to the nature of economic relationships in capitalist societies, rather than specifically 'human' problems. Marx argued that the organisation of the economy and economic relationships – what he labelled the 'mode of production' – formed the material base of society. To give a contemporary example of what is meant by the mode of production, today the West lives in an age when the economy is still largely based on the mass production of manufactured goods and services. Capitalism is built upon the principles of private ownership of property and the pursuit of profit. Most people go to work every weekday in shops, factories or offices, producing goods and services for the 'boss' (be it a single entrepreneur or huge multinational), which are subsequently sold for a profit in the 'market place'. People do not own the goods and services which they produce but instead are paid a wage for their labour. Moreover, the contemporary economy is characterised by a highly complex division of labour so that the production of a single commodity, like a car perhaps, takes place in a number of factories, in several different countries and involves very many different people in complex relationships, at different stages of the production process. Collectively, the ways in which goods and services are produced (the division of labour, factory production and so on) and the conditions under which they are produced (wage labour) constitute the 'economic base' or 'mode of production'.

In a series of influential essays, Marx developed a 'labour theory of value', which suggests that the 'exchange value' of any good or service (what in capitalist economies is called the 'price') is really made up of congealed human labour. (Marxism identifies three categories: use value, exchange value and surplus value – you might like to follow this up at a later stage.) Marx argued that capitalists paid workers considerably less than the true value of what they produced. In Marx's time employers paid wages which would, perhaps, cover bare subsistence. Marx called the difference between what workers actually produce and what they were paid, surplus value. What we commonly call 'profit' is the surplus value extracted from labour and taken – or in the jargon 'expropriated' – by capitalists. Marx argued that capitalism was driven by the accumulation of surplus value.

The accumulation of surplus value could be achieved in one of three ways: capitalists could search out new markets for the products of labour; they could constantly drive down wages in order to extract more surplus value from their workers; or they could replace labour with new technologies (machines). Marx believed that to some extent these strategies were pursued simultaneously and that sooner or later capitalism would collapse as workers were rendered too poor to provide a market for the goods produced, and as new markets were exhausted. Capitalism was then an exploitative system, riddled with tensions, conflicts and inherent contradictions which would ultimately cause it to collapse.

LITERATURE BOX

The Ragged Trousered Philanthropists

Marx's ideas have been influential in politics, sociology, history, economics and philosophy. However, Marx's ideas have also inspired great works of fiction. Robert Tressell's novel is a moving and informative defence of socialist values with a heartfelt message. The novel is centred on a group of painters who are set the task of renovating a house, owned by a wealthy family. As the novel unfolds, a picture emerges of daily toil, in poor working conditions, for pittance wages, and lives characterised by hardship and job-insecurity, by ill-health and fear. The novel charts the ways in which material conditions of life gradually foster a consciousness of social class and the nature of exploitation. Many of Marx's ideas are explicitly discussed, explained or refuted by the central characters in the book.

Of course human relationships are not just constituted by economic relationships of the kind described above. We interact with other people on a day-to-day basis in the home, in a university, or at church perhaps. Our lives and our relationships with others are profoundly affected by government policies and we have to obey the law. We also 'engage' with others indirectly when we read about events happening away from our locality, or watch programmes on television. Marx believed that the economic 'base' supports a range of other political and social institutions, such as the state, the law courts, the church, the family, the education system, and what we now call the 'mass media'. Contemporary structuralists sometimes refer to these institutions as the 'superstructure' of society. The superstructure is intimately connected with, but conceptually distinct from, the economic base. Marx devoted a great deal of time to trying to elucidate the relationship between the economic 'base' and the political, social and legal 'superstructure'. He believed that ultimately economic forces drove (determined) social and political change, and much of his work was concerned with explaining how and why such change occurred. The relationship between base and superstructure has been much debated within Marxism.

By combining some of Marx's ideas on the historical and changing nature of human societies – known as 'historical materialism' – with Marxist economic analysis, it is possible to construct a coherent analysis of the overall structure of capitalist societies which can then be used to inform our understanding of the individual 'parts'. To simplify, Marx claimed that human societies were made up of various institutions and forms of social organisation which fulfilled a particular function or role in terms of the overall social system. He believed that as societies changed over time, so too did forms of social organisation, practices and institutions.

Marx believed that the dynamic force propelling change of this kind was economic. That is, the dynamic of change was rooted in the particular 'modes of production' of society. Marx believed that productive forces developed over time as humanity developed more knowledge of/mastery over, nature. As modes of production advanced and changed, the superstructure of society also changed. So, at different periods in history we find different modes of production – agricultural, industrial and so on – and a corresponding system of legal and political forms of organisation and social relationships. Marx argued that social relations could be characterised in different ways – feudal, bourgeois and so forth.

Marx was not alone in seeing a close 'fit' or correspondence between the economy, social relationships and political institutions. At roughly the same period of history, 'functionalist' thinkers, like Durkheim, were arguing that the social, political and economic spheres of life were intimately connected. However, whereas functionalists likened society to something like a natural organism, Marx regarded societies as riddled with internal tensions/conflicts. He argued that all forms of social and economic organisation, to date, were based on forms of oppression and exploitation. Moreover, all systems contained inherent contradictions, based on their exploitative nature, which eventually brought about their downfall. Marx believed that this process of historical change was usually violent. During periods of transition, emerging classes struggled for ascendency over the old ruling order and established their own dominance over the rest of society.

From a Marxist perspective, the French Revolution and the subsequent period of social turmoil/political upheaval, were illustrative of a process by which an emerging social class (the bourgeoisie) rose up and displaced the established ruling class (the *ancien régime* or aristocracy). Marxists continue to view classes in terms of their relationship to society's mode of production. So, contemporary capitalism is characterised by a ruling class (bourgeoisie) which owns/controls the means of production, and the working class (proletariat) who must sell their labour to survive.

Before considering how Marx, and Engels, provided a theoretical framework which has been used to develop a structuralist analysis of international relations we need to draw out the ways in which Marx's ideas about the relationship between economics, politics and society are later used to develop an elaborate structural analysis of capitalism (see box).

AUTHOR BOX

Louis Althusser

The French philosopher Louis Althusser is a good example of a structuralist thinker. Althusser argued that capitalism was a system – a set of ordered economic, political, social and legal relationships – reinforced by a range of institutions, like the family, church and education system. The parts of the system can only be understood in relation to the function they fulfil in the system as a whole – thus, institutions and their practices have to be understood in terms of their place in the overall system of ordered relationships. The structure of the capitalist system determines the nature/purpose of the various parts.

Althusser is also known for his work on so called Ideological State Apparatus and Repressive State Apparatus. He argued that the state had at its disposal a number of repressive apparatuses, such as the police or military, who could be used to put down rebellion or quell social unrest. However, physical force was a costly, ultimately inefficient, way of crushing opposition. Therefore, the ruling class attempts to legitimise its rule through a number of ideological state apparatuses (ISAs) which include the mass media and the education system. These ISAs transmit ruling class ideology and convince the working class that their subordinate position is normal, natural and just. The education system, for example, provides workers and managers with the skills necessary to perpetuate capitalism and inculcates a set of values and beliefs which legitimise capitalist class relations (see also Gramscian ideas in chapter 4). If capitalism is an exploitative system, benefiting the interests of the ruling class and detrimental to the interests of workers, to survive, capitalism must constantly reproduce labour power. This involves the production of a technically competent and skilled workforce, which is compliant and submissive.

Marxism is often dismissed as 'ideological', but structuralists make their claims on the basis of what they regard as 'scientific' analysis. Though Marx was unable to allow for many factors (and hence 'wrong'), he was actually trying to suggest that what was happening was based on certain observable, inevitable processes. History was 'determined' in the sense that capitalists could not prevent their own demise and workers were destined to inherit the world and build a better and brighter future. This is a notion reflected in the final words of Tressell's novel *The Ragged Trousered Philanthropists* (see box).

REFLECTION BOX

Human beings frequently think of themselves as living in history. That is, people tend to believe that history is going somewhere and so their lives are likely to be better than their forefathers'. Moreover, both religious belief systems and modern secular ideologies tend to impute a final purpose to life – this is called teleology or teleological. Marxism *is* radically different from liberalism, but have you noticed how both share a view of history *as* progress?

So far we have discussed Marx's ideas about the nature of capitalism as a social economic and political system, and hinted at ways in which Marx's work subsequently influenced structuralist writers. We now turn to the ways in which Marx (and later structuralist writers) developed concepts and theories which can be used to inform the study of international relations.

Marx was interested in the dynamism of capitalism and the ways it was radically transforming the economic, social and political landscape across Europe. He also believed that while the crisis of capitalism would occur in a relatively advanced industrial economy (like Britain or Germany) he was aware that the ramifications would be felt in other countries across the European continent. Marx was also a committed member of the Communist International, an organisation dedicated to the task of raising awareness of transnational working class interests, uniting the working class across Europe and stressing the need for solidarity with the poor and oppressed across the world. However, Marx's ideas contain important omissions if one attempts to apply them to contemporary IR. Marx did not develop a sustained analysis of the state system and did not aim to. What is more important is that his ideas have been utilised by others with a more internationalist orientation.

The work of Lenin is an important stepping stone between Marx's analysis of industrialised capitalist countries in Northern Europe and an analysis of international capitalist expansion and inter-state conflict. Lenin's ideas also draw from the English economist/historian Hobson. We suggested above that Marx believed capitalism would eventually collapse as workers became more impoverished and new markets became exhausted. Hobson, and later Lenin, did not necessarily disagree with Marx's basic thesis, however, they believed that Marx seriously underestimated the ability of the capitalist system to survive in the face of periodic crises. The nature of capitalism, it was argued, was such that it needed to expand in order to find new markets and secure new sources of raw materials and labour.

At the same time, industrialisation furnished the élites of developed European states with the means to undertake campaigns of colonial expansion across the globe. Hobson believed that these campaigns were designed to ensure that rich élites in European states had captive markets and was a form of exploitation. Lenin took this basic idea of expansionism and, using guiding ideas on the nature of capitalism provided by Marx and Engels, developed a more sustained analysis of imperialism as 'the highest state of capitalism'.

CONCEPT BOX

Imperialism and Colonialism

Imperialism means the extension of power through conquest. It refers to the extension of a state's hegemonic power/influence beyond its own borders, so much so that it amounts to an empire – the extension of a state's sovereignty over other countries. Colonialism refers to a situation where a group of people settle in a foreign country, establishing some form of domination over the indigenous population and maintaining close links with their 'mother' country. Since successful imperial domination frequently depends upon the loyalty of particular groups in subordinated countries, in practice, imperialism and colonialism might be closely linked.

Imperialism was said to be the highest stage in capitalist development because it would bring about the total exhaustion of new markets in accordance with Marx's predictions. However, Lenin believed that long before that occurred, capitalism would collapse because the search for captive markets and sources of raw materials was already generating conflicts between imperialist powers. Lenin believed that the First World War was the result of such squabbles and that along with the working class of industrialised countries, subjugated peoples across the world would eventually rise up and throw off the yoke of imperialist domination, as the world descended into vicious war.

Lenin's ideas about the end of capitalism were popular among intellectuals in the inter-war years. However, with the so called golden years of liberalism (that is, the economic boom post Second World War) such ideas quickly became unfashionable, in the West at least, and so structuralist type explanations did not play a significant role in the early development of International Relations. We now turn our attention to two important theories which *have* been influential in developing a structuralist perspective in the contemporary discipline. These are dependency theory and world-systems theory.

It was only in the late 1960s and early 1970s that Marxist-derived ideas were picked up by the International Relations community. Dependency theory and world-systems theory were becoming influential in areas of the social sciences like Sociology just at the time when IR scholars were becoming more keenly interested in the relationship between international economics and international politics. This was, more generally, a time of economic uncertainty and instability. By the early 1970s the international financial community began to entertain doubts about the monetary system underpinned by the US dollar. Oil prices increased drastically and the world economy was subsequently thrown into a deep recession.

At the United Nations General Assembly (UNGA) of 1974, the poorer countries of the world stood together to demand a new, and just, international economic order (NIEO). During the same period, the relaxation of tension in relations between the USA and USSR allowed academic attention to switch to more economics based concerns. We might say that from Marx through Lenin, through to the emergence of the dependency theory and world-systems theory, combined with the waxing and waning of international affairs, structuralism gradually emerged as a distinctive perspective or paradigm within International Relations.

Dependency theory came to prominence in the 1960s. It developed as a critique of liberal modernisation theory (see box). During the 1950s and 1960s developing countries threw off the yoke of colonialism/imperialism; they demanded and achieved independence. However, this was happening in the context of the Cold War (see chapter 1); Western countries were keen to ensure that former colonial states (or third world) did not fall into the hands of communist regimes, and encouraged newly independent states to develop capitalist economies. Walt Rostow's influential text on economic growth/modernisation was subtitled 'a non-communist manifesto'. Developing countries were encouraged to allow free enterprise to flourish and to engage in free trade with the rest of the world to encourage competition, economic dynamism and growth.

 CONCEPT BOX

Modernisation

The concept of 'modernisation' denotes a process characterised by inter-connected economic, technological, industrial, social, cultural, and political change. Modern, 'advanced' societies as opposed to traditional, 'backward' societies, are organised on the basis of secular, individualistic values. In modern societies people are supposedly judged, rewarded and afforded a particular role and status in society according to individual aptitude, achievement or merit, rather than on the basis of family connections, gender or age. Power in modern societies is seen to be exercised through administrative machinery in accordance with abstract rules. Along with the secular institutions like the modern state and legal institutions, bureaucratic procedures and processes are supposed to ensure that people are treated impartially.

In short, modernisation is typically associated with capitalist development and industrialisation, technological innovation, consumerism, the market economy and increases in population. Modernisation is also associated with improved levels of education, an expanding role for the state, the emergence of political pluralism, respect for civil liberties and rights and democratic, as opposed to authoritarian forms of government.

Modernisation theory has been refuted both on the grounds that its empirical and theoretical claims are flawed and on the grounds that it is, at best, patronising and, at worst, a powerful justification for a form of neo-imperialism. First, the major criticism of modernisation theory is that it has not worked, even in societies which have embraced its values and prescriptions. Second, in suggesting that 'they' can become like 'us'; i.e. the poor can become like the rich, in a stroke it dismisses as a mere 'waiting post' the culture, traditions and histories of many 'less developed countries'.

The *Dependencia* School emerged from the efforts of Latin American intellectuals to account for their societies' demonstrable inability to 'catch up' the rich countries of North America and Western Europe, even though they had largely followed the advice of the West and endeavoured to 'modernise' their societies and move to free market economies. Dependency theory attacked modernisation theory, because it was severely misleading in terms of its predictions about the development prospects of the third world. Indeed, with the notable exception of parts of East Asia, by the mid-1960s much of the developing world found that its relative economic performance was extremely disappointing. Although directed at modernisation theory, dependency theory also provides a critique of Lenin's analysis of imperialism.

The economic/political climate of the late 1960s and early 1970s was such that developing countries in particular were receptive to critiques of Western led development models. A key idea of modernisation theorists was that all states would pass through stages of development and that sooner or later all would become advanced, high consumption countries. However, modernisation theory rejected/ignored the possibility that deep structural factors might prevent economic progress, and more importantly, that the nature of the international system itself might be an obstacle to development. Accordingly, dependency theory developed a critique of modernisation theory which emphasised the structural constraints to development in Latin America.

Key writers in the *Dependencia* School, including Andre Gunder Frank, Raul Prebisch and Henrique Fernando Cardoso and Enzo Faletto, undertook a detailed historical analysis of the pattern of growth and development in Latin America and claimed to find that Latin America actually achieved its most impressive levels of growth and development at times when there was a slow down in world trade and trading links with developed countries were disrupted. Taking this empirical observation as a starting point, dependency theorists suggested this was because the basic structure of the global economy was such that it worked to further the interests of the already rich, developed economies of the West (or North) and to progressively impoverish already poor countries (the South or third world). The basic structure of the world economy, the trading regimes that existed, the nature of the markets for basic commodities and so on, fundamentally determined the development trajectory of individual countries. Therefore, even as large parts of the world emerged from imperialism and colonialism, the West continued to dominate the third world – hence the terms neo-imperialism and neo-colonialism. Dependency theory can be considered a variant of structuralist thought because it suggests that we can only understand, in this example, the Latin American part of the world economy, in terms of its relation to the world economic system as a whole.

Dependency theory can also be considered a form of economic determinism, in so far as *Dependencia* scholars frequently suggested that the political institutions and social relations which characterised developing countries were a reflection of the economic 'base' – dominated by élites who actually benefited from this exploitative economic system. Liberal economic theory suggests that successful modernisation depends to some extent upon the growth of an indigenous entrepreneurial class. Accordingly, development strategies frequently targeted resources at a 'modernising élite', believing that as countries underwent industrialisation and economic growth, wealth would 'trickle down' from this élite to the masses. They also believed that this élite would imbue liberal social and political values and these would gradually spread from the 'advanced' middle classes to the rest of society. Dependency theorists contended, to the contrary, that while élites did indeed benefit from their particular position in the system, the promised 'trickle down' did not materialise and was unlikely to do so. In fact, as a country ostensibly 'advanced', the masses became progressively more impoverished.

While dependency theory owes much to structuralist analysis, it also offers a critique of the Marxist notion that certain classes have common interests regardless of their nationality. Dependency theorists recognise that transnational élites share some common interests, but they also argue that to some extent the workers in developed countries, while relatively impoverished and exploited, have actually benefited to some degree from the exploitation of the third world. Earlier theorists of imperialism had recognised that the working classes had rallied to nationalist causes (particularly in war) and were, in some cases, enthusiastic supporters of empire. Taking this further, dependency theorists have shown how the bourgeoisie in the rich countries can exploit the poorer countries and use the profits to dampen the demands of its own proletariat by providing limited welfare for instance. In this way, dependency theorists suggested that there might well be obstacles to worker solidarity, which were rooted in different interests. They have questioned Marx's notion of a simple divergence of interests between the proletariat (all workers) and the bourgeoisie (all owners).

Finally, no discussion of the origins of structuralism would be complete without some reference to the work of Immanuel Wallerstein. Wallerstein is particularly known for his 'world-systems theory' (hereafter WST). As the name suggests, the idea of this theory is that elements of the world-system cannot be understood in isolation and that a holistic approach is needed. The logic of the WST argument is fairly simple to outline. At one time, we could conceive of all societies as mini-systems – self-contained economic, political and social units with a single culture. These societies were characterised by a simple division of labour and all members had a specific, clearly defined role – hunter, farmer, carer and so forth. Today, there are very few examples of these kinds of societies left in the world. Over time they have been swallowed up by larger systems of social, economic and political organisation.

A world-system is the largest and most complex of all and comes in two types – world-empire and world-economy. According to Wallerstein, prior to the birth and expansion of capitalism, there were examples of world-*empires* based on the conquest of, and subordination of, peoples across the world. Clearly, world-empires have been based on both economic exploitation and political domination. Examples of such world-empires are all the so-called great civilisations of pre-modern times, such as China, Egypt and Rome. However, in about 1500 a novel type of world-economy emerged in Europe and gradually expanded across the globe (though you should be aware that not all Marxists/structuralists date the emergence of capitalism from 1500). New transportation technology allowed far-flung markets to be obtained and maintained especially when combined with western military technology to dictate and enforce favourable terms of trade. As this 'capitalism' spread throughout the globe, there developed a 'core', composed of well-developed towns, flourishing manufacturing, technologically progressive agriculture, skilled and relatively well-paid labour, and high investment, and a 'periphery', from which raw materials necessary for expansion and certain key primary goods were extracted. In such a system, it was necessary to coerce labour in order to keep down the costs of production. In such circumstances, the periphery stagnated, its towns withered, and those with money, technology and skills moved to the core.

At first, the differences between the core and the periphery were small, but gradually the gap widened as more and more, the core countries concentrated on the production of manufactured goods and the periphery produced only primary products and basic commodities. Accordingly, uneven development across the world, and the existence of a 'first' and third world is not a consequence of historical lag or a technical hitch to sort out, but actually a function of the capitalist world-system. Unlike the core–periphery model characteristic of dependency theory, WST also posits the existence of a semi-periphery – intermediary societies which play an important role in the functioning of the world-system as a whole (see below). When applied to international relations, what this effectively boils down to is an argument that lower levels (states, communities, individuals) matter, but that the highest level (the world-system) constrains behaviour in all sorts of ways (see box on the structure–agency debate in chapter 4). Therefore, it makes no sense to start from the premise that the state is the basic unit of analysis in IR, or posit that states are autonomous 'actors'. It also alerts us to the degree to which social institutions are constantly changing and adapting over time and in the context of a dynamic world-system.

Assumptions

1. 'Human nature' is not fixed and essential. The human subject is social and historical. However, human nature is conditioned by prevailing forms of social, economic and political organisation. People are products of their society.

2. Subjects can be grouped into identifiable collectivities which might, in turn, be said to have concrete interests. While recognising the historical and changing nature of human societies, this version of structuralism nevertheless claims to be 'scientific' and 'objective', in so far as it claims to have identified certain 'facts' about the world, and objective laws which determine the course of history.

3. 'Structuralism as science', is clearly distinguished from belief systems or ideology, despite the deep moral convictions of many who have used it as an explanatory theory.

4. Structuralists make no clear distinction between the national (inside) and the international (outside). From this perspective the state-system is determined by the international capitalist system, or they emerged together and are thus mutually constitutive.

REFLECTION BOX

Does structuralism deny the possibility of political action or belittle the efforts of heroic struggles throughout the third world?

Themes

The State and Power

The state is a central concept in structuralist theories, but is viewed in a different way from realist or liberal approaches. Structuralists differ over the importance of states in international relations with some arguing that international political and economic analysis would be better focused on social classes and the nature of transnational alliances among élites. However, even those who prefer such a class-based analysis recognise the actual political division of the world into states, and the role that these states play in helping to maintain class-based inequalities.

In a superficial way structuralists resemble realists in recognising the importance of the state in IR. However, rather than seeing the state as a sovereign power representing the interests of the 'nation' in international relations, structuralists hold that the state in some sense reflects the interests of dominant social classes. There is, however, disagreement among structuralist thinkers as to whether the state is dominated by élite social classes, or whether it exercises a degree of autonomy.

In classical Marxism and early structuralist theory, the state was seen as a coercive, repressive apparatus supporting an exploitative social and economic order and reflecting the interests of dominant classes. Marx famously described the state as the 'executive committee of the bourgeoisie'. So-called instrumentalist views are similar to classical Marxism in that they regard the state as a direct instrument of class rule. This school of thought suggests that state policies and actions are designed to consolidate and reinforce the position of the dominant class. In capitalist societies, the political and legal systems support the ownership of private property, including the private ownership of the means of production. Since capitalism generates conflict, an elaborate system must be in place to manage or suppress social conflict. These élite classes exercise power for their own ends, and to the detriment of the vast majority of poorer, less privileged people. Structuralists point to the way in which the institutions of the state – the law courts, the police, the military, the economic system – work to protect the interests of the already powerful. As we saw earlier, Althusser saw the law courts, police force and armed forces as integral parts of a repressive, as opposed to ideological, state apparatus. The state quite literally represented the interests of the ruling class. If the ideological state apparatus failed then the repressive forces under the control of the state would be utilised to quell discontent.

WORLD EXAMPLE

El Salvador

International relations are replete with examples of state repression – what has sometimes been called state terrorism. To simplify a complex history, El Salvador was a close ally of the United States in the Cold War (see chapter 1). However, anti-communist and promarket/US policies in that country created a highly unequal society with a majority of the population living in poverty due to a lack of access to resources or money. By the 1970s and 1980s pro-US right-wing governments were only kept in power by extensive repression of left-wing politics, trade union activity and peasant activism; the military, as it had long done, played a vital role in this repression, sometimes covertly but often openly. Elections were rigged, authorities corrupt and people cowed by fear. The state was, in fact, at the service of an élite few known as 'the fourteen families'.

More recent versions of structuralism hold that the state can have a degree of autonomy from the dominant class. The state certainly is not seen as a 'neutral arbiter', but is considered to be relatively independent of specific interests. States clearly do make choices when formulating policies. Moreover, these same choices are sometimes bound to adversely affect some sections of capital. States might even struggle for more autonomy from dominant classes, in response to democratic pressures, perhaps.

However, even if we accept that the state has a degree of autonomy, the state is, nevertheless, compelled to deal with the political and economic contradictions inherent in capitalism and so is never able to completely escape the constraints imposed by the global capitalist system. In order to formulate autonomous policies the state requires resources, including financial resources which it raises through taxation. Arguably then, the state relies largely on the capitalist class to bring about an acceptable level of economic activity, which it needs to maintain support.

Of course, states can borrow money from banks, or try to attract inward investment from foreign enterprises or investors. This is, in fact, frequently the case with many third world countries. However, reliance on foreign capital brings its own dangers, because while the state might increase its autonomy *vis-à-vis* the dominant class in its own state, it simultaneously increases its dependency on foreign capital. Foreign resources typically come from foreign direct investment, supplied by big multinational corporations, in which case the investor maintains control. The state can, of course, take out loans from private banks or, in certain circumstances, apply for assistance from the International Monetary Fund, or the World Bank. Loans from private banks do not restrict the state's autonomy, although the bank will need to be assured that the money is going to be wisely spent. That said, if the loan proves difficult to service, states can find themselves pushed into a situation of dependency and its choices are then severely curtailed, or the sources of further credit might quickly dry up. Either way, it is clear that even if we agree that the state has a degree of autonomy from dominant classes within its territory, it is still constrained by global economic realities. This means, of course, that government policy, whatever its ideological basis, is profoundly shaped by either pressures from its own élites, or by systemic pressures.

WORLD EXAMPLE

The Debt Crisis

This is instructive of the degree to which developing countries are severely constrained by world market forces, dominant sections of capital *and* international institutions.

In 1973 the oil producing/exporting countries, OPEC, used their collective muscle to drastically raise the price of a barrel of oil on the world market. Since many Western (and indeed developing countries) were dependent upon imported oil for their energy needs, they had no alternative but to pay up. Consequently, many OPEC states found themselves suddenly enriched with a large glut of so called 'petrodollars'. These funds were quickly reinvested in Western banks. At the time, interests rates around the world were low and inflation rates were relatively high. For this reason, many developing countries were encouraged to borrow heavily – under the conditions that existed at the time, they were, in effect, getting interest free loans. Developing countries hoped that these loans would provide a much needed injection of investment in their economies and so fuel economic development. At the same time, Western banks had a large glut of petrodollars and were looking for investment opportunities at a time when Western countries were reluctant to borrow.

However, within a short period of time, global economic conditions had changed dramatically. In the first place, countries which imported oil took measures to protect their own economies and began to look for ways to restrict imports, often developing substitutes for commodities which had previously been imported. Consequently, the world market price of many basic commodities fell. The increase in oil prices also resulted in inflationary pressures in Western economies, and, consequently, interest rates increased rapidly. Many developing countries now found themselves in an extremely difficult position; they had large debts, were facing an increasing tide of protectionism in Western economies, were experiencing deteriorating terms of trade for the basic commodities which they sold on the world market, had to pay the new higher price for oil and also had to pay high rates of interest on their loans. In such circumstances, the level of debt escalated and many countries found that they were unable to repay even the interest on their debt. In 1982, Mexico announced a moratorium on its debt and the financial world was plunged into a crisis.

The inability of developing countries to service existing debt sent shock waves through the global financial institutions. In such circumstances, private banks were reluctant to offer fresh loans and developing countries were compelled to turn to the only real alternative sources of finance, the International Monetary Fund and World Bank. These institutions did indeed provide developing countries with fresh sources of credit but, in return, imposed harsh conditions. Developing countries had little alternative but to accept tough 'structural adjustment' packages which included, among other things, devaluation of local currencies, adoption of export-led growth strategies, and cuts in welfare provision. The debt crisis clearly indicates how state autonomy is severely constrained.

With respect to the overarching global economy as a constraining/determining factor in state behaviour, structuralists (e.g. Wallerstein) make a distinction between 'core' and 'peripheral' states arguing that in the core, the state is relatively strong, but functions to advance the interests of the bourgeoisie by preventing other states erecting political barriers to the profitability of their activities. Core states, then, shape the world market in ways that advance the interests of some entrepreneurs against those of other groups. Core states cooperate to extend and deepen the capitalist world-system. The most powerful states, for example, the United States of America, Japan and Germany work together (and through their influence in international organisations like the World Bank or IMF) to ensure the survival of an international capitalist economy, which benefits élite classes across the globe.

It follows from this that whilst structuralists believe that states are of central importance, the study of international relations must also extend to a range of other 'actors' like the World Bank, International Monetary Fund, and multinational corporations as well. Core states also seek to reinforce the advantages of their producers and to legitimise their role in the world-system by imposing their cultural dominance on the world.

In developing an analysis of the interconnections between states, the state system and global capitalism, structuralists have also elucidated the key concept of power. Power to structuralists is not about relational 'trials of strength' (i.e. who wins the war) but something much more subtle. Power is embedded in social relations; that is, it is a part of the structure. Power thus involves the inequalities of capitalist class relations and core–periphery relations. It also involves less tangible ideas such as persuasion or influence and may be 'invisible'. One person or group may have power over others not just through threats and coercion but via ideology and manipulation. In this way, power relations may come to be seen as such a 'natural' order of things; no one is consciously aware that it is being exercised.

ANALOGY BOX

The Happy Slave

The operation of the global capitalist economy might not always appear conflictual, oppressive or exploitative because these relationships are often not overt or obvious. Although the notion of the 'happy slave' does not originate from Marxist/structuralist thought, it is nevertheless useful in illustrating how power relations can be subtly disguised.

It is possible to imagine a society where slavery is the norm. As the norm, people do not question that slavery is part of the natural order of things. Within this society a particular slave owner may provide their slaves with healthcare, education, food, reasonable accommodation and working hours. The slave, in turn, may be very happy with his/her lot. Though as outside observers we can see a power relationship, perhaps neither the owner nor the slave perceive their relationship as one of power but rather as one of benevolence and mutual respect within the context of an entirely natural state of affairs. To extend the analogy, perhaps power is a facet of all sorts of social relations from the factory owner and worker to the husband and wife? (See also chapter 6.)

Institutions and World Order

It might be argued that Marxism has made no real contribution to IR theory, because Marxism has everything to say about economics and nothing to say about international politics. Marxists reject this idea because economics is not an autonomous sphere of human activity, but is linked to socio-political factors. The economic substructure involves the mode of production and the social relations of production, and the superstructure involves the exertion of (political) power by one class over another. Structuralists follow Marx in insisting that politics and economics are intimately connected. Unsurprisingly then, structuralism has made a contribution to our understanding of world order and institutions. In this section we concentrate on how world order is conceptualised in dependency theory and world-systems theory, then comment briefly on the role of institutions.

As suggested earlier, structuralists conceive of world order as a capitalist system of inter-connected sets of social, economic and political relations which collectively constitute a structure. From a structuralist perspective, modern capitalism has now expanded to become a global system; local, national and regional economies now form part of a much larger interconnected economic system and are conditioned by that system. Similarly, the conditions of life for individuals, social groups and even states, are determined by their place in the overall, global capitalist system.

In essence, structuralists see this global capitalist system as being structured along both a vertical and horizontal axis. Relations between states are structured hierarchically between those who are wealthy and powerful – the core – and those who are poor and without much influence – the periphery. There is also a horizontal structure of class relationships, namely the relationship which exists between élites in both core and periphery countries. Elites in both the rich 'North' and poor 'South', share fundamental interests in supporting this system because they actually benefit from the exploitation of other social groups.

AUTHOR BOX

Immanuel Wallerstein (The Modern World-System)

According to Wallerstein, the concept of a world-economy assumes that there exists an economy wherever there is an ongoing extensive and relatively complete social division of labour with an integrated set of production processes which relate to each other through a market. Wallerstein (though others disagree) believes that a capitalist world-economy has been in existence in at least part of the globe since the sixteenth century. We have now reached the stage of capitalist development and expansion where the entire globe is operating within the frame of a singular social division of labour. It is meaningful, therefore, to speak of a capitalist world-economy.

The major social institutions of the capitalist world-economy are states, social classes, 'peoples' and households. Wallerstein believes that all of these institutions and social

AUTHOR BOX (continued)

relationships are profoundly shaped (or even created) by the ongoing workings of the world-economy. Therefore, we can speak of a 'world-system'. The main underlying dynamic of the capitalist world-economy is the relationship between capital/labour and the extraction of the surplus created by direct producers (labour), or by others (capitalists) either at the actual site of production or, later, when goods are exchanged in the market place. The principle of private property, upheld by the law and enforced by the state, means that appropriators control the capital and that their rights to the surplus are legally guaranteed. Increasingly these 'appropriators' are not individuals but collective entities like multinational corporations.

Whereas orthodox Marxist analysis emphasises processes of unequal exchange between capital and labour, Wallerstein introduces the notion of a 'core' and a 'periphery' in the world-economy and calls the exchange of products containing unequal amounts of social labour a core–periphery relationship. Wallerstein argues that the structure of the world-economy permits an unequal exchange of goods and services such that much of the surplus-value extracted in the peripheral zones of the world-economy is transferred to the core zones. However, unlike dependency theorists, Wallerstein posits the existence of a 'semi-periphery' in the world-economy or world-system. He argues that some states are neither in the core or periphery of the world-economy. Instead they can be thought of as semi-peripheral states. These states are engaged in production activities, some of which are 'core-like' and some 'periphery-like'. An example of these states might be the newly industrialising countries (NICs) in Asia. So, the structure of the world-economy consists of a tripartite division between the core, periphery and semi-periphery. States and social groups can move, slowly, from one category to another but they remain within the overall determining structure of the world-economy.

Dependency theorists argue that the economies of Asia, Africa and Latin America are on the periphery of the global economy and that they are dependent on the capitalist countries of Western Europe and North America at the centre/core of the system. The trade relations and capital flows between the core and periphery of the global economy are asymmetrical, shifting the economic surplus to the core and undermining the resource base of the periphery. Countries in the periphery produce primary products like raw materials – cotton or coffee – not manufactured goods like motor vehicles or electronic goods. This degree of 'specialisation' or division of labour perpetuates inequalities. Surplus flows out of the periphery to the core, in the interests of international capital. Peripheral countries (the South or third world) are not 'catching up' with the core because of their dependence on, and exploitation by, the core (West or North) of the international capitalist economy. Economic growth and development in the periphery is sluggish due to a lack of technology and investment, which again is a consequence of their dependence on the core.

According to world-systems theorists, capitalism is driven by the imperatives of accumulation – each 'entrepreneur', whether an individual or a big corporation, seeks to maximise their profit. For this reason there is an inherent tendency for the absolute volume of production in the world-economy to expand over time, as more is produced to be sold on local, national or world markets.

However, profit can only be made if there is effective demand for the goods and services produced and this is a problem when wages are being driven down. According to Wallerstein, the dynamics of the world-economy ensure that the level of world supply expands at a steady rate, while world demand remains relatively fixed for intermediate periods. This results in reoccurring blockages in the process of accumulation, which in turn generates periods of economic recession and stagnation.

In response to such pressures, capitalists will 'restructure' the network of production processes and underlying social relations in an attempt to overcome obstacles to capital accumulation. Such 'restructuring' might involve attempts to cut the cost of production in core countries by replacing labour with machinery. Alternatively, capitalist enterprises might relocate in the periphery where wages are much lower. Periods of restructuring have a profound effect on class relations both within and between states in the world-system.

Starting from the central premise that economics and politics are intimately connected allows structuralists to make various points about the nature and role of states and institutions in international relations in 'managing' world order (global capitalist relations). Structuralists argue that capitalism is maintained and perpetuated by a range of institutions and practices and by dominant ideologies or belief systems which legitimise the current world order. The fundamental economic inequality which exists between core and periphery determines the nature of the state – put simply core states are powerful and peripheral states are weak. States in the periphery have little autonomy in relation to the global economy in which they are embedded, because ruling classes in peripheral countries are tied by economic interest to international capital and play a managerial or intermediary role within their own countries for international capital by using control of state power to protect the interests of multinational capital. Structuralists believe that major institutions like the UN, the World Bank and IMF and trading blocs like NAFTA are dominated by élite groups and/or hegemonic states. Thus we cannot take statements of the World Bank and IMF about their role in poverty alleviation at face value; these organisations have a role in the capitalist structure which helps to maintain current injustices.

 REFLECTION BOX

How would Wallerstein explain the wide gulf which exists between the rich, industrialised, developed North (the core) and the poor, underdeveloped South (the periphery)?

Inequality and Justice

Whether one adopts a dependency theory or a world-systems approach, it is clear that structuralists see inequality as a fundamental and enduring feature of international relations, because the international system is divided between the 'haves' and the 'have-nots'. The 'haves' are (or live mostly in) the rich countries, predominantly in the northern hemisphere. Structuralists argue that these countries, or their capitalist élites (along with smaller local third world élites), constitute a strong centre or core in the world economic and political order, or world-system. The 'have-nots' are the poorer countries of the South or the down-trodden classes; they are the weak and powerless and make up what is known as the periphery.

By focusing on structures of the international system and world economy, WST puts the experience, and plight, of third world states in an entirely different light from the optimism generated by liberal modernisation theory. For example, the end of colonialism (where third world countries were ruled as colonies of other states such as Britain) cannot be seen as signalling the end of exploitation of the third world states by rich, industrialised nations; the 'end' of colonialism simply changes the nature of colonialism from a direct type, based on military occupation, to an indirect type based on economic structures (that is neo-colonialism).

According to this view, third world interaction with the financial and commercial power centres of the rich states of the first world is undertaken on unequal terms since the rich countries have used their previously existing position of economic dominance in order to structure the international economy to serve their interests and maintain their dominance. Third world states which have tried to 'opt out' of the system have not fared well economically and so, however unfair the existing situation, most third world states are dependent upon (and trapped by) it. This 'dependency' has left most third world states unable to define effectively their own development goals, or to advance the welfare concerns of their populations, because their economies are set up and organised to serve the interests of the industrialised states.

HISTORICAL BOX

The Case of Cuba

Cuba was once a country which sold its sugar to the United States. It was also characterised by oppression and poverty. The revolution of 1959 sought to end such injustice. However, the United States quickly defined the revolution as communist and refused to trade with Cuba. In the context of the Cold War (see box in chapter 1), Cuba was fortunate in that the Soviet Union saw Cuba as an important ally (given its geographical proximity to its ideological enemy) and so stepped in to exchange Cuban sugar for oil, and at preferential rates. Even so, shunned by the international financial institutions such as the IMF Cuba faced big economic problems. These problems were severely exacerbated by the end of the Cold War and therefore the end of subsidised Soviet oil and the loss of its market for sugar. Cuba is relatively isolated from the normal workings of the world economy. Although in a relatively equal fashion, most goods are rationed in Cuba today, and Cuba is struggling to survive in its present form. The case of Cuba suggests that in some senses dependency is a lose–lose situation; states can suffer the injustice of dependent status or fare worse in attempting to set up an alternative. It might be suggested that the only thing worse than being exploited by global economic forces is not being exploited by global economic forces.

Structuralist inspired critiques of this kind raise normative questions about how this exploitation can be ended and what would constitute a just international economic and political order. The relationship between the rich North and poor South (core and periphery) is said to be unequal and exploitative. Despite differences between varieties, fundamental to a structuralist argument is the idea that the rich are rich at the expense of the poor; put another way, some people are able to enjoy life because of others' misery; this is not just a matter of chance. The global economy is structured by class interests to favour some.

 REFLECTION BOX

Structuralists dismiss the liberal pluralist notion of interdependence, arguing that this implies a balance and fairness which does not exist. To what extent do you think that the complex interactions of international relations are characterised by mutually profitable exchange *or* unfair exploitative relations?

Dependence describes a type of relationship between rich and poor which ensures that money and resources are increasingly concentrated with the former because of the way the world economy is structured. For instance poorer countries might export raw materials such as, for example, bauxite and foodstuffs like coffee and bananas, whereas richer countries export manufactured goods, such as cars, fridges and so on. Statistical evidence supports the contention that over the long term the prices of raw materials and food – primary products – tend to decline relative to the price of manufactured goods. This puts poorer countries at a fundamental, structural disadvantage. Furthermore, richer countries are able to perpetuate this situation because despite the rhetoric of free trade, richer countries are able to control prices by trade restrictions. The EU, for instance, strictly controls the importation of bananas. Furthermore, technical innovation keeps pushing the development of better products, which have even higher levels of 'value-added'. Of course, some people, plantation owners in Guatemala for instance, are very rich despite the overall poverty which may exist in their country; this ensures that the system is kept going since there is a commonality of interest between the rich of the core and the rich of periphery.

WST aims to explain the historical rise of the rich countries (referred to as either the North or the West), as well as the continued poverty of the non-Western (Southern or third world) societies. WST, like structuralism in general, demands a fair redistribution of the world's economic wealth. In order that this should be achieved, WST provides support for a new international economic order, often abbreviated to the unpronounceable acronym NIEO. Demands for a NIEO involve fair prices for products produced by the third world and a restructuring of world trade in general. A NIEO can be contrasted with the actual economic order which is a Liberal International Economic Order, or

LIEO. Given that this version of structuralist doctrine emphasises the systematic nature of exploitation, and given the stress on conflicting interests, we can safely assume that the rich are not likely to give up their wealth and privilege without a struggle. Therefore, the challenge for the poor is to break free from the structures which constrain them. How to do this, in theory or in practice, is a different matter.

Identity and Community

Recognition of the significance of gender and racial discrimination was fairly central to the 'post-Marxist' turn which occurred in the late 1960s and early 1970s (see chapters 4–6). However, generally speaking neither early Marxist nor later structuralist writers paid much attention to aspects of identity and community that did not easily fit within the broad framework of a global capitalist order and notions of class struggle. Despite the importance of nationalism, as both an ideology and political force in nineteenth-century Europe, Marx devoted most of his time and energies to exploring the theme of class consciousness, class interests and class struggle.

Given the national and ethnic diversity which existed in the Soviet Union, it is somewhat surprising, perhaps, to find that none of the leading Bolshevik revolutionaries, including Lenin and Trotsky, gave sustained attention to the ideology of nationalism. Moreover, the intellectual and political climate of the USSR during the first half of this century was such that there were no serious challenges to Stalin's rather simplistic view of the world 'community' as being fundamentally divided into two opposing blocs or 'camps'. Throughout the nineteenth and early twentieth century Marxists tended to regard nationalism, or indeed any other form of identification – religious, cultural, ethnic and so on – as a manifestation of 'false consciousness', in effect a distraction from the real class-based structures of politics. This view continues to find echoes in some contemporary Marxist work.

That said, in the 1960s, there emerged many national liberation movements in parts of Africa and Latin America which were left leaning, or pro-Marxist-Leninist, and, for this reason, it became necessary to develop an account of nationalist struggle which was neither dismissive (as in the notion of false consciousness) nor incompatible with the basic assumptions of structuralism. Thus, in Wallerstein's account of the modern world-system, we find some attention being given to nationalism as a powerful source of political identification.

Wallerstein argues that the increasing definition of state structures has led to the shaping, reshaping, creation and destruction, and revival of the idea of 'peoples'. He believes that these 'peoples' come to see themselves (and are seen by others) as controlling state structures. Through this identification of 'peoples' with the state, 'nations' are created. On the other hand, within the boundaries of the 'nation-state', there are significant groups who are not identified as having rights to control state structures or exercise political power directly. These people come to be seen by 'nationals' as 'minorities'. However, it is important to realise that Wallerstein does not regard national identity as rooted in some real shared ethnic heritage or history. Nations are 'solidarity groupings' whose boundaries are constantly constructed, defined and redefined, and nationalism is a device which is used to strengthen and consolidate the power of the state.

WST incorporates an analysis of those forces which work against the system as well as dominant, class based, structures. Thus, it is possible to identify a number of oppositional or 'anti-systemic' forces at work in world politics. Nationalism is not all of one kind. Some forms of nationalism certainly work to consolidate capitalism and disguise the exploitative nature of the capitalist world-system. However, some national liberation movements are clearly anti-systemic. Various groups have an interest in supporting and opposing particular definitions of the 'nation-state' and so, according to Wallerstein, 'nationalism' must be seen as both a mechanism of imperialism/integration *and* of resistance/liberation.

Clearly, here we have an analysis of nationalism which is influenced by the underlying theory of class politics. Indeed, Wallerstein goes on to say that anti-systemic movements are organised in two main forms around two main themes: social movements around class and the national movement around 'nations' or peoples. Anti-systemic (or revolutionary) movements first emerged in organised form in the nineteenth century to promote human equality and so were, by definition, incompatible with the functioning of the capitalist world economy. It was the political structure of the capitalist world economy – a series of sovereign states – which compelled movements to seek the transformation of the world-system via the achievement of political power within separate states. However, because the capitalist world-system is based fundamentally on class division and exploitation, which is transnational or global in nature, the organisation of anti-systemic movements at the state level necessarily has contradictory effects. Nationalism counterposes the logical and ideological necessity of worldwide struggle against the immediate political need of achieving power within one state. Whatever the tactic of a given social movement, they achieve power in a state structure and are then constrained by the logic of the inter-state system.

Structuralists have also endeavoured to give some account of racism and sexism in the world-system. According to Wallerstein racism is a belief system which functions to justify the inclusion of certain groups in the workforce and the political system at a level of reward and status sharply inferior to that of some larger group. Sexism has the same objective, although it is reached via a different path. By restricting women to certain modes of producing income and by defining such modes as 'non-work' (through the concept of the 'housewife') sexism works to reduce wage levels in large sectors of the world economy. According to Maria Mies, in the contemporary global economy, the coercion of women as 'housewives' remains essential for a system which allowed male workers to be free citizens.

However, while structuralists have attempted to give some account of identity, forms of solidarity and types of community (such as nation-states and anti-systemic movements), it is fair to say that this analysis has been profoundly coloured by their basic beliefs about the primacy of social class and class struggle. Indeed, overall structuralists have tended to emphasise class as the coming together of identity and interests.

Conflict and Violence

For structuralists, conflict is intimately connected with the forces of global capitalism. Global economic relations are highly conflictual, because of the tendencies inherent in capitalism – it is built upon and perpetuates divisions between social classes and between core and periphery states. Conflicts between social groups, and indeed states, are generated by the nature of the system itself. Conflict is not then primarily rooted in the nature of the inter-state system, as realists hold, but arises out of the exploitative nature of capitalism. For this reason, attempts to mediate or resolve conflict by well meaning individuals or groups, are unlikely to be effective.

In the sense of direct physical violence, like war, the link between capitalism and conflict can be seen in terms of imperialism and the violent subjugation of those peoples who opposed it. It has also been claimed, by Lenin for example, that capitalist competition leads to inter-state war, though the evidence here is not clear and might even be contradictory (see chapter 2). What is evident is that some conflicts appear to have at least partly capitalist economic motivations. For example, Indonesia's invasion of East Timor was followed by a treaty with Australia on oil exploitation off the Timorese coast. Many observers suggest that US/UN action in the Gulf in 1991 was motivated more by economic considerations than for reasons of protecting democracy, especially given the highly dubious 'democratic' credentials of the Kuwaiti state that was defended.

CONCEPT BOX

Realist and Structuralist Perspectives on Conflict and Political Struggle

At this juncture it might be helpful to compare and contrast structuralist and realist views on the nature of the inter-state system and forms of conflict and political struggle. You will recall that realists regard states as the primary actors in international relations. Moreover, states are autonomous actors – they are able to formulate foreign policy goals and take effective action to realise these ends ('the national interest'). Conflicts arise because states frequently have competing interests, are prepared to use force if necessary to realise their objectives and because, in an anarchic system, there is nothing to prevent it. Moreover, realists recognise that political struggle is not limited to conflicts between states. After all, from a realist perspective, conflict is endemic to the human condition. However, realists tend to concentrate on conflict between, rather than within, states.

The structuralist view of conflict and violence among states is different. Structuralists regard the inter-state system as reflecting the interests of élite groups (international capital), and functioning to manage conflicts that arise from the contradictions inherent in capitalism. Political struggles take a number of forms, but they can be reduced to two kinds. The first kind is conflict and struggle among different sectors of capital – which may take the form of inter-state conflict (war) when nationally based capitalist classes attempt to increase their share of the global product, or their access to resources. The second kind is conflict and struggle among opposed social classes – capital and labour. The first kind of struggle is a squabble (albeit often a brutal and bloody one) over the share of global wealth and resources, which leaves the capitalist system intact. The second kind, however, is a much more fundamental conflict between those who defend the capitalist system and those who want to change it.

Another way of looking at violence is as something indirect or structural. Johan Galtung is particularly known for his work on structural violence, which has made an important contribution to Peace Studies. One can suffer great harm, both physical and psychological, if deprived of social and economic security. To this view 'violence' pervades the structures of society, which oppress the working class and other marginalised groups. The economic structure of capitalism works to damage subordinated groups in many and varied ways; they get less education, poorer healthcare and so on, leading to shorter life-expectancies. Feminists have gone beyond the class based analysis of Galtung's original work to suggest that structures in society also tend to impact negatively on the lives of women (see chapter 6).

Peace and Security

As indicated above, the concept of structural violence has been particularly influential in Peace Studies. More generally structuralist analysis suggests that current patterns of economic organisation generate tensions and contradictions which often result in direct conflict. The possibility of violence and war mean inherent insecurity for large sectors of the world's population. Peace and security, therefore, lie in moving to a socio-economic system which is not exploitative and so lacks the motivations for war.

Summary

1.   Structuralism is a broad perspective drawing upon a Marxist legacy, but also influenced by ideas not directly Marxist in origin.

2. Probably the best known variants of structuralism are dependency theory (*Dependencia*) and world-systems theory.

3. From a structuralist perspective, the contemporary world order is constituted by a global capitalist system and a corresponding inter-state system.

4. A fundamental feature of this order is inequality. Capitalism is based on the exploitation of the poor by the rich. In pursuing their (class) interests, the rich (people and states) are able to maintain their position by their exploitation of the poor. This is due to a fundamentally unjust system, based on structures, and characterised by inequality.

5. In line with Marx, many structuralists therefore see classes as the dominant actors in IR, despite the importance of the state.

6. Structuralists have not neglected the role of the state-system. Structuralists have developed an analysis of the state as either an instrument used to perpetuate the rule of dominant classes; a conduit for class oppression, or alternatively as a relatively autonomous entity which, nevertheless, plays an important role in facilitating capitalist expansion and supporting an unjust order.

7. Whilst the world is divided up into rich and poor countries, an accurate appraisal of IR needs to look at how classes promote their interests and how they use the state to help them.

8. Structuralism looks carefully at the role of institutional actors such as the World Bank and IMF and how these help legitimise and maintain existing structures.

9. Structuralism claims that processes of capital accumulation, the extraction of surplus value and exploitation can be measured objectively. We can understand processes of contradiction, crisis and change by reference to these same economic 'laws'. Therefore, structuralism can be viewed as a 'scientific' or 'positivist' approach within IR (see conclusions).

10. Despite many insights, structuralism has tended to be marginalised in the study of IR, especially in the US version of the discipline.

Criticisms

Perhaps the biggest criticism of structuralism concerns its level of determinism. This means that the theory suggests that the position of actors within the structure determines the way they behave. States are said to have little autonomy in the way they conduct themselves in terms of winning or losing within the international economy. Some authors, such as Wallerstein, have developed a somewhat less deterministic position. However, the whole point of the analysis is to suggest that poorer states have very little possibility to improve their position. This seems to dismiss as meaningless even noble and heroic struggles to overcome such constraints.

This point gives rise to complaints that structuralism is able to outline the evils of international capitalism but has no scheme which will change it. The despair of such a position (which rejects the purely Marxist determinism of inevitable revolution) may be regrettable or frustrating but is again part of the position that the rich countries have things effectively 'stitched up'. Some structuralists, most notably Wallerstein, have sought to fight their way out of this corner but then find themselves in another (teleology – see below).

A further criticism of structuralism is that it is reductionist. That is it reduces all phenomena – war, economic crisis, inequality, aspects of identity and so forth – to the dynamic of social class and class struggle. What this means in practice is that structuralists have failed to ask a whole range of questions about gender, ethnicity and identities of other sorts. That is, they have reduced a highly complex situation to one which is explained by class, when, in fact, patterns of oppression are multi-faceted and overlapping and where even class loyalties are not always easy to ascribe in a way which helps predict behaviour and attitudes. A related criticism concerns the way that interests are understood. Is it really possible that interests are so fundamentally determined by social class? Or that interests are really this fixed?

In adopting the Marxist heritage, which emphasises the oppression of the working class, structuralism (though it may have no road map to get there) implicitly suggests an end point to history. The end point is socialism, at which point the good life will be enjoyed by everyone. Quite apart from the fact that much of what Marx predicted as inevitable has not happened, this teleological position can be criticised because the explanation of what *is* happening (the dynamic of history and social change) is coloured by the assumption that a socialist society will eventually emerge – that is to say, the posited end point colours the explanation of past and present events.

Moreover, not only does it suggest that the 'end point' influences the theory but also has implications for different cultures as temporary stages or impediments, rather than as possessing of intrinsic value.

Overall, however, we might conclude by saying that more thoughtful critics of Marx have recognised the structuralist contribution, as well as noting its weaknesses.

Common Misunderstandings

If classes are the predominant actors then states are unimportant. No, just as realists do not deny the existence of MNCs, NGOs and so forth, structuralists are not oblivious to a world divided into states. Indeed structuralists have attempted to theorise the nature and function of states and other 'actors' in terms of the way they promote certain class interests.

Structuralists have a plan to end injustice. Not necessarily. In fact, a major criticism of some structuralist theories is that whilst they are very good at telling us what is wrong with the world and how this situation came about, they are not very good at telling us what remedial action to take and how the situation is likely to improve.

Structuralism is Marxism. Not so. Although Marx's influence is clear in much structuralist writing you cannot use structuralism and Marxism as if they were entirely synonymous. It is more accurate to say that structuralism is inspired by, or indebted to, Marxism in terms of the way it approaches international relations.

Structuralism is unified. Only in the sense of a concern for the poverty and underdevelopment of the third world. There is, in fact, enormous variety within structuralist literature. Some structural approaches tend to relate to a particular epoch and have been developed for a particular reason (e.g. dependency theory) whereas others, like the work of Wallerstein, are developing in some new and interesting directions, to take account of factors such as the possibility of counter-hegemonic resistance and environmental issues.

Further Reading

NB. The relevant sections of the textbooks outlined in our introduction are probably the best place to start.

Amin, S. (1974), *Accumulation on a World Scale: A Critique of the Theory of Underdevelopment (2 Vols)*, London: Monthly Review Press.
Amin, S. (1990), *Maldevelopment: Anatomy of a Global Failure*, London: Zed Books.

Baran, P. (1957), *The Political Economy of Growth*, New York: Monthly Review Press.

Cardoso, F. and Faletto, E. (1979), *Dependency and Development in LatinAmerica*, Berkeley: University of California Press.
Chase-Dunn, C. (1989), *Global Formation: Structures of the World Economy*, Oxford: Blackwells.

Escobar, A. (1995), *Encountering Development: The Making and Unmaking of the Third World*, Princeton: Princeton University Press.

Frank, A.G. (1979), *Dependent Accumulation and Underdevelopment*, New York: Monthly Review Press.

Galtung, J. (1971), 'A Structural Theory of Imperialism', *The Journal of Peace Research*, Vol. 8, No. 1, pp. 81–117.
George, S. (1994), *A Fate Worse Than Debt*, London: Penguin.

Harris, N. (1990), *The End of the Third World*, London: Penguin.

Kamrava, M. (1993), *Politics and Society in the Third World*, London: Routledge.

Kolko, J. (1988), *Restructuring the World Economy*, London: Random House.

Marx, K. and Engels, F. (1965), *The Communist Manifesto*, New York: Washington Square Press.

McLellan, D. (1977), *Karl Marx: Selected Writings*, Oxford: Oxford University Press.

Mies, M. (1986), *Patriarchy and Accumulation on a World Scale*, London, Zed Books.

Prebisch, R. (1964), *Towards a New Trade Policy for Development*, New York: United Nations.

Rodney, W. (1972), *How Europe Underdeveloped Africa*, London: Bogle l'Ouverture.

Rostow, W.W. (1960), *The Stages of Economic Growth: A Non-Communist Manifesto*, Cambridge: Cambridge University Press.

Said, E. (1993), *Culture and Imperialism*, New York: Knopf.

South Commission (1990), *The Challenge to the South: The Report of the South Commission*, Oxford: Oxford University Press.

Van der Wee, H. (1986), *Prosperity and Upheaval: The World Economy 1945–1980*, London: Viking Books.

Wallerstein, I. (1974, 1980, 1989), *The Modern World-System (Volumes 1 to 3)*, San Diego, CA: Academy Press.

Wilber, C. (ed.) (1973), *The Political Economy of Underdevelopment*, New York: Random House.

CHAPTER 4

Critical Theory

Introduction

Critical theory has become influential in International Relations since the mid-1980s. The label 'critical' is sometimes applied to a number of approaches including feminism and postmodernism, though in this chapter the term 'critical theory' refers specifically to a school of thought which has its intellectual roots in Marxism. Since critical theory and structuralism are both influenced by Marxist thought, you will find some similarities between, for example, critical conceptions of world order and institutions and structuralist accounts outlined in chapter 3. However, critical theory differs in important respects from structuralism and, hence, warrants separate treatment.

As with all 'critical' perspectives, a first encounter with critical theory can be daunting, because it requires us to think deeply about our everyday practices and the relationship between our 'theories' and the way that we act. The central insight of critical theory can, perhaps, be summed up in Karl Marx's famous remark that while 'philosophers have understood the world, the point is to change it'. In simple terms, according to Marx, in all human societies throughout history, there have been rich, powerful people and poor people, who have little control over their lives. Furthermore, in all societies throughout history there have been dominant or ruling ideas or ideologies which have been used to justify this state of affairs. According to Marx, philosophers pondered the purpose of life, but too often have regarded themselves as detached from the preoccupations of everyday existence. Marx, however, believed that it was impossible for intellectuals to be detached or impartial. Philosophies and theories about the world were not based on 'eternal truths', but were reflections of the historical and social conditions prevailing at the time. Intellectuals were involved in the activity of producing knowledge or 'truths' about the world which worked either to support social relationships of dominance or to challenge those of subordination. This included social institutions and practices which created and perpetuated inequalities. In this sense then, knowledge is inherently social and political. Marx expressed moral outrage at the terrible conditions under which many men, women and children were condemned to live. Marx believed that intellectuals should pin their colours to the mast, so to speak, by taking a position on issues of poverty and inequality and by reflecting on how they could help to bring about positive social change.

This notion that there is an intimate connection between theories or ideas and actual social practices is difficult to grasp, so to illustrate this point, we will briefly revisit our earlier discussion of liberalism. Liberals regard the individual as separate from and existing prior to, society. In liberal thought, society is viewed as the product of relationships between individuals which are based on various sorts of voluntary contract such as the marriage contract, the contract between workers and employers and the contract between buyers and sellers in the market place. The economy is thus the product of transactions between individuals made on the basis of choice. Freed from the dictates of traditional duties and obligations, individuals are free to compete in an open and competitive system. In this competition some succeed and others fail, but the outcome is decided by individual skill, aptitude and hard work, and so it is a fair system. It follows from this that the state should, as far as possible, refrain from interfering in society or in economic activity.

What interested Marx was how and why this powerful ideology was taking hold at a time when capitalism was, in fact, creating a grossly unequal society. The emerging new middle class did, indeed, enjoy more freedom, but an increasingly large group of workers were living in poverty and had to sell their labour on a daily basis in order to survive. There seemed to be a contradiction between dominant ideas about the nature of the social and economic system and the actual, or material, conditions of people's lives. From the point of view of the emerging bourgeois class, liberalism did, indeed, seem to describe the reality of their lives. However, if the impoverished working class, or proletariat, were asked to describe the conditions of *their* everyday lives they would be more likely to use terms like, 'oppressive', or 'exploitative' and see themselves as having few choices and little opportunity to exercise any control.

 HISTORICAL BOX

The Condition of Child Labour in Victorian England

Marx wrote much of his best work while living in Victorian England. At this time, it was not uncommon to find children, many as young as five or six years old, working for up to nineteen hours a day and, in consequence, suffering bad health. The following abstract of the evidence of one Samuel Coulson, to the Committee on Factory Children's Labour in 1832, illustrates graphically the harsh conditions of life for thousands of children.

At what time in the morning did those girls go to work? In the brisk time, for about six weeks, they had gone at three o'clock in the morning and ended at ten, or nearly half past ten at night.

What intervals were allowed for rest or refreshment during those nineteen hour of work? Breakfast a quarter of an hour, and dinner half an hour and drinking a quarter of an hour.

Was any of this time taken up in cleaning machinery? They generally had to do what they called 'dry down', sometimes this took the whole of breakfast or drinking and they got their dinner or breakfast as they could.

Had you great difficulty in awakening your children in this excessive labour? Yes, in the early time we had to take them up asleep and shake them, before we could get them off to their work.

Had any of them any accident in consequence of this labour? My eldest daughter caught her forefinger nail and screwed it off below the knuckle, and she was five weeks in Leeds infirmary.

Were her wages paid during that time? As soon as the accident happened, the wages were totally stopped.

(Abstract taken from *The Report of the Committee on Factory Labour in 1832*, reproduced in H. Allsopp, *The Change to Modern England*)

There were then at least two contrasting views of the nature of 'reality', which gave rise to different judgements about the just or unjust nature of the current social and economic order. It followed from this that liberalism did not describe a 'truth' about human nature and society, it merely reflected the point of view of the dominant class. However, liberalism had established itself as a dominant understanding or explanation about the world – a kind of 'common sense' – which in itself was an important factor in consolidating support for the capitalist system.

Clearly, a central concern with inequality and exploitation also informs structuralist thought, so how is critical theory different from 'orthodox' or structuralist variants of Marxist thought such as neo-Marxism and dependency theory? First, while structuralists concentrate on the actual structure and the 'mechanics' of the capitalist system – the processes by which unequal relations between social classes, and indeed, countries are reproduced – critical theorists emphasise much more the importance of culture and ideology in perpetuating certain sorts of social relationships, or conversely, challenging them.

Second, orthodox Marxist thought holds that society can be understood scientifically. This is because the actual processes of exploitation and expropriation in capitalism can be clearly observed and the major inequalities in the distribution of wealth and income which emerge in consequence, can be measured objectively. Moreover, changes in the economic organisation of society are deemed to impel or determine changes in the organisation of societies. For this reason it is possible to understand the dynamic driving historical change and make predictions about what future social and economic order will emerge out of the ashes of the old one. From this perspective, some versions of 'the truth' are better than others, because they are better able to grasp the exploitative nature of capitalism and the forces at work that will eventually lead to its collapse. In contrast, critical theorists hold that *all* knowledge is ideological – intimately connected with social practice and the pursuit of interests. We can only evaluate theories according to how far they capture the mood of the times and the configuration of forces at work in any given society and historical period, and whether they support or challenge the status quo. (However, as we will see, some critical theorists hold that it is possible to establish 'truths' of a kind through the process of inter-subjective dialogue and negotiation aimed at achieving consensus.)

Third, critical theorists argue that our theories about the world and the practices which they support and perpetuate are so intimately connected, that it is meaningless to see theory and practice as distinctive realms of human activity. This notion of the unity between theory and practice – praxis – is difficult to grasp. It expresses the idea that we employ our critical capacities to make sense of our world; on the basis of this 'knowledge' we act, and our actions then have the effect of confirming the 'correctness' of our theory. To borrow an expression from contemporary parlance, we might say we can 'make it happen', providing we have a realistic sense of what is possible in any given circumstance or period of time. At the same time, our action changes existing 'reality' and so has an impact on what we and others come to think of as 'possible'. Contemporary critical theorists believe that social theory – and in this view IR is a kind of social theory – is concerned with understanding the activity of the thinking person, and moments of reflection and self-understanding. The express purpose of critical theory is to further the self-understanding of groups committed to transforming society. Critical theorists have, therefore, reminded scholars that understanding and explaining the international/global domain does not simply involve identifying the structures and processes which will be the object of study, but also reflecting critically upon what can be said to constitute knowledge of the world, and what our knowledge is for. Critical theory is then centrally concerned with human emancipation.

Fourth, critical theorists do not hold such a rigid or deterministic view of the relationship between the economic and social system, or the dynamic of historical change. It may be the case that there is a close fit between economic organisation (capitalism), social relations (the class system) and the kind of political organisation (states) that exists. It is undoubtedly also the case that the broad structure of the economy and the existing class system places important constraints on the degree of change which can be generated by oppositional social groups and through the political process. However, critical theorists view society and the state as having a certain degree of autonomy, reflecting the complex configuration of forces at work in society. Critical theorists believe that while capitalism is an exploitative and oppressive system, it generates certain opportunities for social change that oppositional groups can use to their advantage. So, for example, while critical of the liberal ideology of so called individual freedom and choice, critical theorists, nevertheless, see some value in working for change through the democratic process and certainly in democratic values and practices more broadly defined.

Fifth, some critical theorists recognise that class is not the only form of domination or oppression in capitalist societies. As we will see in chapter 6, some feminists argue that in the eighteenth century, when liberals were celebrating the birth of a new world of freedom, equality and opportunity, women were not allowed to vote and many women were not allowed to own property; they were, in other words, wholly dependent upon men. If we observe societies across the world today, we find that it is not just social class that is a major indicator of social inequality, but also nationality, ethnic origin, race and gender. For this reason, many contemporary critical theorists concentrate on a number of different kinds of social inequality and exclusion. These scholars are sometimes referred to as post-Marxists.

We have already introduced some fairly complex ideas and difficult terminology in this chapter and the foregoing may bear re-reading. Unfortunately this complexity is unavoidable since it is impossible to really grasp the central insights of critical theory unless you have a basic grasp of these key concepts, ideas and terms. However, we will try to simplify the discussion of critical theory somewhat by summarising the main features of a critical perspective thus: (1) the world should be understood primarily in terms of the major economic and social forces generated by capitalism, which are now international or global in scope; (2) states and institutions should be understood primarily in terms of the functions they perform in supporting global capitalism; (3) while a 'real' world exists, our understanding of the world is always mediated though ideas, concepts and theories which are a product of critical thought and reflection; (4) all knowledge is ideological – it is a reflection of the values, ideas and, crucially, interests of particular social groups; (5) culture and ideology are, in themselves, an important and powerful force working to support or challenge the existing economic and social order; (6) international relations (or politics) constitutes a struggle between a variety of social groups and movements – or social forces – some of whom have an interest in supporting the status quo, while others struggle to change it.

Origins

Critical theorists draw upon so called 'early' Marx. For this reason, critical theory is sometimes called open Marxism or Marxist humanism. Contemporary critical theory also owes much to the work of a number of writers in the Frankfurt School tradition, to the Italian communist Antonio Gramsci and the German social theorist Jürgen Habermas.

As we saw in the previous chapter, the later work of Marx was centrally concerned with economic relations and the relationship between the economic 'base' and social and political 'superstructure' of capitalist societies. This has been very important in the development of structuralism. There are, of course, continuities in Marxist thought. Throughout his life, he dedicated his energies to developing an analysis and a critique of capitalism. However, the young or 'early' Marx was particularly interested in how capitalist society affected the human person or subject, particularly problems of human alienation.

Marx believed that people were, by nature, social beings and so needed to live in social groups. Human beings were also creative beings, in the sense that human beings made and used tools which, in turn, helped them to create various artefacts. In a very real sense, human beings created their own social world. Yet, in capitalist societies, human beings seemed to experience a sense of disaffection and remoteness from society because of how it and its methods of production were organised. Marx's theory of human alienation thus suggested that disaffection and a sense of remoteness lay in the particular form of social organisation which existed under capitalism. It also implied that a major purpose of theory was to understand how human beings could overcome such conditions and, in so doing, achieve emancipation.

In capitalist society, the products of human labour – commodities – were no longer produced to satisfy human needs, but were produced in order to be sold on the market at a profit. The profit was kept by the factory owner, who accumulated wealth in this way. Human labour was no longer viewed as something physically and socially necessary for the survival and welfare of the community, but rather as an 'input' into the production process. Under capitalism people no longer owned the means of production, nor the product of their own labour. Labour was rather expropriated – taken – by capitalists, who owned the means of production, paid wages and so claimed ownership of what was produced.

For this reason, society was not experienced as beneficial and necessary to human beings, but as hierarchical and oppressive. The class system was deeply exploitative, allowing some people to benefit by capitalising on others. Marx argued that not only did capitalists own the means of production, but they were also able to rule through the force of ideas or ideology. Marx believed that this was the reason why society and human life were so awful. Human beings had lost their sense of themselves as inherently cooperative beings and experienced a sense of estrangement from others and ultimately themselves.

Marx was not content to merely criticise capitalism, he wanted to see this miserable state of affairs brought to an end. Human nature was not, he argued, immutable. People's characters or personalities – their subjectivity – were created through active engagement in social relationships. Similarly, forms of economic, social and political institutions were the product of such social interaction, established at different periods in history to fulfil certain needs or functions. What we commonly call social 'structures', such as the class system, or institutions like the family, also emerged in particular historical epochs and changed over time. It was, therefore, possible for humankind to be emancipated from repressive social relationships and forms of exploitation. In the early work of Marx, this notion of emancipation was tied to the recovery of one's sense of self, control over one's own life and in enjoying harmonious, fulfilling relationships with others.

CONCEPT BOX

How Do Things Change? The Agent–Structure Debate

The so-called agent–structure debate has been important and contentious in social science. It is not as complicated as it sometimes sounds. Imagine a school. It has procedures and rules. These are the structure. Within this structure teachers and pupils exist and act. Teachers have more power than pupils because of how they relate to the structure (their position in the school – they enforce the rules). Pupils keep within the rules most of the time. However, the rules of the school are not likely to be the same as they were 50 years ago. Circumstances may change rules, and rules might be changed when pupils protest against them, or when they no longer reflect what is happening in society at large. In relation to the school, the agent–structure debate is about whether to look at how the rules (structure) make the pupils act in a certain way or how the actions of pupils are able to shape the rules (do they have agency?), or at least the relationship between these two.

At first sight, there might appear to be an enormous gulf between the school and the capitalist 'world order'. However, the basic idea about structure, agency and the relationship between the two remains the same. Structuralists and critical theorists have rather different views on the relationship between structure and agency. Structuralists regard the overall structure as determining the nature of the 'parts', the implication being that structures determine behaviour. This approach has been described as anti-humanist, because people are portrayed as having little or no ability to change their circumstances. Critical theorists on the other hand, recognise that the opportunities for human intervention or agency are *constrained* by historical circumstance, but are more optimistic about the possibilities of achieving change through political action.

For Marx, it was the job of radical intellectuals (those committed to the cause of human emancipation) to point the way by analysing the nature of social repression – the kinds of structures that existed – and suggesting ways in which social, economic and political systems might be changed (see box above). Marx did not, however, outline any kind of 'blueprint' for a perfect society, or attempt to describe in detail what kind of social order might eventually replace capitalism. Instead, he concentrated on the prospects for change which were emerging in the existing order. That is to say, Marx believed that societies were always to some extent undergoing forms of change and transition. For example, Marx saw in capitalism tendencies which would ultimately bring about the collapse of the system; workers were being herded together into workshops and factories and in this way capitalism was creating the conditions in which they would come to see the basis of their exploitation and alienation and be able to organise collectively to bring about wide-scale social change. If these tendencies were correctly understood, it was possible to intervene and influence, to some extent, the direction of change. Human beings could, then, become conscious agents of social change.

In the twentieth century, the Frankfurt School continued to develop Marx's analysis of capitalism as a social and economic system. Frankfurt School scholars combined Marx's interest in capitalism with processes of rationalisation characteristic of the modern world. (In this respect, Frankfurt School scholars also owed a significant debt to the social theorist Max Weber.) The term 'modern' in this usage, refers to inter-related historical developments such as the secularisation of the political authority in the form of the state, and the development of industrial capitalism. As Marx had observed, modern societies were characterised by a complex division of labour and a high degree of social differentiation. In modern societies, as opposed to traditional societies, people supposedly achieved their social status and were increasingly identified in terms of their occupation. People also increasingly saw themselves as individuals, rather than say members of a particular family, community or religious group. Modernity not only changed the way in which people lived, but also the way in which people thought about themselves and their lives. The modern world was one in which people believed in progress – history was moving forward and they were going somewhere.

It is not surprising then to find that this period of history also produced a prodigious legacy of social and political thought, much of which was universalist, secular and anti-authoritarian, seeing the major sources of social evils in prejudice and intolerance. Enlightenment thinkers concentrated on the possibilities inherent in throwing off the dictates of custom and tradition and organising society in a more rational way, in the interests of human progress and emancipation. In this respect then, Marxism is very much a modern discourse. Indeed, Frankfurt School thinkers recognised that modernity and the Enlightenment represented a major step forward in the development of the human race, because for the first time people were able to imagine the possibility of change and progress and so, potentially, gain some control over their destinies. However, Frankfurt scholars also saw a 'dark side' of modernity. Drawing upon Weber's work, the Frankfurt School developed an analysis of how the growth of large scale economic and commercial enterprises, combined with the increasing reliance upon and deference towards scientific knowledge and technical expertise, was creating a situation in which a sort of 'means–ends' rationality dominated more and more areas of life. That is to say that human knowledge was not being used in ways that advanced the position of human beings generally, but as an instrument of control. In their everyday working lives, busy people were preoccupied with the task in hand, and spent little time reflecting on the ultimate purpose of life, or path to human happiness and satisfaction. In society at large, capitalism manufactured a desire for consumer goods, which meant that people were encouraged to buy into consumerism and seek fulfilment through the ownership of *things*. In such circumstances, the capacity of people to think critically and reflectively was gradually being lost.

As noted above, Marx believed that eventually capitalism would reach a major crisis and collapse. He also believed that the social conditions were emerging which would enable workers to develop consciousness of their exploitation and through the process of revolution take control of their destiny. Frankfurt scholars began writing in the light of one major crisis of capitalism – the worldwide depression of the 1930s. In the 1930s, in some countries, rather than rallying to the socialist cause, the working class had lent their support to right wing popularist, even fascist, movements. In addition, where socialism had triumphed – in the Soviet Union, for example – it had proved to be a travesty of what Marx had envisaged. Rather than realising the conditions for the emancipation of working people, Stalinism was characterised by widespread repression and tyranny. Frankfurt School thinkers were forced to confront these unpleasant realities and to try to explain why working people had failed to revolt against capitalism. In trying to explain the continuation of capitalism despite crisis, Frankfurt School thinkers turned to the crucial role played by the education system and the mass media in consolidating support for capitalism, as well as organisations like the police that were used to forcibly put down strikes or other open displays of revolt against authority and private property. In this way, critical theorists came to understand that while the economic organisation of society was important, other social institutions played a vital role in supporting capitalism. Through the education system and the mass media, for example, people were indoctrinated into accepting 'received truths' about the world which prevented them from understanding the true nature of the exploitation they suffered.

Frankfurt scholars also noted that changes associated with developments of the capitalist economy in the twentieth century had brought about schisms among workers – for example, a gulf between the regularly employed, casual labour and the unemployed. The introduction of labour saving technologies produced mass unemployment in the 1930s, and the lives of the employed were better than those of the unemployed. The unemployed had very little to lose and so were more likely to take risks. However, these groups lacked organisation and consciousness. Class consciousness also diminished as tasks and knowledge became more and more fragmented, because people began to see themselves more in terms of their specialist role or job, rather than as simply 'workers'. Disillusioned with the lack of revolutionary potential of the working class, many Frankfurt School thinkers began to look for other sources of resistance and other possible agents of wide-scale social change. For example, in the post Second World War period there was an explosion of nationalist discontent across areas of the world previously subjected to colonial rule. Later in the 1960s and 1970s, in the wake of a new wave of political radicalism sweeping across the Western world, a number of social movements emerged which organised around everything from ecological issues, racism, human rights violations, civil liberties, sexuality and gender discrimination. Contemporary critical theorists similarly look beyond the industrial working class to the 'counter-hegemonic forces' which frequently take the form of 'new' or 'critical' social movements and who engage in struggles to resist global capitalism and are, as such, potential agents of social change.

Gramsci's work on hegemony has also been very important in critical International Relations theory, particularly in relation to the study of world order and institutions, which will be discussed at greater length below. Gramsci highlighted the central importance of ideology in maintaining class rule and in bringing about social change. Gramsci argued that ruling groups were able to legitimise their rule by persuading people that it was just and fair. He insisted that in order to bring about change, it was necessary to not only win the battle 'on the ground', but also in the realm of ideas. Counter-hegemony involved, therefore, not only social and political struggle against capitalism, but also the development of an alternative set of values, and, crucially, an alternative set of concepts in order to think about and describe the current social 'reality' and possible alternatives.

As we have seen from our brief discussion above, increasingly critical thinkers have become, if not disillusioned, then certainly more circumspect, about the possibility of working class revolution. Moreover, critical theorists have become much more sensitive to the multiple oppression inherent in capitalism. From a critical perspective, capitalism is transforming the world radically, but in the process it is generating major forms of inequality based on class, race and gender. Capitalist enterprises are devouring more and more of the world's precious resources in order to promote mindless consumerism in the name of 'freedom of choice'. Moreover, the search for markets is destroying traditional societies and the way of life of many of the world's peoples.

However, while this more nuanced analysis of the global impact of capital-ism might have more explanatory power, once the analysis of capitalism moves away from a central concern with class, what happens to the project of human emancipation? How can critical theorists develop a conception of a fair and just society, if it is no longer a question of getting rid of inequalities rooted in social class? Who will be the agents of radical change? Moreover, what does it mean to be 'emancipated'? Jürgen Habermas has become an influential figure in critical thought because he seems to have an answer to these questions. In one crucial respect, Habermas's work represents a major departure from Marxist analysis. Habermas argued that hitherto Marxist analysis had failed to pay adequate attention to the central importance of the communication in shaping consciousness and developing understanding of one's self and one's relationship to others. Marx was correct in stressing the inherently social nature of human beings. However, Marx limited himself to analysing the particular kinds of social organisation that existed. The sociability of human beings is, of course, also expressed through language. Habermas argued that the role of language and communication had been neglected in critical thought. According to Habermas, communication – the use of language and the manipula-tion of symbols – allows a sort of collective learning process to take place. Through language and communication, human beings construct inter-subjective know-ledge about the world.

This emphasis on the importance of communication and human under-standing led Habermas to advocate a process of open dialogue and democracy in the interests of furthering human emancipation. Habermas was a very mod-ern thinker in the sense that he valued the modern achievement of being able to criticise, challenge and question authority and existing duties and obligations.

Habermas believed, however, that such criticism was only a prelude to developing a better understanding of what it meant to live in a moral society in which people were treated justly. He argued that the formation of self-understanding, self-identity and moral judgements concerning justice were intimately linked; we became aware of our own self and our own needs and desires by entering into dialogue with others and becoming aware of the needs, interests and desires of others. Habermas also moved away from orthodox Marxist thinking by arguing that social movements promoting feminism or green issues or indigenous peoples also resisted the extension of 'technical' or 'means–ends' rationality into all spheres of social life, promoted alternative values, and so could contribute to an emancipatory politics. However, this emancipatory politics was no longer rooted in the notion of labour free from alienation. Emancipation was about extending the realm of moral understanding and justice in human life. Habermas was committed to the democratic process because it fostered dialogue and this was necessary in order to further develop our moral codes and thinking about justice.

The problem is, of course, that a process of genuine open dialogue is difficult to achieve in a divided society where people have different – even opposing – interests. Habermas recognised this problem, but insisted that it was, nevertheless, an ideal to be striven for. For this reason, much of his early work was concerned with the condition under which it was possible to create an 'ideal speech situation'. In an ideal speech situation, all people would be able to participate in open dialogue, black or white, rich or poor, Christian or Muslim, male or female. In such a situation, people might be encouraged to consider the perspective of the 'other', rather than just their own selfish interest.

Assumptions

From the above we can suggest the following assumptions common to varieties of critical thought.

1. 'Human nature' is not fixed or essential, but shaped by the social conditions that exist at any period in time.

2. Individual people (subjects) can be grouped into identifiable collectivities which might in turn be said to have concrete interests.

3. There are no 'facts' about the world. Our own values influence our interpretations and explanations about the world.

4. Knowledge is intimately connected to a human interest in emancipation.

5. Despite differences – for example, race, ethnicity, gender, class – all human beings share an interest in achieving emancipation. Critical theory is, thus, a universalist doctrine.

Themes

The State and Power

You will recall from chapter 1, that realism takes the nature of state and the state-system as a basic starting point for theorising international relations. In so far as realists are interested in economics, it is only as it affects state behaviour, or constitutes an issue in international politics. From a critical perspective, it makes no sense to treat the state as the basic unit of analysis in international relations, nor does it make sense to separate economics from politics in this way. In the first place, the state is only one form of political organisation to exist among human beings. From a critical perspective, understanding the historical nature of the state and the state-system is crucial, but this historical understanding is lost if we adopt a 'state as actor' approach to international relations.

We suggested above that critical theory is oriented towards the project of human emancipation. It follows from this that when critical theorists engage in the process of thinking about the forms of political, social and economic organisation that exist in the world, they are explicitly seeking to answer the question: How far do existing arrangements constrain or facilitate the project of human emancipation? In relation to the current 'world order', key questions for critical theorists are: What is the state? Why did the state become the dominant form of political organisation globally? What kind of world order might there be in the future? What tendencies can we see in the existing order that point the way to future changes?

Before the world was constituted as a system or society of nation-states, there existed many different forms of political organisation across the world. We have become accustomed to thinking about the state and the state-system as a European invention, but something akin to what we would now recognise as a system of states emerged in Northern Africa between 900 and 1500, closely linked to the expansion of trans-Saharan trade. During roughly the same period, much of the world was divided into large empires, like the Mongol Empire (1206–1405), or the Ottoman Empire (1301–1520). In much of what we now call Western Europe, there existed a system of Feudal Monarchy between 1154 and 1314. What we would now recognise as the modern state system gradually evolved in Northern Europe between 1500 and 1688 and was consolidated by the rise of nationalism in Europe between 1800 and 1914.

At the time that the state-system was emerging, European merchants and traders were embarking on a voyage of 'discovery', seeking out new trading opportunities in the far flung corners of the world. This, in turn, saw the emergence of Spanish and Portuguese colonies in Latin America, parts of India and in South East Asia between 1500 and 1600. Between 1600 and 1713, waves of British, French and Dutch expansion occurred, resulting eventually in the colonisation of territories throughout Africa, the Indian sub-continent, South East Asia and the West Indies. Here the trade in luxury goods like spices was central to the expansion of world trade and the emergence of a new form of political organisation around the world. The industrial revolution only intensified the search for new markets, and generated new forms of political control, as Europe came to dominate much of the globe during the eighteenth and nineteenth centuries. Many former colonies did not achieve formal independence until after the Second World War.

 HISTORICAL BOX

The Trade in Spices

In northern Europe before the invention of winter feed for cattle in the late seventeenth century, many beasts were slaughtered every autumn and the meat was preserved for winter eating, hence the high demand for spices both as a preservative and condiment. Pepper grew in many parts of southern Asia, while cinnamon was found in Ceylon (Sri Lanka) and nutmeg in the Banda Islands. In the sixteenth century, trade in these goods had been organised and shared out among Malay, Indian, Persian, Arab and Portuguese merchants. In the seventeenth century, by a combination of diplomacy and force, the Dutch East India company seized control of the source of many valuable spices and established a virtual monopoly on their trade into Europe. The Dutch East India Company is an early example of a transnational enterprise. (Information from Barraclough, G. (ed.) (1978), *The Times Atlas of World History*, London: Times Books)

We will not labour the historical development of the different kinds of 'world order' here, suffice to say that the state appears to be a particular kind of political organisation, which emerged at a time of early capitalism in Europe and has gradually been adopted all over the world. Regardless of precisely how this relationship is conceived, the close connection between the emergence of the state system and capitalism is central to critical approaches to international relations. The state-system has developed in conjunction with, or alongside, a capitalist world economy and an over-arching culture of modernity. For this reason, from a critical perspective it makes no sense to view economics and politics as distinct realms of human activity – political and economic forms of organisation are intimately connected. Moreover, a critical conception of world order does not begin and end with different types of political organisation. World order also includes economic forms – patterns of trade and commerce and emergent markets – and the particular configuration of social forces – merchants, traders, industrialists and workers – who are all, in some way or other, drawn into this global system.

The state clearly performs a number of roles which are vital for a capitalist economy, including the provision of a system of law to regulate contracts between individuals and companies, and a police force to ensure that society remains orderly. Orthodox Marxists hold that the state mediates conflict resulting from class struggle. In this way, the state legitimises and ensures continuing class rule. The state also maintains conditions conducive to economic growth (capital accumulation in Marxist jargon). While there are some similarities, there are important differences between critical theory and orthodox Marxist views of the nature and role of the state.

First, critical theorists pay much closer attention to the role of ideology in maintaining the rule of dominant groups. The concept of hegemony expresses the idea that dominant groups establish and legitimise their rule through the realm of culture and ideas. That is, hegemony is seen to rest on a broad measure of consent, but, nevertheless, functions according to basic principles that ensure the continuing supremacy of leading social classes, within the state. The stronger the ruling group the less need it has to use force. Hegemony is the outcome of class struggle and serves to legitimise capitalist rule. Gramscians use the term 'hegemonic project' to refer to the way in which classes present their particular interests as the interests of all people – that is, universal interests. In this way, particular classes are able to maintain their power.

Second, hegemony is used in critical theory to describe the dominance of certain major states in the world. Critical theorists argue that while we now live in a state-system in which all members are formally equal, different states perform different functions to facilitate the opening up of global markets and the operations of capitalist enterprises, and have different power and influence. So, for example, in the current world order, the United States of America is the major, hegemonic state which works to ensure that the world is 'made safe for capitalism'.

Third, critical theorists argue that the state does not reflect the interests of dominant social classes in a straightforward way. It certainly plays an important role in supporting an oppressive social order. Gramsci argued that hegemony was exercised by a class via the agency of a party or through the state. Clearly, the historical emergence and evolution of the state and the state-system has worked to ensure that capitalist economic and social relations are fairly securely embedded across the world. However, as noted earlier, contemporary critical theorists regard the state as relatively autonomous. This means that the state reflects both the interests of capital, and also pressures from counter-hegemonic groups.

The degree to which counter-hegemonic groups achieve influence varies over time. In the current period, the globalisation of capital has undermined the autonomy of the state and its ability to meet the demands of its citizens for welfare and economic and social security. The so called 'rolling back of state' which has been a phenomenon across the industrialised world, during global restructuring, must be seen as a means of insulating economic policy from popular pressures, specifically the demands of poor groups. At the same time, trade unions have been weakened and the position of capital in the production process significantly strengthened.

WORLD EXAMPLE

Interest Rates in the UK

One of the first acts of the British Labour Government on assuming power in the summer of 1997 was to hand over the control of interest rates to the Bank of England. Historically, control over interest rates has allowed governments to exercise some influence over other major economic indicators like the rate of inflation. For this reason, it has been considered a vital tool of economic policy for any government seeking to manipulate the economy to achieve certain goals like full employment and the redistribution of wealth through taxation or the provision of welfare goods. In handing over control of interest rates, Chancellor Gordon Brown effectively admitted that government control over the economy was impossible in an age of globalisation, and that henceforth social democratic parties, like the British Labour Party, would have to work with the forces of global capitalism, rather than against them. From a critical perspective, actions like these represent a fundamental shift in the balance of global social forces in favour of capital and against labour. They would probably predict that the likely outcome will be a further decline in wages and working conditions of ordinary people and growing social inequality.

It follows from this discussion of the state-system and world order, that power cannot be understood solely in terms of the military and/or economic might of the state. Clearly, power is exercised directly by states in some situations. In 'making the world safe for capitalism', the United States of America has intervened in conflicts all over the world, in order to try to influence the outcome in ways which favour global capitalism. However, power is also exercised through a range of other social institutions, and works to support a particular kind of social order. The state supports a capitalist order and, in so doing, supports particular kinds of power relations that exist among social groups – the power of business and commerce over workers, the power of multinational corporations over local communities dependent upon the employment it generates, and the power of currency speculators, investors and traders in basic commodities to shape the global economy and the distribution of wealth throughout the world. Power is also exercised more insidiously through the spread of certain ideas and beliefs in society which work to legitimise the existing order.

Institutions and World Order

Unsurprisingly, critical theory has made a major contribution to our understanding of world order and institutions. We have already seen how a critical conception of the state leads to a particular view of the nature of world order. At this point, it is helpful to develop this notion of world order a little further and to attempt to explain how it helps us to understand the role of international institutions such as the International Monetary Fund and World Bank.

As we saw above, in the post Second World War period the state has become 'internationalised' in the sense that it has become the dominant form of political organisation across the world. The state has become internationalised in a second sense; its traditional regulatory functions are now performed by different states and organisations. If we think about the state in terms of what it does, the control and regulation of capitalism, rather than as an entity or 'actor', we see that these functions are now dispersed among different states in the world and among a range of international institutions and regimes.

The Gramscian notion of transnational class alliances and hegemonic domination has been successfully applied to the conception of world order. Critical theorists adapted this idea to suggest that the dominant state in the world order creates order on the basis of ideology. For example, the Bretton Woods System (BWS) which was discussed at greater length in chapter 2, would not have been possible without the support of a hegemonic state – the United States of America. The US played a number of crucial roles in establishing the BWS and making it work effectively. Perhaps most importantly, the US provided vital ideological support for the new world order, arguing that free trade and monetary stability would allow freedom and democracy to flourish throughout the world.

 AUTHOR BOX

Robert Cox (States, Social Forces and World Order)

In 1992, Robert Cox outlined what has become an extremely influential conception of 'states, social forces and world order'. Cox suggested that advances in communications and the globalisation of finance has brought about a radical change in the way production is organised across the globe. In the nineteenth and early twentieth centuries, the production of goods and services was confined to particular countries and products were then traded between countries. However, today the production process is spread across countries. For example, the production of different car components might be spread across a number of countries, and the assembly of these various components to make a car, might take place in another part of the world. This method of production has brought with it a new model of social relations based on a core–periphery structure of production, with a relatively small core of relatively permanent employees, in the North, handling finance, research and development and technological organisation and a periphery consisting of the dependent components of the production process. This has allowed capital to take advantage of a more precariously employed labour force segmented by ethnicity, gender, nationality or religion. To some extent these groups have displaced class as the focus of social struggle, but like the 'old' working class they derive their force from the resentment they feel at the exploitation which they suffer. Disaffected groups must organise transnationally if they are to be an effective oppositional force. However, increasingly, as the economy globalises, major economic classes become organised globally in response, in order to achieve hegemonic domination, while disadvantaged groups are fragmented along the lines of nationality, ethnicity, class and gender.

As is apparent in our earlier discussion, world orders do change, alternative political, economic and social arrangements can and do emerge. Critical theorists are concerned with the nature of such change and the ways in which social forces and social structures enter periods of transition. The existing order is not 'fixed', because social structures comprise institutions, the prevailing socio-economic form of organisation and ideas. Although social action is constrained by structures, these can be transformed by collective action involving leading or subordinate groups in society. Stephen Gill argues that there are new sources of conflict and cleavages that are working their way slowly but surely into the foundations of world politics. Counter-hegemonic forces are challenging pre-vailing institutional and political arrangements. Gill also argues that there is an urgent need for a counter-hegemony based on an alternative set of values, concepts and concerns, coming perhaps from organisations like Amnesty International, Oxfam and Greenpeace. These movements exist within states, but they have grown up in different parts of the world and are transnational in essence. Intel-lectuals also have a role to play in generating change by developing a 'counter-hegemonic' set of concepts and concerns to deal with the problems of militarism and economic and social inequalities.

Identity and Community

So far, in our discussion of themes, we have concentrated on Gramscian critical theory. At this juncture, it is appropriate to consider the ways in which Habermasian ideas have been influential in International Relations. In our above discussion of the state, we tended to concentrate on the roles and functions which it fulfilled for capitalism, but suggested that to some degree the state also reflects the struggle for political influence among oppositional groups. Critical theorists like Linklater are interested particularly in how far the state and the state-system open up or close off possibilities for human emancipation.

Enlightenment thinkers believed that the modern state created the conditions in which it was possible to live under the rule of law and according to principles of justice. Furthermore, people, or at least some people, enjoyed the status of active citizens and played a role in deciding the politics of their country in the public sphere where issues of law, justice and morality were debated openly, rather than as subjects, who simply obeyed the Monarch. In so far as 'emancipa-tion' was closely connected with a sense of autonomy and control over one's life, this was a major step forward for human beings.

The rise of nationalism as a powerful ideology in the eighteenth and nine-teenth centuries, strengthened the claims of the state to be the sole legitimate representative of citizens, in the first place by extending citizenship rights and, secondly, by inculcating a feeling of emotional attachment to the nation-state. As we saw in chapter 1, realists continue to regard the state as the dominant form of community and only significant expression of political identity in the world. In the twentieth century, nationalist sentiment worked to challenge the authority and legitimacy of existing state boundaries. However, radical and secessionist national movements acting under the banner of the rights of people to self-determination, only strengthened the attachment between the individual and the 'national homeland' and thus consolidated, rather than weakened, the state-system. In some respects, the expansion of the state-system can be viewed as a positive development because it extends the principles of self-determination and citizenship to more and more of the world's peoples.

However, at the same time, the nation-state embodies something of a moral contradiction, because it is at once both an inclusionary and exclusionary form of political community. The nation-state is inclusionary, because it is founded on the idea that all citizens are equal. There are certain rights which flow from citizenship and these should be enjoyed by every member of the community. All citizens are, therefore, of equal moral worth. However, the nation-state is by its very nature exclusionary. It discriminates against 'foreigners' on the grounds that they are different. The differences between 'insiders' and 'outsiders' are held to be morally relevant. The bounded community of the nation-state excludes people whose 'difference' is deemed to threaten the state's distinctive identity. International law sets out just what obligations states owe to non-citizens temporarily residing within the boundaries of the state, who, among other things, must be protected from harm; in certain cases states might extend temporary rights of asylum to foreigners who fear persecution in their homeland. Nevertheless, while, say, the British state has a certain obligation to 'foreigners', these are clearly not the same as or equal to the obligations owed to 'nationals'. Moreover, the boundaries of the communities are constantly being policed to ensure against 'invasion' from outsiders, so much so that we regard 'foreigners' as a threat to the extent that we can even debate the morality of the use of nuclear weapons to deter outsiders from encroaching on our 'space'.

The emancipatory project at the heart of critical theory necessarily raises questions about the limits of political community, how boundaries between self and other are constructed and the moral implications of this. Linklater is also interested in how the boundaries of community change over time. So, for example, historically certain groups, like women and working class men, have been denied citizenship on the grounds that they are 'different' – less rational and not up to the demands of active citizenship. Women, for example, were held to be in need of strong moral guidance from their menfolk. Of course, working class men and women have made great strides in overcoming such prejudices against them and now enjoy rights of citizenship in most states around the world, although as we will see in chapter 6, significant forms of discrimination still exist.

Since the UN was established in 1945, there has been a gradual development of human rights law which recognises the equal moral worth of every human being. The widespread commitment to respect human rights seems to suggest that there exists amongst humankind a moral conviction that all individuals belong not only to sovereign states, but to a more inclusive community of humankind even if, in practice, this has been denied to some groups. Arguably, we might now be witnessing the eclipse of the sovereign state-system in favour of more cosmopolitan forms of identity and community. As is evident from our earlier discussion of world order and the increasingly globalised nature of social relations, expressions of loyalty and solidarity can be both sub-state and transnational. Social movements give expression to, or reflect, the plural forms of identity, loyalty and solidarity. These groups express commitment to various 'communities' and, increasingly, these are transnational in nature.

AUTHOR BOX

Andrew Linklater and the Transformation of Political Community

New forms of political identification and expressions of transnational 'community', have prompted critical theorists to pose questions about the extent to which human beings owe obligations to the people of the world rather than simply fellow citizens. Andrew Linklater argues that critical theorists remain committed to the creation of 'the good society' which is not limited to the nation-state. His point of departure is the need for a return to the classical understanding of politics as orientated towards the emancipation of people. The first stage in this project is understanding the way people learn how to include and exclude those deemed to be 'different' and so excluded from the moral community. This necessarily involves moving beyond a conventional Marxist concern with social class to consider how people of different races, ethnic backgrounds and gender have been or continue to be discriminated against.

As well as understanding the dynamics of social exclusion, however, it is also important to recognise the way in which those practices are being challenged, by groups involved in both national and transnational political action. Moreover, there are many arenas in which people have expressed significant political commitment, and in which people think about and debate moral and political issues. Drawing upon Habermasian ideas about the importance of communication and dialogue in achieving an emancipatory politics, Linklater highlights the multiple 'public spheres' in which these kinds of debates take place. He claims that political communities are already being transformed by, for example, struggles over equality, rights, claims to resources and notions of obligations to others, and how they might change more radically in the future.

Inequality and Justice

While there are variations and nuances within different strands of critical theory, all critical theorists share a fundamental commitment to human equality. In contemporary critical theory, other forms of inequality and discrimination, such as sexism and racism, and the denial of human rights to some groups, are also recognised as highly significant. However, once the multiple sources of oppression are recognised, it raises the question of how can a more equal and just world be realised?

Critical theorists are sceptical of liberal schemes because these grant formal equality to people, but also sanction a social and economic order that generates great inequalities in wealth and power. However, they also recognise that while experiments in state socialism have been partially successful in creating a more equal society, this has often been at the cost of widespread oppression and tyranny. The great challenge for critical theorists is to realise an emancipatory politics, which is socially inclusive and democratic. In a world divided along lines of nationality, ethnicity, religion, culture, class, sexuality and gender, how can such a project be realised?

There have been a number of responses to this question. One response is to insist that inequalities and oppression based on social class remain more fundamental or more significant than any other kind. The gist of this position is that while in today's world there are many voices clamouring to be heard, it is the world's poor who are truly marginalised and invisible. A second response has been to draw upon Habermas's notion of dialogic politics, which appears to meet the needs of a world in which the nation-state remains significant, but which is no longer the only site in which debates about equality and justice are taking place, and a time when liberal and/or Western visions of equality and justice have been subject to criticism.

It is recognised that it might not always be possible to reach agreement, especially in situations where societies have radically different forms of government and cultural preferences. Dialogue does not necessarily have to reach consensus. The primary function of global communities of discourse, according to Linklater, is to reflect the heterogeneous quality of international society. However, the commitment to dialogue requires efforts to build wider communication channels. The universal communication community may be unobtainable, but it remains the ultimate standard of social criticism to which we should aspire.

Conflict and Violence

From this perspective, human conflict is not rooted in the problem of anarchy *per se*, but in the nature of global capitalism. The Gramscian variant of critical theory accepts, with some qualifications and modifications, the more orthodox Marxist view that major wars this century have been caused by the search for raw materials and resources and the forcible opening up of large areas of the world to capitalist expansion. On the other hand, many struggles for 'national' liberation have come about in response to forms of colonial or imperialist domination. Capitalism, by its very nature, generates conflict and violence.

A second variant of critical theory, influenced by Habermas has taken the notion of inter-subjectivity, dialogue and negotiation as a starting point for understanding how peaceful change can be promoted. In this way, critical theorists have made some contribution to our understanding of conflict resolution.

Peace and Security

As is evident from our brief discussion of the role of the United States since the Second World War, critical theorists are highly critical of realist and liberal notions of peace and security and how this state might be achieved. International institutions largely reflect the interests of hegemonic states who act to ensure that world markets remain stable, contracts are honoured and open revolt is suppressed. For critical theorists, genuine peace and security will only be achieved when the major contradictions of capitalism which generate economic crisis and instability are overcome, when people are no longer treated as the means (labour) to an end (production for profit) in a thoroughly exploitative and alienating system, and when the earth's resources are no longer squandered recklessly to satisfy the wants, rather than needs, of consumers. Some strands of critical theory inform the developing school of critical security studies within International Relations.

Summary

1. Critical theory was not developed in International Relations but became influential in IR from the 1980s onwards.

2. Like structuralism, critical theory is influenced by Marxism, though more by the early 'humanistic' Marx, in contrast to structuralism which takes more inspiration from later 'economistic' and 'scientific' Marxism.

3. Critical theorists see an intimate relationship between theory and practice.

4. Critical theorists hold that knowledge is ideology, not truth, although some believe that it is possible to negotiate or agree upon propositions.

5. As well as roots in Marx, critical theory has also evolved from the ideas of the Frankfurt School (particularly Jürgen Habermas) and Italian Marxist Antonio Gramsci.

6. Critical theory is very much a 'modern' project, because it aims to further human emancipation. However, critical theory acknowledges and seeks to overcome the 'dark side of modernity'.

7. Many critical theorists recognise that class-based oppression is not the only form inherent in capitalist societies. Other oppressions include those on the basis of ethnicity, gender, nationality and so on.

8. Contemporary critical theorists see 'counter-hegemonic' forces (struggles to resist global capitalism) in terms of new social movements (women, environment for example) and look beyond the industrial working class for potential agents of social change.

9. Critical theory makes us aware of the historically contingent nature of certain features of human life and reminds us, therefore, that international relations are not fixed or immutable.

10. Critical theory makes claims in the name of all of humankind – it is universalistic. For this reason, it questions forms of exclusion or discrimination which make distinctions between different groups of people. This necessarily raises questions about how we define ourselves, and how we distinguish ourselves from others, leading to consideration of how boundaries between communities are drawn and the consequences of this.

Criticisms

There are a number of criticisms that have been levelled at critical theory. In this section, we will briefly outline some of the most important of these. One criticism of Gramscian critical theory is that it concentrates too much on the significance of social class and class relationships and, in consequence, is blind to other forms of inequality and exclusion. As we have seen, this criticism is not entirely justified as many critical theorists do recognise the significance of gender inequalities or that people can be discriminated against, excluded or somehow treated differently according to their sexuality, race or ethnic origins. However, it is fair to say that there is a tendency among Gramscians to continue to concentrate on (or privilege) social class in their empirical work.

A related criticism is that critical theorists also privilege class in their conception of 'interests'. We might regard ourselves as having concrete interests which derive from our gender or nationality. Moreover, our notion of where our interests lie might also change significantly over time. Even within capital, there might be different interests depending on whether the capitalist is an industrialist or involved in commerce and this undermines to some extent the notion of transnational class alliances.

In relation to critical theory inspired by Habermas, critics have argued that the 'dialogic' model is flawed because access – the ability to have one's voice heard – is inevitably restricted by existing inequalities. It is impossible to establish an 'ideal speech situation'. By and large, the poor, those with little education or access to technology, are likely to be seriously under-represented. A related criticism is that the dialogic model of politics fails to take into account the fragility of a moral point of view in a world characterised by massive inequalities. That is to say that the powerful are unlikely to concede their advantage, under critical review, even if 'justice' demands a redistribution of resources and wealth.

Finally, the universalistic aspirations of critical theory have been challenged. For example, postmodernists argue that it is impossible to establish what *is* morally right or just, even through the process of inter-subjective dialogue, because there is no agreement about these issues across cultures. The most likely result of a (critical) project of this kind would, then, be a profoundly

Western, middle-class and gendered conception of a 'good society', masquerading as a 'universal' point of view.

Common Misunderstandings

Critical theorists are so called because they criticise other perspectives like liberalism or realism. No. It is certainly the case that critique and criticism is an important aspect of critical theory. It is only through critique and criticism that the interested, partial and ideological nature of knowledge claims can be exposed. However, critical theorists are also interested in going beyond criticism, and so concentrate mainly on how theory can be used to inform an emancipatory project.

Critical theory is the same as postmodernism. No. As you will see in the following chapter, postmodernism and critical theory are different in many important respects. However, confusion arises because the term 'critical theory' is sometimes used in a generic sense to describe a number of postpositivist approaches including the Frankfurt School, postmodernism, feminism and even Green Thought.

Critical theorists believe that the collapse of capitalism and worldwide socialism is inevitable. No. While this view of history is found in much orthodox, or scientific Marxist thought (see preceding chapter), critical theorists argue that economic, social and political change is something which must be struggled for. A much greater emphasis is placed, therefore, on the need for human intervention – agency – and political struggle, in bringing about change.

Critical theorists argue that there is no 'real world'. No. In contrast to postmodernists (see following chapter), critical theorists emphasise the existence of real material structures and power relations. However, critical theorists contend that our understanding of the nature of this reality is always mediated through ideas and concepts, which are in turn related to concrete interests.

Critical theorists hold that social class is the only significant division which exists in human society. Not quite. Certainly, critical theorists are interested in class divisions and social inequalities rooted in social class. Some might even believe that these are indeed of major significance. However, most critical theorists now accept that there are many forms of social inequality and many forms of oppression, discrimination and social exclusion.

Further Reading

Brown, C. (1992), *International Relations Theory: New Normative Approaches*, Harlow: Prentice Hall.

Cox, R. (1986), 'States, Social Forces and World Order', in Keohane, R. (ed.), *Neo-Realism and Its Critics*, Princeton: Princeton University Press.

Cox, R. (1987), *Production, Power and World Order: Social Forces in the Making of History*, New York: Columbia University Press.

Devetak, R. (1996), 'Critical Theory', in Burchill, S. and Linklater, A. (eds), *Theories of International Relations*, Basingstoke: Macmillan.

Gill, S. (ed.) (1993), *Gramsci, Historical Materialism and International Relations*, Cambridge: Cambridge University Press.

Gill, S. and Law, D. (1988), *The Global Political Economy: Perspectives, Problems and Policies*, Harlow: Prentice Hall.

Gramsci, A. (1971), *Selections from Prison Notebooks*, London: Lawrence and Wishart.

Habermas, J. (1972), *Knowledge and Human Interests*, London: Heinemann.

Held, D. (1990), *Introduction to Critical Theory: Horkheimer to Habermas*, Cambridge: Polity Press.

Hoffman, M. (1987), 'Critical Theory and the Inter-paradigm Debate', *Millennium: Journal of International Studies*, Vol. 16, No. 2.

Hoffman, M. (1988), 'Conversations on Critical International Relations Theory', *Millennium: Journal of International Studies*, Vol. 17, No. 1.

Horkheimer, M. (1972), *Critical Theory: Selected Essays*, New York: Seabury Press.

Linklater, A. (1988), *The Transformation of Political Community*, Oxford: Polity Press.

Linklater, A. (1990), *Beyond Realism and Marxism: Critical Theory and International Relations*, London: Macmillan.

Linklater, A. (1996), 'The Achievements of Critical Theory', in Booth, K. and Zalewski, M. (eds), *International Theory: Positivism and Beyond*, Cambridge: Cambridge University Press.

CHAPTER 5

Postmodernism

Introduction

The student engaging with postmodern thought for the first time encounters a number of difficulties. First, the very term 'postmodern' creates some confusion. It is often wrongly assumed that postmodernity refers to a period in history which succeeds modernity. This misunderstanding is compounded by the fact that many postmodern thinkers are particularly concerned with the nature of late modern or post-industrial societies. Second, postmodernism is very different, and challenges, or subverts, many of the ideas central to International Relations theory. Relatedly, a third difficulty lies in the complexity of the work itself. The student needs a fairly sophisticated understanding of the political institutions, forms of social organisation and social practices associated with modernity, and the philosophical underpinnings of modern social and political thought, in order to fully appreciate postmodern critiques of IR. Finally, there is a question of definition. What *is* postmodernism? Is postmodernism the same as critical theory? Is postmodernism synonymous with poststructuralism? Do these scholars share a distinctive approach to the study of world politics? The problem, as we shall see, is that a simple definition of postmodernism is not possible.

A good starting point for understanding the origins of postmodernism is the wave of political radicalism which swept across the Western world in the late 1960s. Just as post-Marxist critical theory (see chapter 4) was born of the politics of the New Left, the origins of postmodernism can be seen in the identification with a range of disaffected groups such as student protesters, feminists, environmentalists and the gay liberationists. While advocating political radicalism, many on the Left were dissatisfied with the continuing emphasis on the importance of social class in left-wing political movements. They believed that this emphasis neglected other issues such as racial or gender discrimination. As we will see in the following chapter, during this period feminists were drawing attention to the repressiveness of social relations previously dismissed as 'private'. It was also a time of nationalist struggles against colonial and imperialist domination, with people in many parts of Asia, Latin America and Africa demanding the right to self-determination in the name of 'the people', while minorities in Western countries were documenting the ways in which they suffered forms of discrimination or exclusion from the mainstream of society.

Moreover, there were very real dangers in attempting to understand the politics of feminism, for example, or new social movements like the Greens, through the lens of class or class struggle. Oppositional or radical politics involved often novel forms of resistance to myriad practices of domination and exclusion. As we saw in chapter 4, the experience of widespread persecution and political violence in the Soviet Union had generated scepticism towards the promise of Marxism, even amongst those committed to the cause of human emancipation. In attempting to understand social inequality, Marxists had pointed to the divisiveness and exploitative nature of capitalism, and offered up a vision of a socialist society as a panacea for contemporary ills. Many of

HISTORICAL BOX

Enemies of the People

When the Bolsheviks seized power in Russia in 1917, they promised to create an equal society across the territory they controlled, where people were free from want. They also hoped to provide the inspiration and leadership for oppressed peoples across the world. In a few years, that vision had degenerated into a nightmare. Under the rule of Stalin, the Soviet Union became a land of forced industrialisation and forced collectivisation of agriculture. The latter process saw peasants driven from the land or starved into submission. During the same period, religious groups were persecuted for their beliefs and ethnic minorities often treated with suspicion. One of the main pillars of the system of terror and control created by Stalin was a system of forced labour camps made famous in the work of Alexander Solzhenitzyn. At the height of Stalin's reign of terror, some eight million people were held in captivity. Often the captives were intellectuals – writers, scientists, artists and teachers. Each and every one had been labelled a 'counter-revolutionary' or 'enemy of the people' for daring to speak out against communism, or in many cases, for much less (for suggesting that there were problems or shortcomings in this particular manifestation of a socialist society or merely because someone had denounced them). Of course, we cannot blame Marx for deeds perpetrated in his name. Nor can we conclude that this particular experiment in collective ownership 'proves' that communism does not work. However, postmodernists claim that the experience of the Soviet Union during Stalin's reign of terror is a powerful illustration of the uses and abuses of power justified in the name of grand, all-encompassing doctrines like Marxism. Postmodernists are not just suspicious of Marxism, but are wary of all universalist visions which claim to have uncovered the causes, consequences and solutions to human misery and offer a blueprint for a better world. Inevitably, reducing the source of all our ills to a single cause disguises the complex and varied ways in which power operates throughout society and the many different forms of inequality and discrimination that exist. Moreover, such doctrines provide a powerful justification and legitimation for a system of rule in which opposition is suppressed in the name of 'progress' or 'emancipation' and which frequently works to perpetuate the position of a self-interested élite.

the Left began to argue that in their attempt to generate the impetus to widespread social change, Marxists had 'universalised' the conditions of human emancipation, at the cost of marginalising and silencing large numbers of groups and peoples.

Having situated postmodernism broadly on the left of the political spectrum, you should be aware that postmodernism has been described as profoundly conservative. This implied criticism of postmodernism is often unjustified. However, it is not easy to make sense of postmodernism in terms of simple dichotomies like left/right or radical/conservative. This is yet another difficulty that the student must negotiate!

Finally, given that postmodernists express such incredulity towards 'metanarratives' like Marxism – that is to say, that postmodern thinkers have difficulty believing all-encompassing theories or explanations – it would be somewhat surprising to find postmodernists subscribing to a coherent, comprehensive world view or grand vision of international relations. Rather than sketch out a perspective on international relations, therefore, postmodernists prefer to engage in a critique of such projects and concentrate instead on what is different, unique and seemingly defies grandiose forms of theorising. On the other hand, postmodern thinkers welcome the proliferation of perspectives and approaches in IR during the past two decades. Far from seeing this as a weakening or undermining of IR as a distinctive 'discipline', postmodern thinkers argue that scepticism and uncertainty combined with a plurality of world views, visions and voices, is an appropriate response to a highly complex world.

CONCEPT BOX

The Purpose of Critique

Through the critical analysis or investigation of a text or writing, it is possible to draw out the hidden assumptions which underpin attempts to understand or explain certain events. The function of critique is to demonstrate how theories which profess to be based upon universal categories or basic 'truths' about the human condition, inevitably produce a partial or distorted view.

Let's take the example of realism. Realists claim that states, like 'men', are self-interested 'actors'. Moreover, the international realm is like a 'state of nature'. Therefore, states must always look to their own security and act prudentially, which means safeguarding the 'national interest'. In this way, realism makes certain claims about what can be said to exist – what is 'real' or tangible – a system of states, a precarious or stable 'balance of power', genuine threats to security, concrete national interests and so forth. Realists also claim to 'know' something about this world. This knowledge is based on a mixture of age old 'truths' about the human condition which philosophers have recorded, historical analysis (the preponderance of wars, perhaps, or shifts in the balance of power) and empirical observation (we can see people and states behaving like this on a daily basis).

However, if we unpack, or deconstruct each of these assumptions, we find that they are all problematical. For example, states are 'real' in the sense that they are constituted by a territory, government, a people and sovereign jurisdiction recognised by international law.

CONCEPT BOX (continued)

However, the state is not 'real' in the sense of being a unified 'actor' with a concrete identity or single purpose. The state is made up of an array of institutions and bodies, and within those institutions there are very many decision makers. Moreover, within that given territory there might well be numerous groups and individuals who have access to power, or, conversely, are without influence. In order to make the notion of the state as a unified, coherent actor 'real', realists resort to claims about the selfish nature of 'man', but this view is surely coloured by how 'human nature' has been understood in certain cultures and perhaps in different periods of time. For example, some feminists argue that the kind of behaviour realists ascribe to the state as 'man writ large' – aggressive, dominating – is commonly associated with male, and not female, 'nature'.

The notion of threats, danger and an international state of nature is constructed by drawing upon powerful images of anarchy, and metaphors which present the natural world as hostile and disorderly. Insecurity arises from a fear of not being in command or able to control our environment, and in which the body politic is, consequently, in constant danger of being overwhelmed, invaded or otherwise violated. This analogy of international relations as a 'state of nature' is based on a distinctly modern view of our relationship to nature (see chapter 7 for a fuller discussion of this point). While some might argue that the individualism inherent in realism – isolated, bounded, autonomous states – constitutes a rather strange understanding of how people (or, indeed, states) form relationships with others and how they behave towards others. Furthermore, we need only recall our earlier discussion of liberal pluralism or structuralism or critical theory to realise that the nature of world order is disputed – there are many views of what can be said to exist 'really'. Also, the concept of 'national interest' is difficult to pin down. Liberal pluralists, for example, claim that there are always competing visions of what is in the 'interest' of the people or nation, while structuralists argue that the state reflects the interests of élite classes.

We will return to this idea of critique later in the chapter. At this stage, it suffices to say that postmodern critique aims to show how, in this case realism, offers at best a partial view of international relations. At worst, we could say that the claims that it makes about the world are based on the world view of powerful men in the West at a particular period in history and are both distorting and exclusionary.

This is not to say that postmodern scholars simply reject everything as bias, perverse or a reflection of the perspective of the powerful. Postmodernists are not necessarily cynics or nihilists. They are no different from people in general, in that they have certain values and may subscribe to a particular ethical or moral code. However, postmodernists are different from, say, liberals or critical theorists, because they are more willing to admit that ultimately there might not be any solid grounds, or ultimate source of appeal, on which to establish the 'rightness' or 'wrongness' of particular value systems, beliefs, or world views. They certainly do not claim to have an insight into the 'truth' about the human condition, or the inherent virtue or wickedness of a particular action or event.

But we are running ahead of ourselves here. We will return to the postmodern critique of established perspectives or 'stories' of IR and their celebration of value pluralism and multiplicity later. As we continue, if the language is difficult, you will find a fuller discussion of many key terms in the glossary. First though, while recognising that it is difficult to present this collection of approaches, authors and topics as a coherent theoretical perspective, we will endeavour to make good our promise to make the complex accessible. It is no easy task to sum up the essence of postmodernism. Scholars are themselves reluctant to accept pigeon-holing and labelling. Moreover, there is a great deal of diversity in the work of those scholars frequently identified with a postmodern approach. Nevertheless, we will attempt to identify some of the core themes which reoccur in the postmodern IR literature.

From a postmodern perspective, the study of world politics, a term preferred to International Relations for reasons which are elaborated on below: (1) incorporates the study of a wide range of processes, issues and groups; (2) investigates the ways in which power operates in the discourses and practices of world politics; (3) maps the many and varied ways that political space is constructed and utilised by individuals and groups; (4) unpacks the complex processes involved in the construction of political identities; (5) celebrates differences and diversity among people and across cultures; (6) encourages a proliferation of approaches and world views, because this has the effect of displacing or undermining 'orthodox' or hegemonic forms of knowledge and power; and (7) highlights issues or concerns frequently dismissed as trivial or insignificant in order to give a voice to, or empower, people and groups who have been marginalised in the study of IR.

Origins

The body of work labelled 'postmodern' has made an important contribution to the study of International Relations since the early 1980s. However, the intellectual origins of postmodernism are thought to go back much further. A diverse array of thinkers have influenced and inspired contemporary postmodern scholars. In this section we will concentrate on the ideas of just four – Nietzsche, Heidegger, Foucault and Derrida; we will draw out some core themes from this body of work and, where appropriate, make specific references.

It is helpful to think of postmodernism in terms of a critique of modernity and the Enlightenment project. The German philosopher Martin Heidegger developed a critique of the Enlightenment which finds echoes in much contemporary postmodern thought. We will not outline Heidegger's ideas in detail here, but rather the general outline of such postmodern critique.

Surely, one might think, modernity and the Enlightenment are built on a vision of hope for the future of the human race, so why do postmodernists subject these ideas to such intense criticism? In part, this criticism of the Enlightenment project is a consequence of the rise of fascism in the 1930s which plunged Europe into a new 'dark age' characterised by war, destruction

CONCEPT BOX

Modernity and the Enlightenment Project

The term 'modernity' is used to refer to two related processes. First, to institutional trans-formations that have their origins in the West. Second, to a fundamental transformation in political and social thought which occurred with the emergence of modern science. The Enlightenment refers to a period of European history, from the seventeenth to the nineteenth century, during which time tradition and religious doctrine were challenged by the rise of modern science and certain 'enlightened' or progressive views of humankind's capacity for reasoned thought and moral development. Enlightenment thinkers were com-mitted to scientific, logical and rational forms of knowledge. This manifested itself in a scep-ticism towards traditional forms of authority.

Together, these developments gave rise to the 'Enlightenment Project' of human progress and emancipation. The development of modern industrial capitalism allowed for a more rational organisation of society, while modern science held out the promise of a 'science of society', which would lead to the discovery of 'laws' which governed the social world. This kind of thinking implicitly challenged the idea that the existing social and political world reflected a unified moral order ordained by God. However, Enlightenment thinkers were convinced that the steady growth of human reason and the gradual elimination of ignorance and sus-picion would culminate in the moral and political unification of humankind. This Enlighten-ment project rested on a belief in the possibility of discovering universal 'truths'.

For this reason, universalist doctrines, like liberalism or Marxism, hold that it is unfounded to draw boundaries of, say, human rights, or human dignity and respect any narrower than around the whole human race. Therefore, they protest against needless human suffering wherever and whenever it is manifest. So, Enlightenment thinkers challenge practices of oppression inflicted on people in the name of larger orders or a 'common good' – whether it be family honour, or the glorification of God, or the nation or the leader. This is entirely consistent with the rejection of doctrines like the 'divine right of kings' or a heroic view of great warriors, which clearly places greater importance or value on people who embody special qualities which set them apart from the rest of us. Instead history (social change) is driven by the trajectory of the societies in which we live and possibilities which they allow for producing social change and human progress.

One of the most powerful ideas in Enlightenment thinking is that ordinary, everyday life has intrinsic value. For this reason, Enlightenment thought is sometimes referred to as 'human-ism'. You will no doubt recognise these ideas as central to liberalism. The modern person, or subject, is worthy of respect. This gives rise to the liberal notion of the moral autonomy of each individual and the idea that the person possesses certain inalienable rights. It is because people understand rational principles that it is possible to organise society on a rational basis and according to the rule of law. However, structuralism and critical theory also emphasise the dignity and moral worth of ordinary human life. In orthodox Marxism this modern, Enlightenment, view of man as the measure of all things is expressed through a belief in the dignity of work. Indeed, the common working man is no insignificant minion destined to toil, but rather the central actor in a great drama – the unfolding of history and human destiny. As will we see in later chapters, some strands of feminism and 'green thinking' subscribe to an essentially Enlightenment view of progress and emancipation.

stupid.

and horrifying acts of cruelty and barbarism. The experience of a modern nation seemingly submitting willingly to the iron will of the Führer in the interests of the glorification of the Aryan race, wartime atrocities such as those perpetuated at Kerch in the Crimea and the Nazi death camps at Auschwitz and Belzec, seemed to defy the idea of history as progress and cast doubt on the West's claims to be advanced and civilised. In more recent years, the spectre of nuclear war, environmental degradation, and widespread feelings of alienation and hopelessness, which seem to be endemic to advanced capitalist societies have added further to the criticism of the West as a bastion of progress.

HISTORICAL BOX

The Final Solution

The most obvious manifestation of Hitler's fanatical hatred of Jewish people was his determination to exclude them from every area of German society and every aspect of everyday life. At first, this policy took the form of 'voluntary' emigration or forced expulsion. However, as Nazi forces occupied more and more of mainland Europe, Jews had fewer means of escape from persecution and fewer places to hide. A few weeks after the German occupation of Poland in September 1939, Reinhard Heydrich, the head of the Third Reich central security services, issued an instruction that Jews were to be grouped together 'as a means to the final end'. The 'final end' or 'final solution' was the mass extermination of the Jewish people. Initially herded together and held captive in ghettos across Europe, the Jews were transported to camps deep within the occupied territories. Here millions of people died as a result of torture, hard labour or starvation, or by asphyxiation through gassing.

You might object that, however terrible, the experience of Nazi fanaticism and the spectre of concentration camps is an aberration in European history and so cannot be taken as evidence of the bankruptcy of the Enlightenment project. Moreover, is not fascism a rejection of everything the Enlightenment holds dear, the intrinsic value of the human person and moral dignity? This would certainly be one interpretation of events. However, postmodernists hold that far from being a deviation, the final solution is the logical consequence of trends set in motion by modernity – the rational organisation of society, the prevalence of 'means–ends' instrumentalism, the existence of social hierarchies and chains of command, the means to transport people across vast territories, and the factories of death in which people were systematically killed and their remains efficiently disposed of. From this perspective, the Nazis saw the final solution merely as a technical problem and industry and the rational organisation of society allowed a technical solution.

You will recall, no doubt, that this stark realisation of a 'dark side of modernity' was also central to the 'critical turn' in Marxism in the 1930s, which gave birth to the Frankfurt School. Frankfurt School scholars understood the danger of an all pervasive technical, means–end rationality. It was necessary, therefore, to return to the vision at the heart of the Enlightenment – human emancipation – and reflect critically on how current conditions facilitated or threatened the realisation of this vision. Critical theorists believe that it is still possible to salvage an emancipatory project through a reformulation of

Marxism. Greens also have much to say about human faith in the possibility of technical solutions (chapter 7).

So, what is different about postmodernism? Postmodern thinkers are profoundly sceptical of any such scheme. Moreover, postmodern thinkers have argued that all attempts to establish the universal conditions for human freedom and emancipation will inevitably be used in practice to subordinate and marginalise those who are deemed 'different'. This is because, as Foucault held, power/knowledge relations, which we discuss in greater detail below, are always at work in social relationships. To illustrate this point, postmodernists point to the ways in which liberal ideas about rationality, civilisation and progress have also been used historically to divide up and categorise the world's people as 'advanced' or 'backward', 'civilised' or 'barbarian' according to what were actually European (or Western) social, political and cultural values. They pointed out that the Enlightenment period was accompanied by the widespread oppression of many peoples in the cause of spreading the benefits of civilisation.

 HISTORICAL BOX

The White Man's Burden

An obvious manifestation of the European sense of superiority which accompanied colonial expansionism in the nineteenth century, is the powerful image of the 'dark continent' of Africa and the necessity of taking on the great burden of leading these strange, exotic people out of barbarism and into a civilised future. The struggle for Africa and the subordination of many peoples to colonial rule was made possible by the great advances in technology, which allowed organised political action, the manufacture of guns, the technology to transport goods and people across the world, and was a powerful discourse which justified such actions in the name of human progress. In more recent years, the discourse of modernity has been used by Western élites to justify modernisation projects which seek to rebuild the so-called 'third world' in the image of the West. In contemporary parlance, the term 'modernisation' is broadly understood as the transition from simple, homogeneous societies to complex, highly differentiated, advanced ones. In reality, 'developing states' in the so called third world, have been subjected to forms of Western colonial and neo-colonial domination and now many years later are no closer to 'catching up' with the West.

The implication of the critique of the Enlightenment developed by Heidegger and others, was that while the Enlightenment has been presented as a period in which mankind has been liberated from ignorance, the discourse of rationalism characteristic of the 'modern' age has been imbued with bias. Postmodern thinkers argue that there are varied forms of social organisation and many different kinds of cultural practice. These are not inherently 'good' or 'bad', 'progressive' or 'backward', though they are often adjudged as such by reference to some supposedly superior model – the Western world. Similarly, the model of the rational subject, held to be a universal characteristic of 'man', actually described a particular kind of view of human 'nature', or subjectivity, which was European, bourgeois and masculine – the new élite which emerged from the ashes of feudal society. Any manifestation of human life and being which seemingly confounded this view, has immediately been labelled as alien, ignorant and, more importantly, threatening.

Postmodern thinkers have drawn heavily upon the work of the French philosopher Michel Foucault. Foucault's work is extensive, so here we will concentrate on just a few central ideas – Foucault's view of the power/knowledge relationship, his ideas about discourse, and his conception of the human person, or subject. Following Nietzsche, Foucault developed the idea that power produces knowledge. What this means is that there are no undisputed 'truths' about human 'nature' or human life. Everything that we think we 'know' for sure is merely an expression of dominant modes of thought or explanation. We 'know' because we believe these things to be true. We believe these things to be true because we are taught in schools, or told by scientists, technical 'experts', bureaucrats and policy-making élites. Since societies are always organised on the basis of hierarchy and inequality, we cannot accept that what passes as 'knowledge' is disinterested and impartial. The most powerful people in society are in a much better position to have their views accepted as 'truth', and are able to dismiss or trivialise alternative views. Indeed, the very fact that we usually make a distinction between canons of 'knowledge' taught to us in schools and universities and myths, stories, narratives and the kind of 'common sense' which is passed down in families and local communities, is itself a consequence of modernity and the Enlightenment. The rejection of tradition, myth and superstition, coincided with consolidation of a powerful new class of bourgeois men who used 'knowledge' to legitimise their privileged position.

Foucault argued that there was no pure form of knowledge. All knowledge about the world was constructed from a particular point of view. In this respect, postmodern thinkers share some common ground with critical theorists in the Marxian tradition. However, as we saw in the preceding chapter, critical theorists hold that through dialogue aimed at consensus we might at least arrive at 'truths' of a kind, even if they are always open to refutation. Postmodern thinkers, on the other hand, argue that such a project will only replace the hegemony of one 'orthodoxy' with another. We can never be free of the power/knowledge nexus – it permeates all aspects of our day-to-day life. Knowledge then presupposes power relations and so we can only ever adopt an attitude of scepticism and critique. From a postmodern position, whenever we are confronted with a 'story' about the world, we must ask: Who has power? How is it exercised? To what end? How are particular configurations of power relations implicated in this view?

According to Foucault, the idea of a rational, autonomous human subject is also a fiction. In his earlier work, Foucault presented a view of the human subject as a body, an empty vessel, a product of the power relations to which we are all subjected throughout our lives – in sexual relationships, in the family, in the school, by exposure to media and communications, by conscription into the armed forces perhaps, by the regulation and supervision carried out by the police force and law courts, by the discipline we are subjected to in the workplace and so forth. Unsurprisingly, this view of the human subject has been criticised as anti-humanist and profoundly pessimistic. If we are only ever the product of discipline and punishment, how can we ever escape? Towards the end of his life, Foucault began to change his views somewhat. Certainly, most

---

 CONCEPT BOX

Telling Stories . . .

Postmodern thinkers influenced by Jacques Derrida, claim that in a sense we can think of the social world as being like a book. We use our critical faculties to 'read' and interpret the world, just as we would read a book. The world is like a text because it has no meaning independent of this interpretation. You might object that a book *does* have a meaning. The meaning of a story or an account is invested in the work by the author. For example, we are the authors of this book. We are endeavouring to convey something of the world of international relations. As readers, you are attempting to discover something about international relations by interpreting the meaning of words, analogies and examples that we have used. But are you learning anything about the world of international relations directly? Are you not learning about perspectives? Interpretations? Or, even, our interpretation of various works and perspectives? And are not these interpretations based on other sources – the works of philosophers, claims of science and so on? This is not necessarily problematic, if you believe that this process of interpreting 'texts' culminates in some sort of collective wisdom or understanding and, so, takes us closer to the truth of the world. However, once we introduce questions of power/knowledge into the equation, it becomes highly problematic.

As we noted earlier, postmodern thinkers reject grand theories or metanarratives, including the idea of God or Rationality or any other authoritative voice. The world has no 'author'. God did not create the world in six days; this is only a story about the world gleaned from the Bible. History is not the history of class struggle; this is an interpretation of history that comes to us through the pages of *The Communist Manifesto*. There is no hidden meaning of life which we can one day hope to discover. Postmodernists often speak of the 'death of the author' to convey the contested nature of knowledge, meaning and interpretation. We can only 'read' and interpret the world, or read and interpret other interpretations.

There are some similarities here with the interpretative or hermeneutic tradition of thought. However, postmodernists do not accept the proposition that there is a single world which we are all interpreting. In so far as we have *shared* meanings these must be understood as inter-textualities, rather than 'truths' arrived at by a shared understanding of events, processes and practices 'out there' in the real world. There are very many different stories or texts, and many different interpretations of dominant texts. Indeed, meaning is derived from the interaction of the reader with the 'text'. Since the social world is made up of such interpretations or discourses, we could say that interpretation constitutes the social world.

What this implies, of course, is that to all intents and purposes we can make no distinction between a great work of history or science or social science, and a work of fiction. We may believe that Darwin's *Origin of Species* or de Beauvoir's *The Second Sex* has more insight into the human condition than, say, *Reservoir Dogs*, but ultimately we cannot claim this with any degree of certainty.

contemporary postmodernists do recognise the capacity for resistance and empowerment. If this was not the case, we would not find examples of opposition, or different perspectives and 'stories' about the world. Indeed, postmodernists see inherent value in a multiplicity of approaches and perspectives on world politics, not because collectively they will increase our stock of knowledge and take us closer to the truth, but because they allow us to see the world through different lenses, enable us to hear diverse voices articulating various issues and concerns, and so undermine the truth claims of orthodox or hegemonic world views.

In developing this critique of the Enlightenment, postmodernists also develop a critique of philosophy. In so far as philosophers have sought to understand the truth about the human condition and speculate about the ends of human life, philosophy is rejected on the grounds that there can be no single truth and no one conception of the good life.

Derrida was critical of Western philosophy because it is phonocentric – centred on one authoritative voice. It was also logocentric – committed to a belief in some presence, or reality. Derrida argued that this occurred because of the human desire for certainty, the need to posit a central presence – something or someone there at the beginning of time and whose idea or will is being played out throughout history. If Enlightenment thinkers were concerned to challenge the one authoritative voice of God, they were never able to quite give up on the idea of a point of origin and ultimate destination – the human subject, human progress and a better future for the world.

Indeed, postmodern thinkers criticise this view of history as 'progress'. Human history should not be viewed, as some Enlightenment thinkers have suggested, as a gradual journey, or unfolding of events which is destined to culminate in a more rational world and freedom for the human race. Postmodern thinkers argue that there is no overall pattern, no end point or destination in history. Foucault was also deeply critical of the idea that human history should be seen in linear terms – as the logical and necessary progression of the human race. Foucault criticised traditional history which interpreted historical events in terms of some grand explanatory system as teleological. That is they attempted to track and interpret events, in accordance with some preconceived ideas about the overall direction and pattern of history.

Foucault used a method called genealogy to trace the discontinuities and ruptures in history in order to emphasise the singularity of events, rather than seeking to identify historical trends. In effect, to show that history had become accounts of the powerful. In so doing, Foucault was attempting to show what had been marginalised or neglected in traditional accounts of history. If traditional history focused on the big events, or the heroes and villains, and, say, Marxism focused on history as the history of class struggle, Foucault's genealogy was designed to show what and, crucially, whom had been neglected in these accounts and so, effectively, denied a history. In so far as the legitimacy of the current social and political order is embedded in certain interpretations or stories about the past, in this way it was possible to delegitimise the present social and political order and expose the current configuration of power relations.

To return to our notion of storytelling and interpretation, many postmodern thinkers believe that a central characteristic of modernity is that people develop a coherent sense of themselves as subjects, by being able to recount a narrative or story about themselves. In modern subjects this typically takes the form of a story of a life in which the subject has a history, is able to locate himself/herself in the present and is able to envisage a future. So, for example, you might 'know' that you are a person with a real existence because you were born in a certain year, in a particular geographical location (say London), that you had friends and siblings, you had birthdays, progressed through school, you are now a full time student, but one day you might become a teacher. This conception of self has also been formed by what other people have said about you and how you have been treated. This is similar to the Habermasian view of identity. However, unlike Habermasians who believe that the inter-subjective nature of identity formation made it possible to achieve a consensus about 'reality' and 'truth', postmodernists believe that power relations are always being played out in encounters or dialogues. Foucault was fascinated by mental 'illnesses' like schizophrenia because here was a concrete example of people who manifested 'split' or multiple subjectivities and who were often not able to locate themselves in time or space, in the way that our hypothetical person from London could. It is important to understand Foucault did not regard these people as 'mad', because the notion of 'madness' was another manifestation of intolerance and the desire by the powerful to marginalise, or incarcerate the 'different'.

Foucault is also important because of his work on discourse. This notion of discourse is intimately connected with the power/knowledge nexus. Foucault suggested that the production of knowledge was bound up historically with specific 'regimes of power'. According to Foucault every society produced its own 'truths' which had normalising and regulatory functions. It was the task of the genealogist of discourse to trace out the ways in which these discourses of truth operated in relation to the dominant power structures of any given society. Power and knowledge were intimately connected; so much so that Foucault consistently referred to power/knowledge in his writings. Discourse was never innocent. The 'truths' of those in positions of power were more likely to be accepted because they were powerful. At the same time knowledge constituted power.

If there are many different kinds of human knowledge, then we need to critically assess the nature of knowledge, the ends to which it is used and how power relations are implicated it the construction of theory. In this respect Foucault's ideas about knowledge/power and discourse are similar to the Marxist view of knowledge as ideology – the world view or 'truth' of the powerful which masquerades as 'common sense'. However, postmodern thinkers do not presuppose any direct connection between power/knowledge and social class. Power is seen as multi-faceted and, as Foucault held, everywhere. Also,

CONCEPT BOX

Discourse

According to postmodern thinkers, a discourse is not an account or a story about something or somebody. Discourses are practices that systematically form or create the objects that they speak. This is a complex idea, so let us try to unpack it further by taking the concrete example of discourses on 'women'. Throughout history, in works of art and pornography, in literature and folklore, in philosophy and science, there has been a great deal written on the subject of 'women'. People called 'women' have been variously represented as virtuous goddesses or treacherous witches, as caring wives/mothers, or scheming whores, as autonomous individuals each possessing free will or naturally subordinate and suited to a subservient role. So what are we to make of these creatures called 'women'? Do we conclude that the cumulative wisdom tells us that women are goddesses? Or witches? Or paradoxical creatures embodying complex personas?

Feminists would caution that these stories about women do not necessarily tell us anything at all about the 'true nature' or 'essence' of woman, because they have usually been written by men. These are not, then, accurate or even partial, pictures of what women are. How could men possibly know what women are? However, feminists have not been successful in identifying a female 'essence', as we will see in the following chapter. De Beauvoir argued that woman was what she could be, while others have simply concluded that woman is an enigma, a question. However, just because we cannot identify an essence that is 'woman', it does not follow that discourses on women are of no consequence. Claims about women's 'true nature' have informed laws, social policies, institutions and practices throughout history, from, say, marriage and divorce, to 'proper' education and training, to who can or cannot fly an aeroplane or vote in an election. Discourses inform or create concrete practices, or we might say, discourse is itself a practice. A discourse is not about a 'real' thing, or event, or category of person like 'woman'. Discourse creates the thing it speaks, because it invests meaning into an empty term like 'woman' and, in so doing, creates a 'real' category of people whose lives are then profoundly shaped by the concrete practices that flow from this meaning.

as is apparent from the above discussion, postmodernism rejects the division between true and false forms of knowledge.

Postmodern thinkers invoke the notion of 'otherness' to refer to the voice that is silenced, or the experience which is marginalised when the 'truth' is asserted. The concept of the 'Other' is employed to confound the notion that there can be universal rights grounded in a conception of universal reason, that there are universal experiences or universal values. Experiences, values and knowledge claims are always particular. It is simply that, as Foucault held, some groups have the power to make claims in the name of 'humankind' as a whole. Postmodern thinkers embrace and celebrate Otherness because they value the diversity of human experience and differences which exist between peoples. This emphasis on the positive side of Otherness is a major theme of the work of Derrida.

CONCEPT BOX

Poststructuralism

Derrida's work is often referred to as poststructuralist rather than postmodern. Similarly, Foucault can be, and often is, described as a poststructuralist rather than postmodern thinker. Often the terms postmodern and poststructuralist are used interchangeably. At this point it is useful to just sketch out in simple terms the differences between them in the interests of clarity. As we have seen, postmodernism is centrally concerned with the nature and consequences of modernity and develops a thoroughgoing critique of the Enlightenment project. To simplify somewhat, we might say that poststructuralism is more concerned with the nature, role and function of language – how social meaning is constructed through language.

Derrida argued that much philosophical thought was metaphysical. That is, it was a belief system which depended ultimately upon an appeal to an ultimate truth, or a solid foundation. For example, the idea of God, or the human subject. In so far as human language is used to convey these ideas, Derrida called this single 'truth' a transcendental signifier. That is, the definitive word which gives meaning to all others; in the final analysis, metaphysical belief systems are based on a fiction, but a whole hierarchy of meaning is then constructed upon this. Derrida pointed out that many philosophers had used the opposition between nature/culture as basis for theory. The notions of archaic man living in a 'state of nature' and desire to establish 'society' are, by now, familiar to you. The structure of the nature/culture dichotomy repeats itself in other binary oppositions: man/woman, national/international. The first term in each opposition constitutes the privileged entity, the secondary term is always viewed as in some way inferior.

Such binary oppositions are used to draw rigid boundaries between what is acceptable and what is not, between self and non-self, truth and falsity, sense and nonsense, reason and madness, central and marginal. It is from Derrida that we get the notion of deconstruction – a critical method of reading a text to expose the ways in which meaning is constructed. At this stage, it is enough to note that there is quite a lot of overlap between postmodernism and poststructuralism. Postmodern and poststructuralist scholars do not spend a great deal of time agonising over terms and labels and neither should you. It is more important at this stage to grasp the general critique of power relations, dominant forms of knowledge and social practices which arise from both poststructural and postmodern insights.

Assumptions

1. Human 'nature' is not immutable. The human subject is 'open' and malleable, a product of practices of subordination and resistance.

2. Human values, beliefs and actions vary according to the wider social and cultural context. There are no characteristics or values which have universal applicability. The behaviour/actions of people and particular values

can only be understood and judged in terms of specific cultural meanings and contexts.

3. Similarly, we cannot outline any general theory which helps us to 'make sense' of the world, or prescribe a blueprint or scheme for universal human emancipation.

4. There are no 'facts' about the world. All we have are interpretations and interpretations of other interpretations of 'reality'.

 REFLECTION BOX

If you are new to IR and you have read through quickly from the start, you are likely to find postmodernism difficult. Rather than reflect on a specific assumption here, why not go back and read slowly the box on 'Telling Stories' or 'Discourse' to check that you have thoroughly understood it.

Themes

If you are now operating in postmodern mode, perhaps you will have already adopted a certain scepticism towards the study of 'International Relations'! Perhaps, you will ask: How are power relations implicated in perspectives and world views? Which views of the world are accepted as valid and which are not? What other possible stories could we tell about the world? You might also desire to unpack or deconstruct the language, symbols and images which are invoked in particular discourses. Or maybe you want to challenge the very notion of 'international relations'. The conception of the nation-state makes certain assumptions about identity and community, of course. It assumes that we identify first and foremost with members of the national group and owe our primary allegiance to 'our' state. Perhaps you would now argue for a more open, ambiguous and messier notion of 'world politics' on the grounds that it better captures the nuances and complexities of the world you are striving to 'make sense of'? It is in this context that we can focus on how postmodernism critiques existing perspectives on IR and champions radical new ways of thinking about the general domain of world politics.

The State and Power

At first sight, the state-centric orientation of much IR theory is not unreasonable. The nation-state has constituted the dominant form of political organisation in Europe since the seventeenth century. In the European context, the birth of the state as a form of political organisation was closely associated with the rise of nationalism. Forces of nationalism have played a large part in post-colonial and revolutionary struggles for 'national independence' which have, in turn, encouraged the proliferation of the states around the world. Moreover, the defining characteristic of the state is sovereignty – exclusive jurisdiction over a people in a given territory and the right to act on their behalf in relations with others. Is it not reasonable then to start out from the position that the state is the main actor in international relations and acts to secure the 'national interest'?

From a postmodern position we cannot take the state to be our starting point for study of IR for much the same reason as critical theorists reject state-centrism – states have emerged during certain historical conditions. In earlier periods, there were many and different 'sites' of power and authority which claimed the allegiances of peoples. Postmodern scholars also argue that mainstream IR theory, in taking the state as a pre-given entity, neglects to ask important questions about why the world has come to be divided up in this way. That is, state-centric approaches neglect to ask how sovereignty – centralised authority – has been produced and the consequences of carving up political space in this way. It is to these questions that the discussion now turns.

Postmodernists would not deny the importance of the concept of the state in IR. However, they encourage us to think about the state as 'actor' in a radically different way. Rather than taking the existence of the state as given, postmodern thinkers argue that it actually takes a great deal of time and effort to 'make' a state. Not only must the state constantly patrol and police demarcated boundaries (contested or otherwise), but élites also have to expend considerable effort on retaining the allegiance of the people.

The shorthand term for the making of the state is 'state-craft'. In conventional diplomatic history or orthodox accounts of foreign policy, state-craft refers to statesmanship – foresight and skill in the art of government and in conducting relations with foreign powers. While postmodernists would not necessarily contest this definition, they contend that it is mistaken to view diplomacy or foreign policy as the expression or execution of some pre-given national interest. State-craft is an ongoing, dynamic process, whereby the identity of state is actively created and recreated. Every day, political élites are involved in practices such as the making of speeches, the exercise of diplomacy, and the formulation of foreign policy which serve to constantly mark out the boundaries and identity of the state. Rather than viewing the state as an actor with a concrete identity and pre-given interests, postmodern thinkers regard the state as a 'performance'. Through the performance – the acting out – of both foreign and domestic policy, by entering into diplomatic relations with other sovereign bodies and, sometimes, through acts of war, the boundaries of the state are constructed, policed and patrolled. State practices are also legitimised through the articulation of a discourse of national identity, community and interests.

Discourses of Nationhood and National Identity

The idea of investing the state with a concrete identity is difficult to grasp, so let's take the example of how the idea of 'Britishness' is acted out on a day-to-day basis. Nationalists frequently claim that the people of a given land – the 'nation' – have existed since time immemorial. A great deal of academic writing on nations and nationalism, endeavours to trace back the origins of nations in certain ethnic groups or through a historical lineage stretching back to ancient times.

In an influential book Benedict Anderson claimed that nations were not 'real' entities, but 'imagined communities'. That is to say that the idea of nationhood has been constructed through symbols, myths and narratives, which allowed people to imagine that they shared a deep bond based on blood-line and/or a common history, interests and destiny. Anderson claimed that far from being ancient, nations were relatively a recent phenomenon. It was only with the advent of modern transport systems, the imposition of common time zones, the invention of modern print media and the centralisation of authority in the state, that people began to imagine themselves to be a part of one community. State building projects and modern warfare have both manipulated and perpetuated this notion of 'nationhood'.

If we take the example of the British nation, here we have islands comprised of more than 60 million people. Even if we exclude from our definition of 'Britain' the troubled province of Ulster, where contested ideas of nationhood and sovereignty have lead to bitter and bloody conflict, we find that 'Great Britain' is an island of considerable diversity. It is made up of three distinctive countries, England, Scotland and Wales. Many – though certainly not all – Scottish and Welsh people feel themselves to be different from the English and, indeed, may perceive the notion of 'Britishness' to be merely an imposition of some notion of 'Englishness'. This feeling of 'difference', whether it has positive or negative connotations is undoubtedly part of the reason why Scotland and Wales have demanded a greater degree of self rule in recent years. However, the decentralisation of power to Scottish and Welsh Assemblies, has, in turn, increased demands for a greater autonomy in regions of England like the North East and South West, which have been backed by claims of 'cultural differences'. Of course, we cannot prove in any objective way that these claims have any substance, or that perceived differences are based on 'real' differences. The point is that the idea of nationhood and community is contested. Add to this, the very large numbers of British citizens spread across the various territories and regions, who have parents, grandparents, partners or close relatives who were born in the Indian sub-continent, the Caribbean, Africa, the Baltic States or some other European country, and a picture of a diverse and multicultural society begins to emerge.

It is clearly difficult to sustain the notion of a coherent and unified nation in the context of diversity and complex feelings of identity and allegiance, and yet on a day-to-day basis the idea of 'Britishness' is played out, or performed, on the international 'stage'. Politicians debate the implications of European Union for British sovereignty, or the 'problem' of 'bogus' asylum seekers. At the same time, officials and representatives of the British state are involved in diplomatic missions, statespeople take part in international conferences, and British forces patrol the seas and airways, and police territorial boundaries – all in the name of 'British interests'. In all of these ways, the idea of a unified nation and a distinctive 'Britishness' is played out or performed.

WORLD EXAMPLE (continued)

How then is the state made to appear like an entity, a cohesive, purposive actor? Postmodernists argue that the state – in this case the British state – is made to appear like it has an 'essence' by performative enactments of various domestic and foreign policies. Through the performance of both foreign and domestic policy, by entering into diplomatic relations with other sovereign bodies and, sometimes, through acts of war, the boundaries of the state are constructed, policed and patrolled. State practices are then legitimised through the articulation of national identity, community and interests. The state is never finished, statecraft is a dynamic ongoing process. Similarly, the state, and how we think about the state, is always undergoing processes of transformation.

Of course, you might object that while closely connected, the concepts of state and nation are distinct. Realists would contend that, notwithstanding the diversity within the citizen body, the concept of 'national interest' is valid because ultimately the state guarantees the security of the citizen body. Some realists prefer not to rely on arguments about nationhood to justify their position and contend that we obey the state because it is prudent to do so – the state protects us; if we betray the state (treason) we can be killed. Moreover, the world is divided up into entities called states and the defining characteristic of a state is sovereignty.

Given our earlier discussion of the nature of discourse, we would be surprised though to find postmodern thinkers being lulled into a conversation about the so called 'objective' characteristics of the state, or the ultimate foundation of sovereign authority. The postmodern perspective on sovereignty shifts the focus from the 'objective' characteristics of sovereignty onto how the discourse of sovereignty has profoundly shaped our thinking about political life. In concentrating on discourses of sovereignty, the aim is not to define sovereignty or pin down the essence of sovereign power. Adopting a genealogical

---

AUTHOR BOX

Simulating Sovereignty

Postmodern thinkers like Cynthia Weber often refer to the notion of 'writing' the state, or simulating sovereignty. To go back to our earlier metaphor of the world as a text or book, this notion of 'writing' conveys the idea of inscribing modes of representation. That is, meaning is inscribed in a text through the act of writing – the use of words, signifiers, symbols, metaphors and images, which we read, interpret and, at some level, understand. Similarly, concepts, ideas and fictions – the state, or security, or sovereignty – are portrayed or represented to us as having a concrete existence or 'truth'. To write the state is to give the state an 'essence' or, more properly, a presence – a concrete identity or existence. Having established the presence of the state, certain practices are then infused with meaning and, thereby, legitimised – the policing of boundaries, acts in the name of 'national security', the crime of treason and so on.

method, it is possible to show how the meaning of sovereignty has changed over different historical time periods and according to the context in which the term has been evoked. This implies that we need to understand how different configurations of power/knowledge have shaped our understanding of sovereignty.

Peace and Security

Drawing upon the work of Derrida particularly, many postmodern thinkers have argued that the 'making' of the state necessitates the construction of a hostile 'Other'. A discourse of threat or danger is central to the making of identities and the securing of boundaries. Thus, the political cohesion of the United States of America relies on the construction of hostile 'others'. During the Cold War period in US foreign policy, the Soviet Union was constructed as a unified and cohesive actor – a 'red menace' bent on world domination. The Soviet Union covered a large geographical area and embraced a vast array of peoples of different classes, genders, nationalities and cultures, but was presented as an entity with cohesive identity and purpose – or subjectivity.

Adopting a postmodern position on security, foreign policy and diplomacy, gives us a much more fluid and dynamic understanding of politics, and the power relations which underpin dominant discourses of political space and identity, than that provided by state-centric perspectives. It allows us to see that these practices effectively carve up political space on a global scale and determine what constitutes 'threats'. Not only does this serve to legitimise high levels of expenditure on armaments and political violence in the defence of the nation and its boundaries, but also disguises internal division and dissent. Far from being politically, socially and culturally cohesive units, 'nation-states' are frequently rent by internal turmoil; legally recognised but lacking domestic legitimacy. However, sovereignty confers on the state ultimate power over the citizen body.

AUTHOR BOX

David Campbell, *Writing Security*

David Campbell's book *Writing Security* shows how US foreign policy has relied on so called discourses of danger. Such discourses have been able to 'create' enemies externally as well as externalising internal dissidence/difference. As Campbell himself puts it 'the ability to represent things as alien, subversive, dirty or such has been pivotal to the American experience' (p. 2). He argues that this was not just some Cold War necessity but is an ongoing feature of US politics; thus, just as 'women, blacks, foreigners, radicals, the "insane" and the sexually deviant were often the targets of anti-communism's discursive practices' so anti-narcotics discourses of danger in the post Cold War period 'have identified the same groups as of concern' (p. 205).

It has been suggested that the state requires this 'discourse of danger' not only to secure its identity, but also to legitimatise state power. Some writers argue that modern state-craft is built upon a set of practices that work to subdue resistance. The consequence of this is that citizenship is equated with ultimate loyalty to the nation-state and the elimination of all that is foreign. Threats to security are seen to be in the external realm and internal dissent is quelled.

Conflict and Violence

From a postmodern perspective, violence is not, then, endemic to international relations because of conditions of 'anarchy' or because states constantly face real threats to their security from hostile foreigners. The construction of the 'outside' as hostile and threatening, legitimises violence in international relations. Furthermore, violence is actually central to the very constitution of the state. The state is, to borrow Max Weber's phrase, that institution which holds a monopoly on the legitimate use of force. The state exercises authority through the political and legal system, but this is backed up by the coercive arms of state power, the military and internal police forces. At the very heart of the state are discourses and practices of violence. This casts considerable doubt on the claim that the state is a 'progressive' form of political organisation.

Identity and Community

If, however, the state is a 'problem', how might we re-articulate or revise conceptions of community and belonging? Postmodern scholars accept that the nation-state is an important expression of political community. However, they point out that it is certainly not the only significant expression of identity or community. The problem is that when we study international relations, we necessarily privilege citizenship over and above other expressions of identity and community. That dominant ideas of identity and political community are confined to identification with the nation-state is in no small way a consequence of the way in which the creation of state boundaries in Europe was closely linked with the rise of nationalism as a powerful discourse and political force and war as an all too frequent expression of this. However, if we focus solely, or mainly, on the nation-state, we may well miss other significant expressions of community and identity. State-centric models of international relations marginalise the political significance of social movements which identify on the basis of class or gender or are organised around specific issues, such as the environment.

Postmodern scholars embrace the idea of globalisation, not because it necessarily captures real material processes or developments, but because it represents a powerful challenge to state-centrism in IR. That said, in true Foucauldian spirit, postmodernists are also sensitive to the power relations which underpin discourses of globalisation. That is to say that globalisation is itself a contested term for a contested process. It is important to realise, therefore, that postmodernists see value in any idea or perspective which encourages us to think about the world differently, but are, as always, alert to the particular interests and motives which inform claims about the world. Nevertheless, globalisation might be encouraging new forms of identification and expressions of identity and solidarity which cut across state boundaries. Therefore, the concept of globalisation opens up possibilities for revisioning identity and community.

 REFLECTION BOX

Hybridity

The notion of hybridity implies mixing of different elements of identity to form something new. The concept of hybridity is particularly associated with the ideas of Homi Bhabba. In order to flesh out the concept of hybrid identities, it is helpful to consider further the ways in which globalisation is relevant to the study of identity. Globalisation implies increased travel, the growth of media and communication and a generally 'smaller' world. In a globalised world, therefore, cultural encounters and mixings are likely to become the norm. For example, it is *possible* that somewhere out there is a Bangladeshi woman. She is the daughter of a Bangladeshi man and an American woman, herself the daughter of German Jews who fled the Nazis. This hypothetical woman grew up in Turkey, though she was educated in English. If this person exists, the only people to share her particular mix of identities are likely to be her siblings who even then will be unique perhaps due to gender, sexuality and so on.

It is interesting to speculate on what all this means. But perhaps hybridity, mixing and transmission of ideas mean more than anything else that the stereotype is increasingly hard to 'hold on to'. Are the reinforcement of ideas such as the 'American Way', the remodelling of ideas in say 'Cool Britannia' or attempts to deny or frustrate global trends by say 'protecting' the French language from Anglicisation worthwhile projects or discourses of the powerful?

Postmodernists are interested in social movements because this is a politics which challenges the rigid inside/outside boundaries of state-centric analysis. Innovative new technologies like the internet are being used by a wide variety of social movements to network, campaign and articulate dissent and resistance. All of this political activity is being carried out in a particular 'space' – cyberspace – which is outside the jurisdiction and control of individual states though, ironically enough, vulnerable to hacking and virusing by individual people. Postmodern scholars argue, therefore, that we need to radically rethink our conceptions of global political space.

AUTHOR BOX

R.B.J. Walker, *One World, Many Worlds*

Walker has been an influential figure in the development of postmodern/poststructuralist thought in International Relations. In this work, Walker outlined how he saw the significance of new social movements, in relation to questions of identity, solidarity and political action.

Their special significance lies in the way they sometimes respond to the challenges they identify. They find new spaces in which to act, thereby challenging the prevailing topography of political life. They discover new ways of acting, thereby challenging the prevailing conceptions of how people ought to behave towards each other. They extend the horizons of what it is possible to know and to be as human beings, thereby challenging the boundaries of received ethical, aesthetics, and philosophical traditions. Critical social movements struggle in particular circumstances, and yet they also recognise that specific struggles require new forms of interaction between peoples, new forms of human community and solidarity that cut across social and territorial categories established under other historical conditions. (p. 115)

Inequality and Justice

This concern with novel forms of identification and expressions of community, necessarily raises questions of how we conduct our relationships with others. Given the central concern with the power/knowledge nexus and general scepticism towards Enlightenment discourse, we might expect to find postmodern scholars adopting a rather cynical approach towards questions of justice and moral right. No doubt, some postmodern thinkers are sceptics in this respect. However, this is far from true of all postmodernists working in the field of IR. Some postmodern scholars attempt to go beyond critique, and suggest that postmodern insights are helpful in addressing a range of human problems and concerns. Postmodern thinkers are interested in questions of justice and concrete inequalities. However, postmodernists tend to concentrate more on the moral and ethical implications of a diverse, culturally heterogeneous world. That in turn raises questions of morality and ethics in world politics.

Questions of morality and ethics cannot be understood purely within the boundaries of nation-states. As was suggested above, Enlightenment thinkers saw the human race as engaged in an effort towards universal moral and intellectual self-realisation and as the subject of a universal historical experience. The nation-state was seen by many as a political space in which ethical behaviour was possible. However, as critical theorists have pointed out, there is a moral paradox at the heart of the nation-state – excluded 'others' are not regarded as equal to insiders. So, here 'difference' is dealt with through processes of exclusion and unequal treatment.

As we saw in chapter 1, realists believe that the central difficulty in international relations is that under conditions of anarchy, ethics or morality does not and cannot provide the impulse and rationale of foreign policy; it must be based on self-interest. The moral ties and obligations which tie together the national group are absent in relations with external others. For this reason, relations with outsiders are always underpinned by the ultimate threat of violence.

This is not to say that all IR scholars have dismissed the possibility of moral or ethical behaviour among states and other 'actors' in international relations. As we saw in chapter 2, liberals hoped that it might be possible to realise the rule of law in relations between states, while critical theorists, following Habermas, argue that by engaging in dialogue we might be able to establish just and moral standards applicable to all of the world's peoples.

A second problem with approaching questions of justice or ethics from a state-centric perspective is that, as we will see in chapter 7, the nation-state is ill-equipped to cope with the many problems facing humankind. The state provides no secure boundaries against the threat of global economic crisis, environmental pollution or nuclear attack. Moreover, when this orientation towards the other is coupled with radically different conceptions of political community and political space, it becomes clear that demands for justice can come from above and below the state. Ethical issues and dilemmas arise in a range of contexts. That is, questions of justice and ethics necessarily arise in the practices of the World Bank, United Nations, or a multinational corporation, for example, and also from the demands articulated by, for example, minorities, social movements or indigenous peoples.

Postmodernists are, of course, at pains to point out that power is everywhere and power relations can never be completely overcome. However, the response has been to argue that we must, nevertheless, try to conduct our relations with others on an ethical basis. One of the central questions in traditional IR theory is what do 'citizens' owe to others? A postmodern ethics refuses to start out from the assumption that we are above all else citizens of pre-given states. Rather it suggests starting from the question: What do I as a subject (however that subjectivity is constituted) owe to others? So, postmodernism begins from the position of the Other. Postmodern thinkers ask: How does recognition of, and respect for, the Other make certain claims or pose specific obligations on me?

Recognition of the inadequacy of the state and calls to rethink our approach to questions of identity and community, necessitates rethinking what it means to have solidarity with Others, and in what it now means to behave in an ethical and just way towards Others. For this reason many postmodern scholars are interested in discourses on ethics and moral obligation found in, perhaps, writings on human rights. However, it is important to recognise that postmodern thinkers do not start out from the abstract notion of universal reason as a basis for rights claims. Rather they are interested in how we can develop an ethics based on respect for concrete others out of discourses and practices which already have some currency. At the same time, postmodernists want us to rethink the basis for 'rights' claims, or notions of morality and ethics, so that they are sensitive and responsive to differences.

Summary

1. Postmodernism is not easy. It challenges many ideas central to International Relations.

2. Postmodernism is not simply about the period of history following modernity, but provides ways of thinking about the consequences of modern thought and practice.

3. Despite some leftist origins, postmodernism has been accused of profound conservatism. Its questioning attitude is just one reason why it is impossible to politically categorise.

4. Postmodernism enquires into multiple power/knowledge relationships.

5. Postmodernists have been concerned with drawing out hidden assumptions (making visible the invisible) by a process of critique.

6. Postmodernism does not mean a person can have no values or should believe in nothing, more that they should be tentative about the grounds for the claims they make based upon these.

7. Particularly important authors are Jacques Derrida (b.1930), Michel Foucault (1926–84), Martin Heidegger (1889–1976) and Friedrich Nietzsche (1844–1900), but postmodernism is much more difficult to pigeon-hole than say realism.

8. Postmodernism uses various methods including genealogy. This seeks to highlight the singularity of events rather than trends, in order to reveal the idea that all history is written by the powerful.

9. In undermining much of IR, postmodernism might be considered better taught *before* students have inculcated the discipline's 'truths'. For this reason it appears in this book despite its difficulties.

Criticisms

Some critics have argued, often in a very hostile manner, that postmodernism has no real 'relevance' to IR. That is to say that postmodernism is not policy orientated and so cannot be used to inform the conduct of international relations. This can be contested on the grounds that many postmodern ideas, for example, on ethics, can inform policy. Moreover, this kind of criticism is based on a rather narrow definition of what constitutes international relations or international politics.

The postmodern suspicion of metanarrative and grand theory has led some critics to argue that postmodernism will merely generate endless empirical studies, in which the scholars admit to doing no more than 'interpreting' or 'telling stories' about discrete areas of interest. However, such criticism neglects the importance of critique in postmodern thought. Moreover, it implicitly assumes that grand theories and metanarratives are useful or insightful.

A further criticism often levelled at postmodernism is that it gives us no way of distinguishing between 'good' and 'bad' forms of knowledge. A related criticism would be that if we cannot grasp life from a single perspective, and power is everywhere, ultimately this means we cannot judge the validity of different discourses. An extreme example of this, in more senses than one, would be that postmodernism cannot judge the validity or prove the falsity of a text like *Mein Kampf*. Again, denying the ultimate foundation or 'truth' of particular world views or values or texts, does not necessarily mean that we cannot be opposed to some positions. Indeed, critique and deconstruction can be important political tools in themselves, revealing the partiality and bias of a particular position or doctrine and so undermining its claims to be based on a truth.

This criticism of postmodernism is, perhaps, based on a misunderstanding of 'responsibility'. Having no 'universal truth' or 'universal agent' does not mean that postmodernists do not have to take responsibility for their actions. Moreover, one can criticise *Mein Kampf* as 'morally wrong' or 'politically exclusionary' without recourse to a universalist position.

Postmodernism has been described as a profoundly conservative position. This criticism arises in part because of the intellectual debt to Nietzsche who has long been considered an important influence in fascist thought. As we pointed out in our introduction to postmodernism above, it is not easy to categorise postmodernism as either 'right wing' or 'left wing'. It might be that some postmodern thinkers are profoundly conservative. However, it does not necessarily follow that all postmodernists want to preserve the status quo. Indeed, as will be apparent from the above discussion, many postmodernists identify with oppositional groups.

A related criticism is that postmodernism is a convenient way of evading political questions. If there is no truth, then we are ultimately prisoners of our own discourse. Also postmodernism has no theory of freedom or emancipation, seeing the project of social transformation as either vain or, more worryingly, a reflection of dominant power/knowledge relations.

Postmodernism has also been criticised because it attacks Marxism, but has paid little attention to the violence and oppression inherent in capitalism. In their defence, postmodernists might point out that while Marxism has indeed been a target of critique, many postmodern scholars have also attacked neoliberalism and contemporary approaches to modernisation because they legitimise dominant economic projects.

Postmodernism has been criticised as profoundly disempowering, because it has no real conception of agency. It is sometimes suggested that postmodernism even in its 'oppositional' mode, rejects the notion of a subject with a voice, and so undermines the ability of marginalised groups to articulate their experiences. However, some postmodernists are sympathetic to human (subject)

centred analysis and seek to retain, or salvage something of the humanist tradition characteristic of the Enlightenment.

Finally, if power is everywhere, but we cannot identify structures of power,
for example, patriarchy, or capitalism, who or what are we supposed to be resisting? Moreover, if postmodernists are sceptical about the existence of material
interests rooted in, say, class or gender, what grounds, if any, are there for collective action? Marxists and some feminists have contended that postmodernism
uses the language of dissidence, exile and marginalisation, but has nothing to
say about how political action can be used to make the world a better place.
The postmodernist 'defence' is that emancipatory projects imply a coherent
plan; since power relations are always implicated in visions of emancipation,
we can only be vigilant and ask: Whose conception of emancipation is this?

Common Misunderstandings

Postmodernism is the same as poststructuralism. No, but there are similarities. See
box, p. 138.

Postmodernists think that there is no 'real' world. It would be plainly absurd to deny
that there are, for example, real wars and that real people get killed. However, we
can never understand the world directly, so we rely upon interpretations of events
rather than the actual events themselves for our knowledge of the world. Moreover,
in the contemporary age, as often as not, those interpretations come to us through
the media and mass communication. In a sense, we usually find ourselves interpreting images and stories that come to us through foreign correspondents and/or
television news bulletins which are necessarily selective and, perhaps, biased in their
coverage of events/issues. In such circumstances, it is perhaps wise to ask what picture of the world is being presented to us? Whose world view is this? What sort of
interpretation of 'what happened' and 'why' is it being offered to us here? This is not
to say that an interpretation can be contrasted with what really happened. All we
ever have are interpretations in which the 'reader' infuses any event or process with
meaning.

Postmodernists are all relativists. Not necessarily. Certainly, postmodernists concede
that there is no ultimate foundation for a knowledge or a belief. Therefore, we cannot say categorically that some cultural values and practices are 'bad' and others are
'better' or 'right' (but see below).

Postmodernists are nihilists who have no values. Not necessarily. We cannot say
categorically that some cultural values and practices are 'bad' and others are 'better'
or 'right'. However, this position is not inconsistent with preferring one set of values
to another, it is simply a matter of on what basis we justify those preferences.

*Postmodern thinkers deny the possibility of human emancipation, therefore, they
are unlikely to oppose oppressive practices or systems of rule.* No. Postmodern
thinkers eschew the term 'emancipatory' politics, preferring to speak instead of
'interventions' or 'sites of resistance'. The notion of emancipation is too closely tied
to the language of old ideologies such as Marxism which have frequently engaged in
repression when they have succeeded in gaining political power. It does not follow
from this that postmodernists will be silent or timid in the face of aggression or

oppression, as should be apparent from the earlier discussion of Stalinism and the Nazi persecution of Jews and other minorities.

Further Reading

For some of the authors cited here, these selections represent only a tiny part of their published works.

Ashley, R.K. and Walker, R.B.J. (1990), 'Speaking the Language of Exile', *International Studies Quarterly*, Vol. 34, No. 3, pp. 259–68.

Campbell, D. (1998), *Writing Security: United States Foreign Policy and the Politics of Identity* (revised edition), Manchester: University of Manchester Press.
Connolly, W. (1993), *Political Theory and Modernity* (2nd edition), Ithaca: Cornell University Press.

Der Derian, J. and Shapiro, M. (eds) (1989), *International/Intertextual Relations: Postmodern Readings of World Politics*, Lexington, MA: Lexington Books.
Derrida, J. (1978), *Writing and Difference*, London: Routledge and Kegan Paul.
Devetak, R. (1996), 'Postmodernism', in Burchill, S. and Linklater, A. (eds), *Theories of International Relations*, London: Macmillan.

Edkins, J. (1999), *Poststructuralism and International Relations: Bringing the Political Back In*, Boulder, CO: Lynne Rienner.

Foucault, M. (1979), *Discipline and Punish: The Birth of the Prison*, Harmondsworth: Penguin.
Foucault, M. (1989), *The Archaeology of Knowledge*, London: Routledge.

Heidegger, M. (1969), *Identity and Difference*, New York: Harper & Row.
Heidegger, M. (1993), *Basic Concepts*, Bloomington: Indiana University Press.

Nietzsche, F. (1954), *The Portable Nietzsche*, New York: Viking Press.
Nietzsche, F. (1990), *Unmodern Observations*, New Haven: Yale University Press.

Rosenau, P. (1991), *Postmodernism and the Social Sciences: Insights, Inroads and Intrusions*, Princeton: Princeton University Press.

Walker, R.B.J. (1987), *One World, Many Worlds: Struggles for a Just World Peace*, London: Zed Books.
Walker, R.B.J. (1993), *Inside/Outside: International Relations as Political Theory*, Cambridge: Cambridge University Press.
Weber, C. (1995), *Simulating Sovereignty: Intervention, the State and Symbolic Exchange*, Cambridge: Cambridge University Press.

CHAPTER 6

Feminist Thought

Introduction

Most definitions of feminism centre on the demand for equality between the sexes or equal rights for women. For this reason, students new to the study of feminism and IR often assume that it is about women. As we will see below, feminists do have much to say on the topic of sexual equality and women's rights. However, this rather narrow definition does not fully reflect the richness and breadth of feminist thought. Equality and equal rights issues have never been the sole focus of feminism. Furthermore, as with other perspectives, there are different 'strands' of feminist thought and this is reflected within what might be broadly termed 'feminist International Relations'.

In this chapter, we do not intend to gloss over the differences in feminist thought completely. On the contrary, we emphasise the different intellectual roots of feminist thought in the origins section and, periodically, draw your attention to differences within feminist thought in the sections on assumptions and themes, when it is useful and appropriate to do so. However, as in other chapters, our aim here is to simplify as much as possible. At this stage we will only try to provide you with a basic vocabulary which will equip you to undertake more in-depth study. While standpoint feminist and postmodern feminist ideas are drawn upon throughout the chapter, for the most part the discussion is informed by liberal and critical feminisms. However, we hope that in this way, by the end of this chapter, you will have some sense of the nuances of feminist thought and its overall critique of traditional approaches to IR. Through your further reading you will gain a better understanding of the commonalities and differences in different strands of feminist thought and how these are reflected in the feminist International Relations literature.

While acknowledging that feminism is something of a 'broad church', we suggest that it is possible to construct a feminist 'perspective', in a limited sense of the term. The term 'perspective' can be used to describe a way of looking at the world which prioritises certain features, issues or processes. Historically, the point of departure for feminists in constructing knowledge about the world has been women's everyday lives and experiences. Feminists ask, what might the world of international relations look like if we made women's concerns central rather than marginal? How might our understanding of power be revisioned if we considered the ways in which women experience forms of domination, or empowerment? What would we see as vital to the achievement of security if we prioritised the things that women fear most? Feminists have concentrated on women, because they believe that women have been subjected to discrimination and unequal treatment. Feminism is, then, a 'bottom-up' view of the world, constructed from the point of view or experiences of a marginalised group.

INFORMATION BOX

A Feminist Lens on International Political Economy

For a long time, women were ignored or marginalised in the study of International Relations. It was generally believed that the position of women fell outside the realm of the study of international relations, because it was not relevant to relations between states. Even the 'sister' discipline of International Political Economy was, initially, largely concerned with the study of states and markets. Far from being irrelevant, the position of women is, on the contrary, central to international political economy.

For example, structural adjustment policies foisted on indebted states by the International Monetary Fund often require governments to increase exports and cut back on domestic social and welfare spending (see chapter 3). This is justified by neo-liberal economic ideology which emphasises the efficacy of the free market (see chapter 2). As providers of basic health and social welfare needs, the effects of debt and structural adjustment fall disproportionately on women. When the state withdraws from health and welfare provision it usually falls upon women to provide these services. Women's labour is expected to 'stretch' in order to compensate for cuts in public services. The burden of debt and economic policies, which are themselves largely conditioned by the global economy and international institutions, are having particular effects on women in countries throughout the world and, this in turn, has a profound impact on children and the future health, welfare and stability of whole societies.

In contemporary feminist theory, the focus is no longer solely on the lives of women, but rather extends to an analysis of gender. Gender describes the relationship between the sexes in any given society or culture. If gender is socially or culturally determined, it follows that gender is related to, but not the same thing as, biological sex. If there are no innate or immutable male or female natures rooted in sex differences, the question arises: Why are values or traits held to be essentially 'masculine' or 'feminine' ascribed to biological males and females respectively?

While there are differences in emphasis, in analysis and in the explanations they produce, there is also widespread agreement among feminists that gender is best understood in terms of power relationships. During the late 1960s and early 1970s, during the 'second wave' of feminist activism in the

REFLECTION BOX

Are Men from Mars?

In everyday usage, the term gender is used to describe essential differences between men and women. The idea that gender differences are rooted in biological sex differences and are 'natural' remains prevalent in popular culture. For example, the premise of a recent best-selling popular book, entitled *Men are From Mars: Women are from Venus*, is that gender differences are rooted in biological sex and that recognising/accepting such differences is the first stage in achieving harmonious relationships. However, those same characteristics which are held to be essentially 'male' or 'female', for example rationality or emotion, competitive or consensus oriented behaviour, aggressiveness or submissiveness, vary in different societies and across cultures. The social meanings ascribed to sexual differences also change over time. Since prevailing beliefs about gender vary across societies, cultures and across time, it is difficult to substantiate the argument that gender differences somehow reflect essential differences. Feminists are interested in gender because it seems that across countries and cultures, values, characteristics or roles regarded as 'masculine' tend to be more highly regarded than those which were held to be 'feminine'. Certain ideas about gender have been used to justify different and usually unequal treatment between men and women. Feminists ask: Who has the power to decide what is an essentially masculine or feminine trait or role? Who has the power to decide the social rewards attached to such roles? You might usefully reflect here on your own assumptions about what is 'masculine' and 'feminine' behaviour and whether you believe such views fit exactly those of people in other societies. Can you think of examples of differences?

West, feminists developed an analysis of gender and power relations. This in turn led to a greater appreciation of the degree to which women's lives were embedded in a whole range of social practices and shaped by social and political institutions and prevailing ideas about the naturalness or rightness of sexual inequality. So, while many contemporary feminists prefer to concentrate on gender rather than women *per se*, questions of power and inequality remain central preoccupations in feminist thought.

In keeping with our objective of providing an introduction to each perspective, in this chapter we will limit ourselves to sketching a 'feminist position' on key areas long recognised as central to the study of International Relations. Feminists have written on the subject of conflict and violence; have contributed to debates on peace and security; undertaken a critique of the state; conceptualised power; suggested alternative visions of identity and community, and developed an analysis of world order and institutions. In all of these areas we will try to demonstrate how starting from the position of women's lives leads to a different perspective on the nature of, say, identity, or the problem of achieving security. However, we will also endeavour to 'go beyond' this concern with women's lives, to explore the significance of gender and gender relations in international relations. This necessarily involves addressing issues of power and inequality.

In summary, we suggest that a feminist perspective: (1) employs gender as a central category of analysis; (2) regards gender as a particular kind of power relationship; (3) draws attention to the public/private division as central to our understanding of international relations; (4) traces the ways in which ideas about gender are central to the functioning of major international institutions; (5) suggests that gender is 'embedded' in international order; and (6) challenges dominant assumptions about what is significant or insignificant, or what is marginal or central, in the study of international relations.

Origins

The openness of theoretical debates in International Relations in the late 1980s, created a space for feminist scholarship in a discipline which had, hitherto, largely ignored gender. However, feminist International Relations draws upon a rich and varied tradition of feminist thought, stretching back to at least the eighteenth century.

CONCEPT BOX

When is a feminist not a feminist?

Some of the origins we refer to were 'feminist' in the sense that they raised issues which have influenced subsequent feminists and provided 'feminist' insights. However, just as Thucydides (see chapter 1) did not refer to himself as realist, not all the thinkers referred to here called themselves feminists. However, just as what Thucydides wrote influenced realism, these thinkers can be regarded as influential in feminist thought.

There are many ways of categorising feminism. In this section, we will follow a conventional form of categorisation which divides feminism into liberal, Marxist, radical, standpoint, critical and postmodern strands. However, we will also try to historicise feminist thought and practise by sketching the relationship between feminism and Enlightenment discourses of social progress and human emancipation. In this way, we hope to draw out not only key differences in various strands of feminism, but also some common assumptions.

Feminism can be seen as a distinctly modern phenomenon. At this point it might be helpful to refer back to our earlier discussions on the nature of modernity (see chapters 4 and 5). The modern notion that human societies could progress, along with the emphasis on science and knowledge rather than superstition and belief, allowed liberals like Elizabeth Stanton (1815–1902) to argue that 'social science' showed that the status of women was a measure of the progress and civilisation of any given society. Although not explicitly calling themselves 'feminists' (see box) women like Stanton gave voice to a set of concerns and demands which we would clearly identify as feminist. For example, she claimed that the position of women was not ordained by God or determined by nature. From a liberal perspective, participation in public life was the key to advancing the status of women. Liberals claimed that women, like men, were capable of intellectual development and moral progress. This meant that women, like men, were rational creatures and so had the right to participate in public life – to contribute to debates about political, social and moral issues – rather than being confined to the private sphere of the home and the family, represented by the male 'head of the household'.

AUTHOR BOX

Mary Wollstonecraft

The English radical thinker and writer Mary Wollstonecraft's feminism was fostered by her own experiences of discrimination. Passionate on the subject of education for girls, Wollstonecraft published a book on the subject *Thoughts on the Education of Daughters* in 1787 and helped to establish a girls school at Newington Green. However, she is most famous for her 1792 treatise *A Vindication of the Rights of Woman*, in which she used liberal arguments to make the case for equal rights and opportunities for women. The book caused quite a stir at the time, as did Wollstonecraft's unconventional lifestyle. Indeed, to some extent, Wollstonecraft suffered the fate which befalls many women, in that her work was not judged on its merits alone, but rather in the context of her own appearance and behaviour. She was dubbed, among other things, 'a hyena in petticoats'. Wollstonecraft refused to bow to the pressures on women to conform to conventional notions of 'femininity', by being demure, modest and, above all, deferential to men. She enjoyed several adventures and love affairs, before eventually agreeing to marry William Godwin, after she became pregnant. Wollstonecraft died in childbirth in 1797. The child grew up to achieve her own fame as Mary Wollstonecraft Godwin Shelly, the creator of Frankenstein. (Information from: Tuttle, L. (1986), *Encyclopedia of Feminism*, London: Arrow Books)

However, at the very time that liberal feminists were rallying around the cause of women's rights, Marxists were arguing that equal rights would not lead to women's emancipation. From a Marxist perspective the notion of 'rights' was rooted in a very individualistic, anti-social view of human nature. Moreover, the end of religious dogmatism and traditional beliefs would not necessarily bring the end of women's inequality, because capitalism created new forms of social subordination. In the next century, Marxist-feminists developed a more sophisticated analysis of the relationship between capitalism, the prevailing sexual division of labour, and women's inequality.

The gist of the Marxist-feminist position was that the emergence of capitalism as a social and economic system brought about a clear distinction between the public world of work and the private realm of the home and the family. This led to particular ideas about what constituted 'work' and 'production' and in this process 'women's work', came to be denigrated and undervalued. Women's labour was constructed as a labour of love which did not require pecuniary reward. The male head of household was the 'breadwinner' who provided for his family. Marxist analysis showed how the home and the family had come to be viewed as 'private' areas of human life; clearly separate and distinct from the public realm. Here human relations were supposedly based on affection, and particularism. A man's relationship with his wife and family was not then subject to the rather more abstract and universal principals of justice and equality that governed the public world.

However, this idealised view of the family disguised the reality of power relations and inequality that permeated both the public *and* private realms. The construction of a public/private division effectively served to reduce women, and children, to the private property of men. It also rendered invisible the vital role that women's unpaid labour in the home made to the capitalist economy. Women, quite literally, reproduced the labour force, provided essential support services for capitalism through their labour in the home and served to ameliorate the competitive, alienating, stressful and exploitative nature of 'men's work' by providing a 'haven in a heartless world'. The 'privatisation' of women allowed their labour to be exploited, while at the same time disguising this exploitation behind a veil of ideas about the 'naturalness' of the sexual division of labour and women's dependency on men.

These concerns – women's contribution to the global economy, prevalent ideas about the naturalness of gender roles, and the separation of the public and the private – are central to contemporary critical feminism in IR. The emphasis on the exploitative nature of capitalism has led Marxist (and contemporary critical) feminists to conclude that women share certain common interests despite their differences. As this illustration of married life in the 1950s makes clear, the construction of women as people who achieve true fulfilment through the performance of their nurturing, caring and supporting roles, prevailed until well into the twentieth century.

LITERATURE BOX

Married Life

1. Have dinner ready. Plan ahead (even the night before) to have a delicious meal ready on time. This is a way of letting him know that you have been thinking about him and are concerned about his needs. Most men are hungry when they come home and the prospect of a good meal is part of the warm welcome they need. 2. Prepare yourself: take fifteen minutes to rest so you will be refreshed when he arrives. Touch up your make up, put a ribbon in your hair and be fresh looking. He has been with a lot of work weary people. Be a little gay and a little more interesting. His boring day may need a lift. 3. Clear away the clutter. Make one last trip through the house just before he arrives, gathering up school books, toys, papers, etc. Then run a dust cloth over the tables. Your husband will feel he has reached a haven of rest and order and it will give you a lift too. 4. Prepare the children. Take a few minutes to wash the children's hands and faces if they are small, comb their hair and, if necessary, change their clothes. They are little treasures and he would like to see them playing the part. 5. Minimise the noise. At the time of his arrival

eliminate all noise of washers, dryers, dishwashers or vacuums. Try to encourage the children to be quiet. Be happy to see him. Greet him with a warm smile and be glad to see him. 6. Don't greet him with problems and complaints. Don't complain if he's late for dinner – count this as minor compared with what he might have gone through that day. 7. Make him comfortable. Have him lean back in a comfortable chair, or suggest he lie down in the bedroom. Have a cool or warm drink ready for him. Arrange his pillow and offer to take off his shoes. Speak in a low, soothing and pleasant voice. Allow him to relax and unwind. 8. Listen to him. You may have a dozen things to tell him but the moment of his arrival is not the time. Let him talk first. 9. Make the evening his. Never complain if he does not take you out to dinner or to other places of entertainment. Instead try to understand his world of strain and pressure, his need to be home and relax. 10. The goal: try to make the home a place of peace and order where your husband can relax. (Taken from a *Home Economics* manual, published in 1950)

The construction of women as the gentler, weaker, nurturing sex reduced women's labour – cooking meals, washing the children, and clearing away the clutter – to a 'natural' extension of their caring role. Moreover, women's needs have clearly been regarded as less important then men's. However, in the 1960s, such idealistic notions of women's nature and family life were subject to profound and wide-ranging criticisms during the so called second wave of feminism; for example, Betty Friedan's *The Feminine Mystique* articulated the deeply unsatisfying and unfulfilling position of the middle class, educated American woman confined to the 'private' realm in her roles as housewife and mother.

Radical feminists took this insight into the nature and significance of the public/private division further, arguing that the 'personal' was, in fact, profoundly 'political'. That is to say that for radical feminists areas of life conventionally held to be characterised by particularism and affection, were actually characterised by processes of subordination and domination. From this perspective, women's liberation would only be achieved through a transformation in the most private and intimate spheres of human relationships. However, radical feminists also developed the concept of patriarchy to explain the institutionalisation of male domination over women, and so demonstrate that gender was not just a question of individual identity, or sexuality. The structure of gender relations in any given society was determined, in large part, by prevailing social institutions and practices, like for example, the institution of marriage, or the family, or the education system which served to reinforce relations of inequality and subordination.

Critical feminists would later develop this insight into the patriarchal nature of social and political institutions. However, critical feminists also emphasised the importance of ideas about gender in legitimising and perpetuating this form of social inequality. Radical feminists criticised liberal feminists and Marxist feminists because they saw both as encouraging women to emulate men and what were seen to be 'male values'. This necessarily served to devalue 'feminine' characteristics, values and roles. Radical feminists argued that the feminine should be celebrated. Moreover, women's experiences of nurturing and caring should be recognised as central to the shaping of a particular feminine experience and, perhaps, a distinctive viewpoint.

CONCEPT BOX

Standpoint Feminism

Contemporary feminist standpoint theory draws upon the radical feminist notion that women have different characteristics and values as a consequence of socialisation, if not by 'nature'. Standpoint theorists in International Relations place emphasis upon different ways of viewing the world, our place in it and our relationship to others which emerge from distinctly male and female experiences and their implications for how we construct knowledge about the world. This involves moving women 'from the margin to the centre' as the subjects of knowledge. In adopting a feminist standpoint the first aim is to reverse the usual understanding of events, and reveal hidden assumptions in dominant theories or 'common sense' views of the world. Standpoint thinkers have, for example, noted the failure of social scientists to address issues of sexuality, procreation, child rearing and socialisation practices as definitively human problematiques and argued that this failure reflects the 'male as norm' standpoint. The lack of men's awareness of this particular bias reflects their privileged position. However, while standpoint feminism has proved useful as a mode of critique, exposing the gender bias in much IR theory, it has been criticised on the grounds that there is no essential 'woman's nature' or universal experience of 'womanhood' which can be used to reconstruct theory. We return to this point below in our discussion of postmodern feminism.

So far, our story of the history of feminist theory and practice has concentrated on feminism in the Western world. However, both the theory and practice of feminism have been shaped by developments in non-Western societies. Over the past two centuries, non-Western societies have also experienced radical social, political and cultural transformations, which have, in turn, impacted on the lives of women and men and on gender relations. In the post Second World War period, many societies across the world adopted 'modernisation' strategies, which had a profound impact on the social and economic order and politics of many countries.

Since the UN Decade for Women in 1975, UN development agencies have included sections that are specifically charged to advance the position of women in the development process. However, modernisation strategies, based on predominantly Western, liberal values, and moves to incorporate strategies for the advancement of women around the world have created some tensions and contradictions. On the one hand, women's and men's lives have been transformed by modernisation, and more recently, globalisation, but they also continue to be enmeshed in a whole series of practices and informed by prevalent ideas about gender in any given culture or society. While it does appear to be the case that in cultures and societies around the world, women do not enjoy equal status with men, it is also clear that women's particular location within a culture or society and the meaning attached to 'femininity' in that context might serve to give women access to resources and a certain amount of social power. At the same time many countries in the so called developing world have a history of colonial or imperialist domination and, unsurprisingly, are sceptical of the idea that progress and freedom will come from following the Western model of social and economic development.

There is a strong anti-universalist theme in postmodern feminism. Post-modernists are interested in gender relations as a particular manifestation of power relations. However, postmodern feminists do not rely upon some notion of women's liberation or emancipation derived from a Western experience as a prescription or model for women's emancipation. Instead, postmodern feminists concentrate on incremental changes and socially contextualised activities and strategies which women use to improve their social position. So, for example, a postmodern feminist scholar will eschew forms of theorising based on pre-conceived ideas about 'women's interests' or 'emancipation' and concentrate instead on concrete day-to-day practices and how these allow or close off access to resources in any given situation or society.

Moreover, postmodern feminists argue that it is wrong to simply equate culture with 'backwardness'. The strategies employed by the liberal 'Women in Development' movement (which has worked within the UN system to advance the status of women) have been profoundly influenced by Western ideas of what constitutes progress. However, to assume that women in the 'undeveloped' world are uncivilised, oppressed and powerless is both ignorant and arrogant. Nor should we assume that women are always 'victims' of oppressive practices. Discourses of gender might be used in certain circumstances to proscribe what women (and indeed men) can and cannot be or do, but women are not without power. Often women will exercise power and influence through the traditional roles ascribed to them in particular societies. Women will also use all available re-sources to achieve a degree of control over their own lives and to influence others.

An increased sensitivity to gender, culture and difference has meant that since the 1980s, postmodernism has become an important influence on femin-ist thought. As we saw in the previous chapter, postmodernism can be seen as constituting a radical critique of all metanarratives of human progress and emancipation, which are, in reality, based on a particular Western experience. Postmodernism also places much more emphasis and value on different expres-sions of identity and culture. Postmodern feminist thinkers argue that there is no authentic 'women's experience' or 'standpoint' from which to construct an understanding of the social and political world, because women's lives are embedded in specific social and cultural relations. Moreover, a person's understanding of what it means to be 'masculine' or 'feminine' is constructed through language, symbols and stories that are woven into the fabric of every-day life in different societies.

By way of concluding this section on origins, it is helpful to draw out the commonalities and differences in different strands of feminist thought. While liberal, Marxist and radical feminists disagree about how women can best chal-lenge and overcome inequality and subordination, they have tended to hold a fairly optimistic view of the possibilities of human progress. Moreover, it is vital that people become active agents in the process of realising social change. In contrast, postmodern feminists argue that no one group possesses a blueprint for universal, human emancipation. This is not to say that postmodern feminism simply defends the status quo. Power relations are embedded in certain cultural and social practices, so in any given culture, dominant groups will be able to impose definitions and construct meanings and, in so doing, legitimise gender inequalities. It is possible to explore how dominant discourses about gender serve to legitimise particular social practices and how these are, in turn, resisted, but the emphasis is always on the local and the specific context.

Assumptions

1. Feminists do not regard human nature as immutable.

2. From a feminist perspective, we cannot make a clear distinction between a 'fact' and a 'value'.

3. There is an intimate connection between knowledge and power and between our 'theories' about the world and our practices – the way we engage with our physical and social surroundings.

4. Postmodern feminists apart (postmodernists reject universalistic claims), feminists share a commitment to the idea of social progress and the liberation or emancipation of women.

 REFLECTION BOX

- Do you agree that women and men are basically alike and that any perceived differences are simply the effects of discrimination? (liberal feminism)

- What do you think are the main implications of advancing a view of gender as: (a) a specific form of inequality constructed as a socially relevant difference? (critical feminism) or (b) a term which is used discursively to ascribe socially relevant differences to men and women? (postmodern feminism)

Themes

The State and Power

As is evident from the above discussion of origins, liberal feminists are interested in improving the status of women around the world, increasing women's participation in public life and gaining access to power. While working within a basically liberal pluralist framework, liberal feminists highlight the absence of women from mainstream analysis. Liberal feminists ask the questions: Where are the women in international relations? What is the status of women around the world? How far are women represented or under-represented in international relations? What are the best strategies for overcoming discrimination against women and giving women more control over their own lives and destinies?

'Bringing in' women is a first stage in developing feminist insights into the nature of the state. Looking at the world through a liberal feminist 'lens' allows us to see that the world of international relations – international politics, security, foreign policy, diplomacy and international political economy – is a man's world. The state's representatives are mainly men. Women have historically been excluded from political power and today remain heavily under-represented in the 'high politics' of state-craft. From a feminist perspective, very few women are involved in the making of foreign or defence policy, so the 'national interest' is always defined by men of state-craft.

As we saw in chapter 2, liberals view the state as a neutral arbiter between competing interests in an open and pluralistic society. Liberal feminists recognise that, historically, the state has not been equal and impartial in its treatment of women. However, for liberal feminists, male domination is largely explained by historical circumstance and accident. Given opportunities, women can prove that they are the equals of men. In this way, women can gradually overcome prejudices. A central question for liberal feminists is: Given that the state is now the dominant form of political organisation around the world, to what degree can it be viewed as a vehicle for women's liberation? For liberals, 'women's liberation' involves a multi-pronged strategy of gaining the vote, then gaining equal opportunities in education, in social institutions and in the workplace. From this point of view the state can be seen as a vehicle for the advancement of women.

Liberal feminists also argue that male domination of public international life has implications for women's status as citizens. Liberal feminists have thus contributed to a debate on the state and power in international relations, but this has largely been confined to a discussion of the implications of continuing discrimination for the status of women as citizens. Liberal feminists believe that extending rights to women, gives them a stake in the political order and 'national community'. Indeed, during the first wave of feminist activism in the nineteenth century, the movement for women's suffrage and citizenship, was at the very forefront of feminist campaigns. In more recent years, liberal feminists in the United States have used this argument in their campaign for the right to fight in combat roles in war.

One response to liberal complaints about under-representation and discrimination, is to suggest that ultimately the phenomenon of male domination of international life is explained by women's special responsibilities in the 'private sphere' of the home and the family. In order to demonstrate the relevance of gender to international relations and counter this legitimation of the existing

HISTORICAL BOX

The Suffragettes

The term 'suffragette' was originally used as a term of abuse against British women who advocated radical action in the cause of women's suffrage (the right to vote). The movement originated in June 1866 when Emily Davis (1830–1921) and Elizabeth Garrett (1836–1917) presented a petition demanding the right to vote, signed by 1499 women, to John Stuart Mill, who agreed to present it to Parliament. The action was not successful. Between 1886 and 1911, a number of Bills came before the British Parliament, but were all defeated. Frustrated by the lack of progress, Emmeline Pankhurst (1858–1928) and her daughters waged a militant campaign to bring the issue to the attention of the wider public, which included chaining themselves to the railings in Downing Street, refusing to pay taxes and even going on hunger strike. One member of the movement, Emily Davison (1872–1913) became a martyr to the cause of women's right to vote when she was killed after throwing herself under the king's horse at the 1913 Derby horse race. The suffragettes called a temporary halt to their campaign at the outbreak of the First World War in 1914. In Britain, women over the age of 30 were given the vote in 1918. It was another ten years before women achieved equal treatment with men by being given the right to vote at age 21. (Information from: Tuttle, L. (1986), *Encyclopaedia of Feminism*, London: Arrow Books)

order, we need to unpack the significance of the public/private division in supporting and legitimising male dominance. A second stage in developing a feminist perspective on the state is, then, to make visible the gendered power relationships which permeate all aspects of international relations, but which are rendered 'invisible' by powerful ideologies or discourses on the 'naturalness' of the sexual division of labour or the 'socially relevant difference' justification for gender inequality.

In our brief outline of a feminist perspective in International Relations we have suggested that: (1) gender is employed as a central category of analysis; (2) gender is a particular kind of power relationship; and (3) the public/private division is central to our understanding of international relations. How do these propositions inform a critical feminist analysis of the state and power? Critical feminism takes as its point of departure the notion of a patriarchal state. The state can be seen as patriarchal to the extent that it supports institutions like marriage and a specific form of household – the family – which both reflect and sustain a male dominated social order. The state also engages on a day to day basis in ideological activity on issues of sex and gender, from birth control to the policing of sexuality, support for heterosexual marriage, to forms of labour legislation and taxation, which institutionalise gender relations. The state may condone gender-differential terms by sanctioning or turning a 'blind eye' to differential wage differences.

Moreover, states are involved in regulating what are often held to be 'private' decisions, concerning, for example, who one can marry and the legal status of children. Although gender relations appear locked into the private sphere they are determined by the modern state through taxation, social security, immigration and nationality law, all of which retain elements of the husband/master legacy. The construction of women as 'dependants' who are identified only in terms of their relationship to men, as wives and mothers, plays a role in limiting rights of citizenship. Obviously, actual laws relating to rights of citizenship vary from state to state, but the point is, all states take an interest in who their citizens choose to marry and the implications of extending citizenship rights to 'outsiders', so these decisions cannot be regarded as entirely a matter of individual choice and inclination. We will return to this critique of the state and citizenship in our discussion of identity and community below.

CONCEPT BOX

Gender-based Persecution and Asylum

The widespread acceptance of the idea of universal human rights since the Second World War has meant that a wider range of crimes and forms of persecution have been recognised as grounds for asylum. Persecution is frequently seen as perpetrated by states against a particular social group defined, perhaps, by ethnic identity or religious belief, or is deemed to have occurred in cases where states have failed to protect such a group.

Gender based persecution takes many forms and occurs on a daily basis in countries across the world, for example forced marriage, forced abortion or sterilisation, or severe punishment for disobeying restrictive religious doctrines or cultural practices. Sometimes such repressive practices are sanctioned by states, but often they are ignored because 'private' or 'cultural' matters are seen to be outside the domain of state intervention. The construction of women as dependants of men, rather than fully fledged, independent citizens in their own right is common today. The 'people' of the nation are still often assumed to be men. Consequently, the particular kinds of violence, fear or persecution that women suffer are still frequently regarded as cultural or private and so not recognised as human rights violations, crimes, or grounds for asylum. For this reason, historically, women have not been recognised as a 'social group', for the purposes of granting asylum.

There is some evidence that this is beginning to change, thanks largely to the efforts of feminist groups around the world who have been actively networking and lobbying to influence the political process, in this case by having women's rights recognised as human rights. As early as 1984, the European Community admitted that gender based persecution might be recognised under the category of membership of a particular social group, and the United Nations High Commission for Refugees quickly followed suit in 1985, although neither the EC/EU nor the UNHCR have moved to have gender recognised as a category in itself. This development gives some grounds for optimism, marking as it does, a significant breakthrough in determining refugee status which could potentially allow many women protection under international law.

This brief account of feminist perspectives on the state, challenges the idea that gender relations and the 'private' realm have nothing to do with politics, less still international politics. In seeking to 'make sense of international politics' feminists start out from precisely those areas of life usually regarded as 'private'. It also demonstrates how power relations permeate down from the policies of the state and are an integral part of state building projects. However, it should be noted that critical feminists view the state both as a set of power relations and political processes in which patriarchy is both constructed and contested. From this perspective, feminists can work *through* the state to try to achieve positive changes for women.

Identity and Community

Some of the most interesting feminist work in IR is being done in the general area of gender, sexuality and sexual identities. This is part of a much broader critical interest in sexualities and identities in contemporary International Relations, which is not exclusively feminist. Feminists have drawn upon some of this work in order to develop a critique of gender bias and the profoundly masculinised and feminised imagery which is employed in orthodox (realist) IR discourse. We have referenced some key texts at the end of this chapter and would encourage you to engage in further reading in this area. At this juncture, however, we will concentrate on the implications of feminist work on the state for conceptions of community and identity in International Relations.

We have seen in our earlier discussion of postmodernism that war, foreign policy, diplomacy and other powerful representations of 'national identity' and 'national interests' are all central to the demarcation of the boundaries of 'community'. At the same time, nationalist ideologies have been used to foster a sense of distinctive identity and cohesion to 'insiders' and served to exclude others. Of course, nationalism and state building projects do not exclude women. On the contrary, in the West and more recently in many post-colonial countries, the struggle for popular sovereignty and national independence has stimulated demands for citizenship rights, and women have often benefited from this. Moreover, it is clear that women, like men, frequently have a very strong sense of identification with the nation. However, adopting a feminist perspective on state-building projects around the world reveals that even while granting women formal rights, nationalism can work to institutionalise male privilege and so impinge upon women's citizenship.

WORLD EXAMPLE

The Nicaraguan Revolution

The revolution of 19 July 1979 was a profoundly anti-imperialist and nationalist one. At the same time it also sought to address the situation of women in a society profoundly influenced by machismo (macho behaviour) and set up specific women's organisations. The revolution did not succeed, certainly not in terms of rectifying profound gender imbalances in Nicaraguan society, but has stimulated debate about issues such as the double work day and domestic violence which had previously been regarded as in some sense 'normal'.

As we saw in the previous chapter, national identities – such as 'Britishness' – are not homogeneous and stable, but rather constructed. Essential in the process of establishing a sense of identification with the nation and inculcating a nationalist consciousness is the telling of a particular story about the nation and its history. Ideas about gender and women's roles are often a central and powerful part of the 'story' told about the nation, its history and its distinctive identity. The idea of the nation is constructed out of an invented inward looking history; a 'cult of origins'. Women are often held to be the guardians of national culture, indigenous religion and traditions. These same traditions and values are used to justify imposing particular constraints on women's activities, thus keeping women within boundaries prescribed by male élites.

Women's behaviour might therefore be policed and controlled in the interests of demarcating identities. The incidences of rape in the armed conflicts that frequently accompany independence struggles, have to be seen as political acts through which the aggressor attacks the honour of other men, and through this breaks the continuity of the social order which it is women's responsibility to uphold. Moreover, if women challenge their ascribed duties and roles they can find themselves accused of betraying the nation, its values, culture and ideals.

So far, our discussion of identity and community has been limited to the nation-state and state building project. However, along with liberals, critical theorists and postmodern feminists also recognise other significant expressions of community and identity. The privileging of nationalist constructions of identity is problematic because it renders invisible the multiplicity of identities which co-exist within this particular 'political space' and the transnational dimensions of political identification.

In some senses we are influenced by events happening well away from the immediate context of our day-to-day lives. Transnational NGO networks are emerging and social movements are now organising globally. The globalisation of communication technologies has facilitated the growth of transnational networks among NGOs and social movements. For example, over a period of twenty-five years, women's groups have taken advantage of the political space opened up by the UN Decade and more recent UN conferences, and networking opportunities to engage in dialogue with women from across the world of diverse backgrounds and cultural experience. Increasingly, women are making use of opportunities provided by communications technologies like the internet to facilitate transnational networking, to further empower women and to increase the influence which women can have in international politics. There is now an emerging literature on women's use of the internet, which again is included in the further reading section of this chapter. The use of communications technologies like the internet was very apparent at the Beijing conference discussed further below. With respect to questions of identity and community, it is interesting to speculate on whether globalisation, the use of communications technologies and the expansion of transnational feminist networks can be taken as evidence of an emerging global feminist consciousness and sense of 'solidarity' and community which transcends state boundaries.

Institutions and World Order

The shift from international to transnational or global relations is an appropriate starting point for outlining feminist contributions to our understanding of institutions and world order. From a feminist perspective, not only is the private public, but increasingly, the private is global. Gender is then a central factor in understanding world orders, old and new. Unsurprisingly, given the emphasis on gender as a specific form of inequality which is supported and perpetuated by social institutions/practices and ideologies, it is critical feminism which has most to say about world order and the nature and purpose of international institutions. What does the world order look like when viewed from a feminist perspective? How do the policies of international organisations and institutions like the UN, the World Bank and the International Monetary Fund affect gender relations in countries across the world?

There is a growing critical feminist literature on gender relations, which is integrated into and informed by an analysis of the changing 'world order'. Of course, in Marxist terms, 'world order' is constituted by global capitalism and the states and institutions which provide a framework in which capitalist economic and social relations are 'managed'. 'Women's work' is frequently unpaid and so not deemed to be part of the activities of states, markets and international institutions which collectively constitute world order. However, not only is the contribution of women's labour highly significant in national terms, but increasingly so in global terms.

AUTHORS BOX

Marianne Marchand and Ann Sisson Runyan (eds), *Gender and Global Restructuring*

Increasingly women are making a significant contribution to the global economy. This text draws out the interconnected material and discursive dimensions of global political economy. The contributors present convincing evidence to suggest, among other things, that economic restructuring on a global scale, and the burden of debt, has a significant impact on women and gender relations in countries across the world.

Gender is also an observable and significant factor in the current global division of labour. Since the 1970s and 1980s, across the world, employers have sought to undermine trade unions in order to achieve maximum labour flexibility. Some employers have relocated abroad in order to enjoy the benefits of cheap labour – frequently this labour force is made up of women. Some employers who could not relocate, have moved to feminise their workforce. Women are paid less, because women's work is constructed as bringing in a second wage. This has been at a time when the number of female headed households is actually rising. The impact of neo-liberal development strategies such as structural adjustment is one example of how international institutions both reflect and perpetuate gender inequalities. Reform of the General Agreement on Tariffs and Trade (now superseded by the World Trade Organisation) and privatisation have all become global gender issues in recent decades.

AUTHOR BOX

Sandra Whitworth, *Feminist Theory and International Relations*

Whitworth's book addresses both material and ideological aspects of international relations in ways that draw out the relevance of gender. Ideas about gender inform and are reproduced by the practices of actors, institutions and, indeed, international organisations. Ideology plays an important role in naturalising and legitimising unequal social relations. Dominant ideas about the naturalness of gender relations and the focus on the family as the basic unit of analysis in the economy, legitimise the appropriation of women's labour and the exploitation inherent in the current world order. Whitworth questions the meaning given to the 'reality' that constitutes gender and asks how ideas about gender are expressed in both national and global social and political institutions.

As we have been at pains to point out, women are not simply helpless victims of forces beyond their control. 'World order' is also constituted by oppositional or 'counter-hegemonic' social forces. Women are organising to resist the undermining of labour rights, to fight for better working conditions and, in so doing, draw attention to the particular problems they face as both paid and unpaid workers. Through political struggle, women can and do play a role in resisting dominant power relations and bringing about change. Women's struggles typically involve going beyond narrow demands for higher wages and better working conditions. They also highlight the particular problems they face as women who must not only juggle the competing demands of work and family, and also face sexist discrimination.

Since the beginning of the UN Decade for Women, women have been organising across national boundaries to raise issues of sexual equality and discrimination against women. In the 1990s, feminist organisations have pushed to have gender issues and concerns incorporated into the mainstream of policy making. The gradual 'mainstreaming' of gender in other areas of the UN work has resulted in the emergence of an international women's regime, which has brought pressures to bear on states, resulting in a flood of gender focused policies over the past three decades. In this way too, feminist organisations are actively working to 'engender' our understanding of institutions and world order.

REFLECTION BOX

Critical Feminists

Critical feminists clearly believe that there are important structural constraints on women's activity: (1) What might these 'constraints' be? (2) What possibilities exist for people to effect changes in the existing 'world order'?

Inequality and Justice

As is evident from the above discussion, issues of inequality and questions of justice have been central to feminist theory, and, from the eighteenth century onwards, feminists in the West have asserted the equal moral worth of women and men and demanded equal rights and justice for women. Unfortunately, there is no space here to engage in a detailed discussion of gender and human rights; suffice to say that in the early twenty-first century, liberal feminists are continuing to fight for women's rights. In so doing, liberal feminists are not only internationalising the issue, but are also encouraging an active debate on what should be recognised as a 'human right'.

Not all feminists favour a rights-based strategy to address gender inequalities. Rights discourse is rooted in a Western tradition, grounded in an abstract, 'universalism' and embedded in Western ideas about 'progress' and emancipation. Postcolonial feminist thinkers have argued that all too frequently criticism of cultural practices is based on misunderstanding and misrepresentation. Women in the non-Western world are not passive and voiceless 'victims' of uncivilised societies and 'backward' cultural practices, but non-Western societies have been viewed through the eyes of Western social and political values and condemned for their ignorance and barbarity. Furthermore, where rights have been connected to the ownership of property, a traditional source of European Law exported through colonialism, the ramifications for women have been enormous, serving sometimes to displace women from land they had previously controlled or from other resources which confer a certain amount of social power on women.

These historical examples illustrate, perhaps, the dangers inherent in advocating strategies to address inequality which have been developed in a specific historical context and which may not be appropriate in another. For this reason, some writers, particularly in Islamic countries, argue that it is more appropriate to return to traditional sources of authority such as the Koran, to see if there are 'human rights' which might be derived from the Islam akin to human rights enshrined in International Law, rather than simply embracing Western traditions. Muslim feminists have traced back a debate about women's rights as far as the 1880s with the appearance of Qasim Amin's book *Women's Liberation* (quoted in Mernisi, 1987).

Some feminists reject rights discourse because they believe that the notion of rights is highly individualistic and based on a male, bourgeois experience. Standpoint feminists have thus argued that we need to develop a different conception of justice, which is rooted in women's experiences, rather than extend the rights tradition to include women. Standpoint feminists argue that women's psycho-socialisation leads them to adopt a moral code which is different, though not inferior, to the moral code adopted by men. Whereas men are socialised to adopt an ethic of justice or an ethic of rights based on abstract concepts of autonomy and rationality, women adopt an ethic of care or ethic of responsibility (duty). The ideals of reciprocity inherent in the ethics of care can be used to forge political relationships of mutuality and respect in the midst of differences and particularities and in so doing provide a fundamentally different conception of justice and ethics.

Conflict and Violence

It was suggested above that the institutionalisation of gender is central to state power. Historically, the state has armed men and disarmed women, who have been constructed as the 'protected'. Moreover, the diplomatic, colonial and military policies of major states have been formed in the context of ideologies of masculinity which put a premium on toughness and force. In the 1980s the feminist anti-war movement often treated the state's military apparatus, especially nuclear weapons, as an expression of male aggression and destructiveness. Ruddick argues that across the world it is men who predominate as police chiefs, spies, judges and governors who construct a peace-time order guaranteed by the threat of violence. The world of generals, negotiators and chiefs of staffs is still a man's world, and it is usually men who make battle plans, invent weapons and supervise their construction. Therefore, feminists refuse to view violence as individual acts committed by states. That is not to say that feminists are not concerned with the problems of conflict and war, but rather that they see such violence as part of a complex which involves institutions and the way they are organised.

Feminists argue that violence is not endemic to international relations because of conditions of 'anarchy' or because states constantly face real threats to their security from hostile foreigners, as realists would contend. At the very heart of the state are discourses and practices of violence. Acts of violence are deeply embedded in power inequalities and ideologies of male supremacy. The most obvious manifestation of this is militarism. What is distinctive about

---

REFLECTION BOX

Militarism and Structural Violence

Feminist scholars have also pointed out that our understanding of 'violence' should not be limited to direct acts of violence between states. Violence can be structural, embedded in unequal social relations which determine access to resources. Like direct violence, structural violence does great harm to people, and might also lead to premature death. Feminists claim that militarism and structural violence are linked. The higher the levels of military expenditure worldwide, the less resources are spent on food and welfare. Feminists also argue that the transfer of resources from the military to the civilian sector of the economy would, in all countries, reap social and economic benefits for all people, but especially women. Resources devoted to arms expenditure could be spent on health, education, development and in this way the most vulnerable people would derive immediate benefits. In this view, therefore, rather than providing protection from the violence of excluded 'others', the military–industrial complex actually does great harm to the 'vulnerable'!

feminist theorising about militarism is that it posits gender, that is the social construction of masculinity and femininity, as a critical factor in the construction and perpetuation of militarism and therefore the possible reversal of the process. Cynthia Enloe (see box) has argued that it is not capitalism nor the state alone, but masculinity that links the military and industry. Male employees in weapons factories may work against their own class interests because they perceive themselves as doing important 'men's work'. Government and military officials are affected by their own perceptions of 'manliness' and 'femininity' and design policies to ensure that civilians and soldiers relate to one another in gendered ways that ease the complicated process of militarisation. The patriarchal assumption that they are really doing men's work then reinforces the militarisation and the hegemony of the 'military industrial complex' in ways that may be crucial for the maintenance of such an alliance.

Peace and Security

The feminist critique of conventional approaches to war and conflict and the emphasis on structural violence, leads to very different conceptions of peace and security. Adopting a feminist perspective not only challenges the view of the military as a defender of a pre-given 'national interest', it also demonstrates that the degree to which people feel, or actually are, 'threatened' varies according to their economic, political, social or personal circumstances. In the contemporary world, the security and well-being of human beings is affected by a whole range of factors: the stability of the global economy, poverty and malnutrition, global warming and climate change, ethnic conflict, political oppression, human rights abuse, and persecution on the basis of religion, ethnicity or gender. Gender hierarchies and inequalities in power constitute a major source of domination and obstacles to the achievement of genuine security.

AUTHOR BOX

Cynthia Enloe

Enloe is widely accredited as being the first author to attempt to 'make feminist sense of international relations'. In her book *The Morning After: Sexual Politics after the Cold War*, Enloe shows how the notion of a New World Order (see introduction) can disguise the existence of enduring institutions and entrenched power relations. As Cynthia Enloe puts it, 'Any post-war time is fraught with questions. These post-Cold War years are no different. The first is always: what has changed? . . . The formal ending of the superpower rivalry doesn't look like the dawning of a brand-new day in the ongoing evolution of sexual politics . . . We are still living in a time when grand politics and the politics of everyday life continue to be defined in large part by the anxieties and aspirations of the Cold War. This continuity is especially evident in the reluctance of governments and of many ordinary citizens to make their militaries less central to their gendered notions of security and even identity'.

Liberals often argue that we cannot achieve truly comprehensive and global security, either in theory or in practice, unless we recognise that security is fundamentally a question of human rights. Indeed, in a global age, when the nation-state as the basic form of political community is subject to multiple challenges, human rights remains the most fruitful way of approaching security. Liberal feminists have stressed the importance of not only civil and political rights, but also economic and social rights in achieving security, and argued that women's human rights must be recognised as central to achieving genuine security. However, many feminists would support the position that the attempts to build global security upon the basis of a bourgeois human rights tradition based upon rational interest, egoism and the defence of property are fundamentally flawed. Indeed, many would argue that non-Western traditions which see the individual as part of the social whole and emphasise human dignity and development are more fruitful starting points for developing alternative conceptions of security. Others have noted affinities between feminist revisions and 'people centred approaches' which simultaneously argue for the equal importance of all people and their security needs, and stress the importance of the collectivities in which people are embedded.

WORLD EXAMPLE

Albanian Refugees

There is still a long way to go in achieving security for women, as evinced by the plight of women who are ostensibly viewed as refugees working as prostitutes in Italy. Fleeing poverty in Albania, such women are frequently controlled by 'fellow' Albanians, 'auctioned' to the highest bidder and 'rotated' from area to area to ensure new faces for clients. Such women frequently suffer for fear of gang reprisals against their families back home.

No discussion of feminist contributions to IR would be complete without some discussion of feminist approaches to peace. Most feminist work on peace draws from radical or standpoint positions. Historically, and in many different cultures, there has been a long association between women and peace. For example, the women's suffragette movement in Britain argued that women's maternal urges made them different from men, but that women's peacefulness was evidence of moral superiority rather than inferiority. (Women peace activists sometimes claim a 'natural' peacefulness on the part of women, whilst some eco-feminists extend the argument to include non-violence towards the planet.) Others, while rejecting biological or essentialist accounts of apparent gender differences, have noted the close association with peace and the 'feminine' and have argued that the experience of maternity on the part of the vast majority of women and women's historical exclusion from public power means that women do have a special relationship to peace.

This idea has found echoes in the calls by 'moral feminists' in the 1980s and 1990s for the inclusion of women into government élites because the inclusion of women would change the foreign policy of states. Feminist discourse on peace emphasised human connectedness, dialogue and cooperation over dominance and violent confrontation. In this way, by taking a more powerful place in the political arena, feminist peace activists are changing the terms in which public discourse is conducted.

Summary

1. Feminism is a broad church with many different strands. There are important differences in feminist theories, but also commonalities.

2. Contemporary feminist theory does not focus solely on the lives of women but is an analysis of the socially and culturally constructed category 'gender'. Feminism thus challenges the argument that *Men are From Mars, Women are From Venus.*

3. A great deal of feminist scholarship is concerned with practices of discrimination and exclusion. However, feminists do not regard women as 'victims'. Feminism is also concerned with uncovering and highlighting ways in which women are empowered to achieve positive changes in their social position.

4. Contemporary feminism does not regard 'women' or, indeed 'men' as a single category, but is sensitive to the nuances of gender identities. Given the great variety of women's experiences and in gender relations it is clear that oppression takes many forms.

5. Feminism has gained influence in International Relations theory since the 1980s, though the scholarship which informs it has a much longer history.

6. Feminist scholarship has made a valuable contribution to very many areas long held to be central to international relations.

7. At the same time, feminism challenges conventional ideas about what is central or marginal, important or unimportant in IR.

8. The central insight of feminism is, perhaps, the way in which the notion of a clear private/public distinction renders invisible a particular set of power relations. From a feminist perspective, the private is not only political, but increasingly international or global.

Criticisms

One criticism which could be levelled is that while ostensibly concerned with gender relations, feminists tend to concentrate on women, in their empirical work particularly. This is probably an accurate observation, although work is now appearing on masculinities in IR. Many feminists would counter that they are interested in gender relations because they explain how women are locked into unequal relationships, or indeed, how ideas about gender are used to legitimise the unequal status accorded to women.

Another potential criticism is that while offering important insights, feminists have failed to construct a coherent account of the nature of international relations, akin to, say, realism or liberalism. Certainly, there is no one 'feminist paradigm' or feminist theory of IR. However, many postmodern feminists working in the field, would contend that the construction of one coherent world view is neither possible nor desirable (see chapter 5).

It might also be argued that feminism doesn't take into account other major divisions between women based on, say, social class or ethnicity. This is a criticism which has been levelled at liberal and radical feminism particularly, with some justification. Most contemporary approaches to gender, attempt a more nuanced analysis which explores the ways in which culture, class, race, and so on intersect and cut across gender divisions.

Another possible criticism is that feminism relies ultimately upon the notion that there is a universal category – 'woman' – and that women share certain common experiences or interests. In reality, gender relations, 'women's experiences' and the social meaning ascribed to gender difference differ from society to society and culture to culture. This criticism is central to postcolonial and postmodern critiques of Western feminism. Again, the response has been to try to develop a more nuanced understanding of how female (and indeed male) subjectivity is constructed. However, while accepting that difference must be taken seriously, many feminists in the critical and standpoint traditions maintain that this concern with difference should not obscure the continuing existence of stark gender inequalities and the degree to which women are discriminated against in *all* cultures and societies.

Common Misunderstandings

Men cannot be feminists. Some feminists hold that ultimately one's identification with feminism arises out of personal experiences of discrimination and a feeling of solidarity and common interests with other women. In this view, men cannot be feminists, but only sympathisers and supporters. In contrast, liberals would hold that feminism is a demand for equal rights, and would be happy to attach the label 'feminist' to men who support the cause of equal rights for women.

Gender is the same as sex. No. Sex describes the anatomical, or biological differences between men and women. Gender describes the social significance or meaning ascribed to those differences.

The study of gender in IR is about women. Although many feminists tend to concentrate on the position of women (see above), the main focus of contemporary feminism is in gender identities and gender relations. The position and status of women cannot be understood without some reference to prevailing ideas about gender and how gender relations are organised in specific societies.

The study of gender and IR is only of interest to women. No. The study of gender in IR requires men to reflect on questions of masculinity, masculine identity and power as well as female identity, femininity and inequality. Many feminists would argue that the often trite dismissal of feminist analysis as 'marginal' or a 'women's issue', both reflects and reinforces the dominant social position of men and their refusal to engage with any discourse or practice which threatens their privileged position.

Feminism is another world view or paradigm. No. See above.

All feminists are lesbian man-haters. This 'criticism' is sometimes levelled at feminists by those who for whatever reason – ideology or personal insecurity perhaps – are strongly opposed to feminist beliefs and practices. The equation of all feminism with lesbian separatism and/or man-hating is without foundation. Feminism is above all about understanding and combating specific aspects of power and inequality rather than closed minded condemnation.

Further Reading

Enloe, C. (1989), *Bananas, Beaches and Bases; Making Feminist Sense of International Relations*, London: Pandora.

Enloe, C. (1993), *The Morning After: Sexual Politics after the Cold War*, Berkeley: University of California Press.

Grant, R. and Newland, K. (1990), *Gender and International Relations*, Milton Keynes: Open University Press.

Harcourt, W. (ed.) (1999), *Women@Internet*, London: Zed Books.

Marchand, M. and Runyan, A. (eds) (1999), *Gender and Global Restructuring*, London: Routledge.

Mernisi, F. (1987), *The Veil and the Male Elite: A Feminist Interpretation of Women's Rights in Islam*, New York: Addison Wesley.

Meyer, M. and Prugl, E. (1999), *Gender Issues in Global Governance*, Oxford: Rowman and Littlefield.

Peterson, V.S. and Runyan, A. (1993), *Global Gender Issues*, Boulder, CO: Westview Press.

Pettman, J.J. (1996), *Worlding Women: A Feminist International Politics*, London: Routledge.

Robinson, F. (1999), *Globalizing Care: Ethics, Feminist Theory and International Relations*, Oxford: Westview.

Schneir, M. (1972), *Feminism: The Essential Historical Writings*, London: Vintage.
Steans, J. (1998), *Gender and International Relations*, Oxford: Polity Press.
Sylvester, C. (1994), *Feminist Theory and International Relations in a Postmodern Era*, Cambridge: Cambridge University Press.

Tickner, A. (1992), *Gender in International Relations*, New York: Colombia University Press.
True, J. (1996), 'Feminism', in Burchill, S. and Linklater, A. (eds), *Theories of International Relations*, London: Macmillan.
Turpin, J. and Lorentzen, L. (1996), *The Gendered New World Order: Militarism, Development and the Environment*, London: Routledge.

Weber, C. (1993), 'Good Girls, Bad Girls and Little Girls', *Millennium: Journal of International Studies*, Vol. 22.
Whitworth, S. (1994), *Feminist Theory and International Relations*, Basingstoke: Macmillan.

Zalewski, M. (1993), 'Feminist Theory and International Relations', in Bowker, M. and Brown, R. (eds), *From Cold War to Collapse: Theory and World Politics in the 1980s*, Cambridge: Cambridge University Press.
Zalewski, M. and Enloe, C. (1995), 'Questions about Identity', in Booth, K. and Smith, S. (eds), *International Relations Theory Today*, Cambridge: Polity Press.
Zalewski, M. and Parpart, J. (1998), *The Man Question in IR*, Oxford: Westview.

CHAPTER 7

Green Thought

Introduction

During the past two decades, there has been growing awareness of problems of resource scarcity, acid rain, ozone depletion and global warming. In response, we have been exalted to 'think green' – to reflect upon the impact our everyday lives and actions have on the environment. Environmental concerns have also begun to permeate International Relations. In this context, 'thinking green' in IR has resulted in environmental concerns being incorporated into existing branches of IR theory like liberalism or structuralism. In this chapter, we make a distinction between 'thinking green' – in the sense of incorporating environmental issues into existing perspectives, and Green Thought, which can be considered as a perspective in itself.

Before looking at exactly how, we need to pause to reflect on the meaning of some key terms. First, what does the term 'environment' mean? Though this might seem like a very obvious question the answer is not as simple as it might at first appear. The term 'environment' can be used in a very general sense to describe where we are and what surrounds us. In everyday language, the 'environment' is frequently used interchangeably with the term 'nature'. The meaning of the term 'nature' is not self-evident. Nature can be used to describe the essence of a thing, such as 'human nature', or to distinguish plant life, animals and insect life from the human world. Wild and dangerous nature, is sometimes contrasted with the order and safety of culture or civilisation. While closely linked, the terms 'environment' and 'nature' are not synonymous. Furthermore, the meaning of the terms 'environment' and 'nature' can differ according to the context in which the terms are used. The relevance of such distinctions is worth bearing in mind.

Environmental concerns themselves are not especially new. There has been a long history of environmental disasters and environmental laws to prevent such disasters reoccurring. The Greek philosopher Plato complained of soil exhaustion due to agricultural practices, the people of Easter Island turned their well-resourced island paradise into a cultist, cannibalistic nightmare whilst British and US history are full of examples of anti-pollution concerns and laws. It is, perhaps, with the industrial revolution of the nineteenth century, and the increasing concentration of people in cities, that we see the beginnings of a popular consciousness regarding the environment. This has burgeoned, along with the exponential reach of technology, in the latter part of the twentieth century.

We will need to consider briefly, what exactly led to the particular perception of a 'problem' in the contemporary world to understand why this chapter has a place in a book devoted to International Relations theory. It is also helpful to pause here for a moment and consider the ways in which environmentalist and ecological approaches to the environment have been shaped by anthropocentrism, or conversely, a rejection of anthropocentric values. Anthropocentric (the opposite is ecocentric) is a somewhat cumbersome label for indicating a human-centred approach to the human–nature relationship. In looking at this, and nature-centred ecocentrism in more detail, we will be able to suggest the ways in which various strands of green thought can inform our study of international relations.

Accordingly, we will make a distinction between 'thinking green' in the sense of incorporating environmental issues or concerns into existing perspectives and Green Thought. We will use Green Thought in a more precise way to refer to a radically different way of thinking about the human–nature relationship, the problematic nature of modern forms of life and contemporary social practices, and the limitations of scientific knowledge in 'solving' human problems. In this chapter, we will take these insights as our starting point for constructing a Green perspective in International Relations. This distinction between 'thinking green' and Green Thought has been described by some authors as that between 'environmentalism' (incorporating the environment into other anthropocentric ideologies) and 'ecologism' (which is said to be an ideology in itself and may be ecocentric or at least radically anthropocentric).

Despite the influence that various environmental events, reports and books were having amongst the population at large from the 1960s onwards, in the very tense times of the Cold War, all this had little impact in IR which was dominated by a concern with power politics (realism) and later the international economy (liberal pluralism and structuralism). It was not until the end of the Cold War that IR really began to think about environmental issues and environmental philosophies in a more serious way. Although valuable work has been done, the interest of IR scholars in the environment has been regarded, in some quarters, as something of a 1990s 'fad', associated with the end of the Cold War. There has also been a tendency to treat environmental concerns as an 'issue' in international relations (thinking green) rather than regarding Green Thought as an approach to the whole enterprise.

The way that 'the environment' has been incorporated into International Relations is such that introductory texts tend to nibble at it in some or other way. For example, realists look at the possibility of wars over natural resources. Sometimes, the environment is viewed as an aspect of North–South relations;

so, neo-Marxists might focus on the close links between poverty, inequality and ecological breakdown, or perhaps suggest that a consideration of the environment raises certain problems for orthodox liberal economic theory. Liberal pluralists, on the other hand, have drawn attention to the complex interactions surrounding environmental regimes. Environmental concerns like acid rain, resource depletion, soil erosion, food shortages and global warming, even when acknowledged to be a threat to the entire planet, can be viewed as simply 'issues' which are now pushing their way onto the international agenda, or 'problems' which can be 'solved' by international cooperation.

CONCEPT BOX

'Thinking Green'

With regard to what we have termed 'thinking green', perhaps the only shared assumptions are that: the world faces serious environmental problems; the environment is important because, in some sense, continuing resource depletion, global warming, environmental degradation and pollution, all constitute a threat to the well-being of the human race; given the global nature of many environmental 'problems' or 'issues', it is appropriate that they are addressed by International Relations scholars; and global environmental problems can be solved, or at the very least managed, through cooperation in existing, or reformed, forums including global institutions.

In a broad sense, all of the above might be pointed to as examples of 'thinking green'. In this chapter, we will spend some time considering such ways in which focusing on the environment as an issue can enrich our understanding of some quite 'traditional' areas of concern such as the state, power and so on. As such, sections of this chapter are closely inter-linked with earlier chapters. However, our discussion of the environment as an issue or discrete problem, whilst congruent with the approach taken elsewhere in the book, is relatively brief. This is because we would contend that raising environmental concerns in the context of International Relations theory takes us beyond a focus on the environment as an 'issue' or 'problem'. 'Thinking green' in the limited sense of incorporating environmental concerns or issues into other theoretical perspectives is not the same as engaging in Green Thought.

Green Thought (ecologism) represents a fundamental challenge to the 'issue' or 'problem solving' approach to the environment. Furthermore, from such a perspective, the contemporary state-system, the major structures of the global economy and even global institutions are seen as part of the problem. In addition, modern science and technology, which is drawn upon extensively in 'problem solving' approaches to the environment can, to some degree, be viewed as much as a cause of global environmental degradation as offering a solution to the crisis!

Since the 1960s there has been a more serious interest in the environment, among academics in the West at least. At the heart of such interest has been a (re)consideration of the 'human–nature' relationship. Put simply, academics with green sympathies have looked to challenge a view of nature as something external to human beings which is hostile and dangerous. A view which suggested that our natural environment should be conquered and subdued rather than respected and lived with. From these deliberations on the human–nature relationship, a more critical perspective has emerged. For our purposes, we will use the term Green Thought to distinguish such critical approaches to the human–nature relationship, from the more limited and reformist forms of 'thinking green'.

The inherent optimism of some 'problem solving' approaches is rejected. Those who adhere to what we call Green Thought argue that the relationship between humans and nature largely explains the current environmental crisis and that various facets of this relationship need to be fundamentally restructured, if the planet and all its inhabitants are to enjoy a secure future. We will discuss this view of modernity, science and the exploitation of nature at greater length below. Greens have a very particular understanding of the nature of the current environmental crisis. At the heart of this understanding is a belief that the world is composed of a series of inter-related ecosystems. Human beings are also embedded in ecological relationships. For this reason it is not possible to make a real distinction between humans and other living things. Green Thought offers a 'holistic' world view which highlights the intimate connection between human life and the global ecosystem. We will aim to show, therefore, how Green Thought encourages a fundamental shift from a focus on the 'international realm' to a conception of the 'global' in contemporary theory.

 HISTORICAL BOX

First Pictures of the Globe from Space

The first pictures of the earth from space had a profound influence on people's perceptions of the planet. From space the earth is clearly whole; a blue/green planet. In this view invisible political and territorial boundaries somehow appear insignificant. These images also brought home the global nature of many environmental problems which have no respect for state boundaries.

In summary, Green Thought demands radical changes in forms of socio-political organisation and respect for non-human species. As its proponents have pointed out, Green Thought need not be a fixed position but generally involves: (1) a rejection/renegotiation of anthropocentric world views; (2) a rejection of development strategies which encourage economic growth above quality of life; (3) the belief that human interference in the natural world is currently threatening the survival of both humankind and other species; (4) an insistence on the need for fundamental changes in social, economic and technological structures and ideological/value systems; (5) a distinction between vital and non-vital needs; (6) an ethics based on a 'green theory of value' which places an intrinsic value on non-human life; and (7) an active commitment towards implementing the changes necessary to achieve a genuinely green future, which includes promoting alternative lifestyles, values and a decentralisation of power.

Origins

Looking at the origins of all types of green thinking we see a mixture of influences. Though these are complex and interlinked, we divide these into three specific areas: scientific origins, philosophical/ethical origins and political origins. Scientific/technological origins refer to knowledge about and awareness of the problem. Here, we find both breakthroughs and setbacks offered by science and technology. Philosophical/ethical origins refer to speculations about the relationship between human beings and the natural world. Philosophy has both contributed to environmental problems *and* raised awareness of the need for different ways of thinking. Political origins refer to prescriptions for the development of action to overcome a perceived crisis. Whilst these distinctions we make are not always clear cut, we hope they will help to make sense of the narrative offered below.

In terms of current interest in the environment, it has become almost a convention to cite its beginnings as Rachel Carson's highly influential book *Silent Spring* (1962). *Silent Spring* was a novel highlighting the dangers of pesticide use. Though the book post-dates a lot of environmental concerns, dating from the industrial revolution, and pre-dates a lot of serious ecological philosophy, it is since this time that the environment has become perceived as vital to the existence of humanity rather than a limitless, often hostile and external, resource to be exploited for the production of human material wealth. In other words, this book did much to encourage the view that humans should be living with nature, rather than triumphing over it.

 REFLECTION BOX

The *Titanic*

Human domination and subordination of nature is encapsulated in the philosophy behind the *Titanic*. The *Titanic* built in the early years of the twentieth century, was felt at the time to be almost the ultimate testimony to humanity's increasing ability to conquer nature. Its alleged unsinkability was typical of the view, questioned from the 1960s onwards, that human ingenuity could always subdue powerful natural forces. The fact that the *Titanic* sank did not, apparently, teach the lesson that it could have done. In fact, it is only now that people are beginning to speak of living with, rather than against, nature.

Various factors have subsequently contributed to growing public awareness of environmental issues. Regrettably these factors include highly publicised environmental disasters such as the melt-down of the nuclear reactors of Three Mile Island, USA in 1979 and Chernobyl, Ukraine in 1986, as well as the human tragedy caused by gas-leaks at the Union Carbide factory at Bhopal, India in 1984. It is only relatively recently that people have had to genuinely worry about immediate environmental threats to the existence of the species. Humanity has been faced with nuclear weapons, greenhouse gases and holes in the ozone layer; posing environmental threats which range from nuclear winter, to global warming, to skin cancer.

Many would date Green Thought itself from the publication of various doom-laden predictions about the future, most notably the Club of Rome's *Limits to Growth* report, published in 1972 (see box). *Limits to Growth* was significant in stimulating discussion, debate and research and in offering an alternative to humanity's predominantly growth orientated attitude. To some degree, the 'limits to growth' argument, combined with a rejection of anthropocentrism, can be seen as the very essence of Green Thought.

LITERATURE BOX

The *Limits to Growth* Report (1972)

Researchers used computer modelling techniques to 'prove' their findings that environmental factors would soon place restrictions on growth and/or lead to disaster. Exponential economic growth and population growth were producing a set of inter-related crises. The world was rapidly running out of resources to feed people or provide raw material for industry. Finally the ability of the environment to actually absorb the waste products of human consumption and industrial output was being exhausted. Human society would collapse before 2100.

But however we think about the origins of 'thinking green', they go back a lot further than the authors' lifetimes. Ancient philosophers as divergent as Plato and Confucius turned their attention to the environment at some point. Furthermore, notions of environmental stewardship are found in many religious and legal systems throughout the whole of human history. To some degree Aristotle, who is widely regarded as a conservative thinker, can be regarded as a 'green', to the extent that he was interested in Greek flora and fauna.

In more recent centuries, we can identify a distinctly 'reformist' strand of environmental thinking which owes much to the utilitarianism of Bentham, discussed at greater length in chapter 2. Utilitarian approaches to the environment prioritise the 'pleasure principle' and the maximisation of individual human material gain. Similarly, it is possible to identify a rather authoritarian strand of environmentalism which evokes Hobbes in calling for a 'green Leviathan' – a centralised power to overcome the ravages of 'natural' economic competition (see chapter 1). Many contemporary green thinkers and activists undoubtedly have some sympathies or affinities with anarchism developed in the nineteenth century. The more romantic versions of anarchism evoke images of people living in small scale communities, which provide for basic needs while eschewing materialism, and finding peace and contentment in this simple lifestyle, which allows them to live comfortably without destroying the environment or exploiting other human beings. As we will argue below, many greens advocate the devolution of power and decision making away from the impersonal, bureaucratic structures of central government, to the local community. Here we find echoes of Rousseau's belief in direct, participatory democracy.

Despite such complex and historical origins, we need to follow a different path in order to really appreciate the contemporary crisis and efforts to theorise it. The term 'ecology' itself is, in effect, a nineteenth-century invention, first appearing in the work of Ernst Haeckl. Haeckl's work is important because it is from this that we get the image of ecosystems as inter-related and of nature as alive. But why would it be necessary to articulate such a view of nature or the environment in the first place? To answer this question, we need to understand Western political and social thought from the sixteenth century onwards, and how modern science in particular has represented the relationship between humans and the natural world. Indeed, having acknowledged the influence of a wide range of diverse thinkers in different strands of 'thinking green', perhaps the most useful starting point for understanding the origins of Green Thought is in a critique of the project of modernity.

The idea that human ingenuity and scientific reason could be used to subdue nature and resolve a multitude of problems, came about with modernity and, subsequently, the Enlightenment. Prior to this modern period, religion played a much more important role in understanding and 'explaining' the nature of human life, forms of social organisation and the relationship between human beings and their 'environment'. For example, in Judaeo-Christian thought, human society was thought to be ordained by God and organised according to His will. This is not to say that religious belief systems necessarily preclude the domination of nature. Indeed, the Old Testament outlines in some detail a 'natural' hierarchy which justifies, to some extent, the exploitation of the natural world. However, this is in the context of an all embracing moral philosophy which encourages respect for all of God's creations and a degree of humility in the face of His omnipotence.

As we saw in earlier chapters, one characteristic of modernity is that secular thought, frequently legitimised by appeals to rationality and scientific 'evidence', played a key role in challenging religious influence in political life. The Enlightenment rested on the belief that the application of science to a range of human problems would much improve the material well-being of humankind. At the same time, the capacity of human beings to understand rational principles would allow for the reorganisation of social, economic and political life. Together, these innovations would allow human beings to continue on an onward and upward path, towards a 'better' life. The 'buzzword' of modernity and the Enlightenment was 'progress'. This new found 'faith' in rationality and science also encouraged a view of humankind as master of, if not the universe, then certainly the Earth.

As we shall see, the environmental problems that face us today have much to do with such optimism. Before looking at the contemporary period, therefore, we need to look at two particular people who were absolutely crucial in changing attitudes from almost deferential and timid in the face of nature, to domineering and confident. Francis Bacon's role in shifting images of nature from the pre-modern to the modern is highly significant. Bacon justified scientific analysis in terms which fitted the religious orthodoxy of the time. For example, he argued that not to look more closely at the world that God had created was actually an insult to God and that scientific method was, therefore, imperative. In suggesting that science was discovering the complex wonders of God's creation, Bacon was able to construct important 'loop-holes' in religious doctrine which allowed the development of science.

However, intellectually, far greater credit in this process is due to René Descartes. From Descartes, we can call this anthropocentric view of the human–nature relationship a Cartesian view.

 AUTHOR BOX

René Descartes

Descartes established two premises of profound influence in Western philosophy. The first was that there was a clear distinction between mind and body and the second, crucial in this context, that the natural world is a machine. In effect, he argued that the understanding of natural processes can be achieved by reducing them to mechanical laws. To Descartes, and those subsequently influenced by him, nature is merely matter in motion. As such it is dead. There is no moral dilemma in using nature for our own purposes and no need to look upon it with mystical awe as had been done in medieval times. The view that nature exists for the benefit of human beings and has no intrinsic value is known as anthropocentrism and has characterised the organisation of human societies in the West since. In other words, it was discovered that human beings could use nature for their own benefit; that it was not necessary to live in fear of nature and that science had the potential to transform societies.

It is worth noting that such a Cartesian view did not entirely replace what went before. Pre-modern conceptions of the human–nature relationship do still exist among small, but significant, groups of human beings, mainly those whose ancestors were not subjected, by some means or other, to European 'civilisation' and a release from 'barbarism'. Nonetheless, though the effects of industrial society have tended towards a process of reverse transformation, which we look at in more detail below, it is the case that anthropocentrism is the generally predominant mind set amongst Western(ised) populations. However, anthropocentrism is now subject to conscious reflection and the physical effects of humans denying and losing sight of how humanity is a part of, and constituted by, nature are becoming increasingly apparent. The debate over whether to resolve a perceived environmental crisis by utilising an adapted anthropocentrism or by replacing it with an ecocentrism (Green Thought or ecologism) is at the base of green theoretical arguments and debates.

LITERATURE BOX

Carolyn Merchant's *Radical Ecology*

This book locates anthropocentrism in the birth of modernity. Anthropocentrism is inextricably bound up with the emergence of instrumental rationality, the subordination or domination of nature (as Merchant puts it 'the death of nature') and the institutionalisation of patriarchal social relations.

Perhaps, we should also note at this juncture that modern discourses about the nature of man as an autonomous, rational being and calls for a more rational or scientific outlook were challenged. As we pointed out in our discussion of feminism, the Enlightenment generated a number of 'counter-discourses'. Much utopian thinking of the time was not concerned with material advancement, but with spiritual matters. However, with the scientific revolution, which sprang from Enlightenment thinking, increasingly the eternal human quest for the 'good life' became associated with conquest of, and dominion over, the natural world in the service of material advancement. As such, many Greens today hold that in the contemporary world, global consumerism, which is destroying the environment, is rooted, ultimately, in an anthropocentric view of nature.

REFLECTION BOX

Greens reject Enlightenment rationality not because it is irrational but because it is not enlightened in an environmental context. Despite the wide-ranging critique of the theory and practice of modernity, you might have detected certain modernist elements in Green Thought. What are they? In terms of attitudes towards the domination of nature for human ends, how does Green Thought differ from critical theory?

As we will see below, Green Thought has an ethics as well as a politics. What is distinctive about Green Thought on justice, morality and ethics, however, is that it attempts to think beyond the boundaries of most discourses, by broadening the concept of 'community' to include animals and other non-human living beings. In many cases, this has essentially involved taking up the theme of egalitarianism from other modern philosophies but applying it to all species, as in animal rights discourse.

Our brief allusion to Confucius notwithstanding, so far our discussion of 'origins' has been confined to Western traditions. However, it is important to note that Green Thought also draws upon a number of non-Western philosophies. Arguments here often focus on environmentally destructive development as part of Western culture and the alleged respect inherent in some other cultures for the natural world. For example, the Gaia notion of the earth as a living being, complex and wondrous, and not just as a source of satisfaction of infinite wants has important spiritual and moral implications. Not only does Gaia (earth) deserve protection, but also we might be signing our own suicide note by continuing with current practices of development based on ever expanding growth and consumption. Greens have engaged with a number of holistic philosophies which start from the premise that the best knowledge comes from understanding entities not as various parts, but as whole systems with parts that interact. The recognition of non-Western influences is important because the Green call to 'think globally and act locally' involves a serious appreciation of how local indigenous knowledge systems have allowed human beings to live successfully with nature for many years and are similarly threatened by the so called 'progressive' forces of modernisation and globalisation.

Assumptions

With regard to Green Thought, it is possible to identify a coherent set of related assumptions:

1. Greens emphasise the global over the international. For example, the importance of global community is recognised as well as the rights of local communities to control their own resources and the existence of bioregional communities as the basic building blocks of the earth.

2. Greens begin from the implicit understanding that current human practices are in some way or other 'out of sync' with the non-human world.

3. Greens stress that modern practices, underpinned by anthropocentric philosophical belief systems, have been critical in causing the environmental crisis.

 REFLECTION BOX

What are the prescriptive implications of this approach?

That is, what does it suggest we do, and what might be the consequences of such action? How far do you think Greens see possibilities for people to effect changes in the existing 'order' and the way they live their lives?

Themes

The State and Power

What are the implications of global environmental problems for the state? Is its autonomy/legitimacy being undermined by the need for global responses to them? If sovereign power must be conceded to global institutions, does co-operation mean that we need to rethink the distribution of power among states and other actors? Is our notion of sovereignty changing? If the state is facing multiple challenges, is this necessarily a good thing?

In the 1970s, liberals linked environmental issues to emerging inter-dependence among states, arguing that this was likely to fundamentally alter the state-system by eroding sovereignty. Today, some liberals contend that environmental problems like ozone depletion and global warming are compelling states to engage in more cooperative strategies, thus undermining the principle of sovereignty. Environmental practices may be leading to new norms of sovereignty.

Litfin argues that political responses to global environmental problems modify the rights and capacities of states. Many third world states lack the capacity to enforce environmental standards; the establishment of international environmental institutions and activities of transnational environmental actors, particularly NGOs and epistemic communities (such as scientists) create new forms of governance and authority. These may not be replacing the state, but they are modifying the character of sovereignty. Similarly, discourses of sustainability compel the state to incorporate some sense of ecological accountability. The growing citizen activism manifested in the proliferation of NGOs and social movements also encourage 'sovereign bargains' to be struck in the form of environmental regimes. NGOs and social movements are, of course, about politics beyond the nation-state, in so far as they provide alternative channels of control and authority and reshape social meaning and beliefs. The cumulative effects of all of these developments may be to alter the norms and practices of sovereignty and create alternative legitimate channels of political activity. Furthermore, the legitimacy of institutions of the state can be seriously undermined by social divisions and conflicts which are, in part, a consequence of deteriorating environmental conditions.

The increasing scarcity of resources can work to increase the state's vulnerability because it weakens the bonds between the state and society. At the same time, the failure of, for example, agricultural crops can increase the demands made on the state by particular social groups. A recent study by the Project on Environment, Population and Security (EPS) concluded that environmental scarcity increases society's demands on the state while simultaneously decreasing the ability of the state to meet those demands.

Realists, of course, see sovereignty as an objective characteristic which entitles states to engage in international relations. Realists might counter that whatever the challenges to the contemporary state, it nevertheless remains the only body which has sufficient legitimacy, resources and territorial control to enforce environmental rules. Only states can formulate foreign policy; international law bolsters the principle of sovereignty, so environmental agreements fortify and reproduce the principle of sovereignty and hence bolster the state system. Furthermore, the state system can actually work to contain economic forces which are encouraging the reckless and relentless destruction of the environment.

 WORLD EXAMPLE

States *have* sometimes gone against accepted economic rules by seeking to limit imports of dolphin-unfriendly tuna and unsustainably harvested timbers on environmental grounds, but the pressures of the liberal free trade system make such resistance difficult.

Even if we are not immediately persuaded by the 'green credentials' of realists, it is important to realise that not all liberal institutionalists see environmental concerns as generating new forms of political activity beyond the state. The state is a key player within new institutions.

These are some of the ways in which 'thinking green' challenges conventional understandings of the state and sovereignty in IR, but is there a uniquely Green perspective on the nature and role of the state? The answer is 'no'. As we suggested in our discussion of origins, there have been strong anarchist influences on Green Thought. These have objected to the state because it is a hierarchical institution which consolidates all hierarchical institutions. Paterson has drawn attention to the state support of patriarchy and other in-egalitarian social relations. The state also supports technological developments and forms of economic organisation that damage the environment. There is, indeed, a very influential strand in Green Thought which advocates the decentralisation of power to small scale communities or larger bio-regional communities. However, support for the state might be forthcoming for pragmatic reasons; some Greens have argued that the state must retain some powers in order to negotiate at the global level. The state can also play a role in redistributing resources from the rich to the poor regions of the world. Indeed, many Greens argue that the environmental crisis is such that reforms must be 'marched through' as a matter of urgency. Only the state can promote effective international action. So, while holding somewhat ambivalent views of the state, some Green thinkers nevertheless regard the state as a necessary institution. At the same time, Greens see an urgent need to decentre power down to local communities and also to centralise power up to the regional and global level. The nation-state is seen to be both too big and too small to deal effectively with environmental challenges and to coordinate responses.

Conflict and Violence

With a realist state-based, instrumental view, the environment is only important in so far as it can be used as a weapon or in so far as a lack of resources
can weaken or strengthen a state's power position/potential. In dealing with
the relationship between resources and power, realists perhaps feel that they
have dealt with the environment as much as they should and that they prefer
to concentrate on the essence of world politics, leaving the environment to bio-
logists, ecologists and other specialists.

However, if realists have displayed little interest in the environment, perhaps
they should? The aforementioned EPS project suggests that global warming
and ozone depletion are unlikely to be the immediate cause of violence, but
over a longer period they might interact with other environmental and demo-
graphic pressures and add to tensions. For instance, although globally there is
more than enough fresh water to meet human needs, many parts of the world
already face water shortages. Poor water resources increase the risk of water-
borne diseases like malaria. In parts of Asia and Africa there is a scarcity in good
quality crop land, while in many places around the world over-exploitation of
fisheries not only threatens ecosystems, but has already produced unemployment
and economic hardship. The EPS report concludes that environmental scarcity
could interact with factors such as these to cause significant social effects; environmental scarcity can exacerbate social divisions or create new forms of social
segmentation, increasing class and ethnic conflict. Although the report explored
the links between the increasing scarcity of renewable resources and the rise
in violent conflict within countries, it has significant implications for relations
between states. As we will see below, the scarcity of resources can generate
conflicts between states, particularly where there are existing disputes about
territory, and 'ownership' and control of resources. Poverty in turn adds to
migratory pressures; people will move to areas where environmental resources
are more plentiful, or to other countries. Migration can generate ethnic tensions, especially where resources are already scarce. Where the ethnic mix of a
country is delicately balanced, an influx of migrants can both increase tensions
and further undermine the stability of the state.

Of course, one does not have to be a realist to recognise the existence of
conflict and violence in human relations; feelings of relative as well as absolute
deprivation, fan the flames of conflict. This is exactly the kind of conflict that
military institutions find very difficult to control, never mind resolve. In many
parts of the developing world, where civil society is weak and democracy fragile,
worsening environmental conditions can further undermine the legitimacy of
government and social institutions. If the political opportunities available to
people to change their situation decline, then political violence is much more likely.

It would be appropriate to finish this section by mentioning how Green
Thought actually challenges our perception of the meanings of terms like
conflict and violence, though this is not exclusive to Green Thought. Conflict
need not imply only physical violence; conflict means differing points of view

each committed to resolving a difference in its favour. In this sense, there exists a fundamental conflict in human societies between advocates of environmentally destructive industrial society (a growth paradigm) and those who would challenge this way of organising society (a limits-to-growth paradigm). According to such an interpretation, what has been called the 'mega-machine' of industrial society (capitalist or socialist) has been inflicting great violence to the planet; to its features and its creatures.

Institutions and World Order

In this section we outline briefly some of the ways in which environmental problems have led to the setting up of new regimes or have forced their way onto the agenda of international organisations like the UN. We then attempt to go beyond this narrow concern with green issues and institutions, and consider briefly how Greens critique the existing world order and attempt to re-vision a world order based on environmentally sound principles and practices.

The international dimension of the environment has come to the fore since the early 1970s. It was at that time that the United Nations Conference on Human Environment took place in Stockholm, explicitly linking environment and development themes for the first time. Since then, the environment has been regarded as another manifestation of interdependence in international relations and another reason why states are compelled to engage in cooperation to 'manage' the problem. Put simply the message of the Stockholm conference was that how countries got rich (or stayed poor) could have environmental consequences. This stimulated a great deal of discussion among International Relations scholars.

Until relatively recently, the solution to environmental problems has been based upon a basic faith in the possibilities of development. Liberals, for example, were highly optimistic about the possibility that guarding against environmental catastrophe and safeguarding natural resources were examples of common interests that could lead to cooperation in the search for solutions. Liberals were the first to suggest that environmental regimes could be used to work out win–win scenarios in order to correct environmental imbalances (see chapter 2). Here, we simply outline some of the institutions and regimes which have grown up in response to the perceived problems of sustainable development.

LITERATURE BOX

Ben Elton on Progress

As well as writing the novel *Stark* to highlight the potentially disastrous consequences of human impact on the earth, Ben Elton's stage show also contains some eco-conscious material such as his comment that 'develop' is such a nice word – a quaint euphemism for 'bugger up'!

This notion that the environmental consequences of development, industrialisation and growth can be 'managed' has been much criticised by more radical Greens. Greens believe that many of the UN conferences and the regimes and institutions which have grown up in consequence all start out from the basic premise that the effects of industrialisation can be dealt with, allowing human society to 'progress' in much the same way that it has been doing. This managerialism assumes that development is not a problem in itself, but that minor modifications to development strategies are definitely needed to make things run smoothly. To draw a simple analogy, a car engine which is perfectly designed but which has a small oil leak will blow up sooner or later if action is not taken to correct the leak, but such action is entirely possible. 'Shallow' environmentalism is frequently used to justify reforming existing relationships, whereas some Greens argue for a radical decentralised, non-hierachical form of social organisation.

The United Nations Conference on Environment and Development (UNCED, 1992), which is sometimes referred to as the Earth Summit or just 'Rio', was a pivotal event in the concept of 'global governance'. UNCED sought to resolve emerging conflicts between the development aspirations of humankind and the need to preserve the earth's finite resources. However, the concept of 'sustainable development' which came out of the Rio Summit similarly assumed that the fundamental tenets of the development discourse did not have to be rethought, but managed rather differently. Sustainable development was popularised in 1987 when the World Commission on Environment and Development (the Brundtland Commission) defined it broadly speaking as development which meets the needs of the present without compromising the needs of future generations. This definition is so vague, and open to such a variety of political interpretations, that it means everything and nothing. It is difficult to disagree with, though imprecise, and hides many different positive and negative ways in which such a term might be understood. Whilst many act as if sustainable development is obviously good (only the exact means may be subject to limited debate), politicians similarly act as if they are faced with a single 'green lobby' and that this lobby is broadly supportive of current patterns of consumption but pleads for moderation.

Perhaps we should be a little more generous in our assessment of the Earth Summit and the various agreements it has led to. The wide-ranging scope of Rio's sustainable development agenda did require policy makers to rethink the entire web of relationships that connect humans with their environment and in turn with their local, national, regional and international institutions. Much of the text of Agenda 21 focuses on local environmental issues, such as land use, drinking water and air pollution. International institutions can play a role in responding to challenges at both local and global level, whenever international cooperation is required. International institutions take up environmental issues in response to threats to the global commons and the allocation of shared resources, transboundary spill over and externalities and disparities in financial and technical capacity. Institutions can fulfil a number of functions, including raising awareness and setting agendas, collecting, processing and disseminating information, setting international standards and regulations, providing technical and financial assistance, avoiding and settling disputes.

INFORMATION BOX

Agenda 21

This is the shorthand term used for the extensive framework document adopted at the Rio Earth Summit to guide policy makers into the twenty-first century. It is 800 pages long, partly as a result of the complexity of the issues it is addressing but also because it seems to many like a very long wish-list. Critics have suggested that rather than a radical blueprint for action it is simply details of those problems which exist and which we would like to resolve. Agenda 21 makes no attempt to answer the politically contentious issue of which problems are most important and therefore in what order we should go about resolving them.

In response to Rio and the Agenda 21 initiative (see box), it has been proposed that new institutions be set up. The Commission of Global Governance made up of twenty-eight world leaders has similarly called for the establishment of an apex body, an Economic Security Council which will provide leadership in the economic, social and environmental fields. There have also been calls for a Global Environmental Organisation. More pragmatic approaches point to the less formal but fairly extensive webs of relationships between localities, states and international organisations that already exist as examples of environmental governance. In all these ways increasingly we are getting what Werksman has called the 'greening' of international institutions.

However, it has also been suggested that UNCED should be seen as a failure rather than success. Rio used environmental groups to legitimise a project which supports developmentalism. MNCs were heavily involved and presented themselves as having the expertise to solve the crisis. This shallow environmentalism manifested itself in International Relations theory in a number of ways. For example, liberal economists conceded that their failure to incorporate environmental factors into their analysis was a weakness in classical economics. However, they do not argue that this weakness invalidates their basic premises; simply that as with other inputs and outputs a price must be attached to environmental goods if they are to be used efficiently. Liberalism is anthropocentric when dealing with the environment. It does not question the goal of human progress, or even the basic means to achieve this; it merely suggests, returning to the car analogy above, that we fix the leak. Similarly, contemporary liberal theories assume that the states can respond effectively, through the facilitation of regimes and institutions.

For Green Thought on the other hand, there is a need to challenge this view and reclaim a set of beliefs about the nature of the ecological crisis; to suggest that radical changes are necessary in order to respond to problems. From a Green Perspective, world order, as it is currently constituted, is based upon capitalism, industrialisation and a consumer culture. These dominant forms of social and political organisation are built upon and perpetuate oppressive social relationships – class inequalities, patriarchy and the destruction of indigenous peoples and communities. Modern social practices and forms of organisation across the globe are also damaging to the environment.

Ecocentric perspectives, in making us aware of physical limits, are urging us to think beyond mental barriers and our addiction to the 'mega-machine' of industrial society in order to create a radical green society. Green Thought envisages a world which would create regional bio-communities organised radically differently from the present. An ecological future would require, amongst other things, a fundamental transformation of our spirituality regarding the planet. This would lead to a de-emphasis on material things and liberal individualism and a (re)emphasis on living within limits. Over time populations would have to drop, and peoples would live in sustainable decentralised communities, similar in some respects but culturally diverse.

Beyond these arguments, we may have grounds for optimism that shallow and deep ecology need not be envisaged as simply a stark contrast between rich world tinkering and rich world dreaming respectively. The 'shallow' lifestyle changes made by many ordinary people (recycling, car-sharing and so on) may be regarded as part of a broader movement towards popular involvement in politics as well as the beginnings of the development of a deeper ecological consciousness. Initiatives like Agenda 21 can play an important role in raising consciousness among people at the local level and they will, perhaps, go on to make important connections between the everyday practices of their locality and the global nature of environmental problems.

Greens recognise that some advances have been made through initiatives like Agenda 21. At the same time, they also believe that it is important to continue to develop a critique of the shallow environmentalism inherent in such approaches. Thus Greens adopt a strategy of lobbying political élites at local, national and global levels in an attempt to influence decision making, but also believe that it is important to avoid cooption and maintain a critical distance from élites and existing institutions. In making sustainable development a self evident truth and reducing the Green movement to a friendly, yet wagging finger the Green movement has been robbed of its critical potential.

Peace and Security

In previous chapters, we have drawn a distinction between positive and negative conceptions of peace and security. Since the birth of International Relations as a discipline, scholars have recognised that security involves more than simply the absence of war. Liberal idealists believed that security required the construction of institutions and the conduct of international relations according to principle not power. In the 1970s and 1980s liberals argued for a strengthening of institutions and forums in order to bring much needed stability and facilitate cooperation in our dangerously interdependent world. Despite the long period of realist domination in the discipline, and the scepticism and cynicism of the Cold War era, this view of security has re-emerged from time to time. A turning point in the history of East–West relations, for example, was Mikhail Gorbachev's call for a new conception of security which recognised the interdependence of all peoples, economies and environments. This proclamation of interdependence, which implied an urgent need to move beyond the nation-state and achieve global security through extensive cooperation, ended the Cold War rhetoric of 'two camps' and inevitable ideological, political, economic and military conflict between capitalism and communism.

In earlier chapters we argue that both structuralists and feminists have developed important critiques of militarism and 'negative' conceptions of security which inevitably fuel militarism. Consciousness of environmental degradation has encouraged research which measures the impact of militarism on the environment, and covers both the aftermath of past wars and ongoing problems caused by current conflicts. The diversion of resources from social groups to the military can exacerbate poverty, which in turn has a negative impact on how scarce resources are utilised. The crisis of legitimacy which many states currently face is also destabilising. Conflicts cause both biological and physical damage to the earth, as does weapons testing, including nuclear testing in peace time. The proliferation of nuclear technologies and the development of chemical weapons all threaten potential disasters in the future.

Environmental disasters resulting from the Gulf War pushed the environment as a security 'issue' onto the security agenda. Through these, and less publicised but numerous 'accidents', it is becoming increasingly apparent that life is characterised by risk and that environmental risks are particularly associated with the current way in which the global economy and societies are organised. Rising sea-levels threaten many small island states who contributed nothing to the problem! More generally we are all vulnerable to a wide range of risks, including environment-related risks, over which we have no control.

Greens then join with feminists and some liberals in arguing for a positive conception of peace and security. Some Greens have explicitly adhered to principles of non-violence, or suggested that violence emerges from environmentally destructive ways of organising societies. Furthermore, debt and development are very relevant to debates about security and, for this, reason, Green thinking about security also involves a critique of dominant modes of political economy. Since capitalist economies assume and require ongoing economic growth, this has profound implications for ecological systems. In short there can be no lasting peace unless oppressive social practices are ended and injustices eradicated. As you can see, in developing a critique of capitalism, Greens share overlapping concerns with structuralists, critical theorists and feminists. For Greens, though, peace also involves establishing a harmonious relationship between human beings and other living entities. From a Green perspective, therefore, achieving 'security' requires nothing less than a change in world view.

REFLECTION BOX

(1) Political economy and the theme of inequality is clearly important in Green Thought. How does this compare with structuralist views of inequality, especially dependency theory? (2) The links between some structuralist writing and deep green critiques are apparent. For example, they share a common concern with 'over-consumption' of resources by the North. In what ways do they differ?

Inequality and Justice

We have made the point that inequality exacerbates environmental problems. We have also indicated that ending unjust and oppressive relationships is a fundamental tenet of Green Thought. It follows that engaging with Green Thought necessarily entails addressing issues of inequality. Environmental degradation of various kinds brings about a decline in the quality of human life, but clearly the weight of hardship is not carried equally by people across the world, but is felt disproportionately by some social groups within countries; usually those who are already disadvantaged suffer the most.

The 1992 United Nations Conference on Environment and Development explicitly linked the environment and development, based on scientific evidence that environmental degradation linked to absolute poverty put pressure on marginal land and advanced desertification. Reduced agricultural output and economic production can be a cause of social deprivation and increase already existing social inequalities. The enclosure of agricultural land during development processes concentrates more resources and power in fewer hands. Since Rio the link between the environment, sustainable development and inequality has continued to be emphasised. This immediately raises questions of social justice – how do we decide how resources are distributed?

In a recent book, Dobson has argued that we cannot assume that justice and sustainable development are complementary. That is, a government could devise a perfectly sustainable society but one which was based on inequalities or where some people had less than most basic needs. Similarly we can envisage 'just' societies which are heading towards environmental collapse.

Problems of justice at the international level are not obvious. Let's take the specific example of global warming. At first sight, this seems to be a relatively easy problem to identify and, with sufficient political will, to solve. Identify the 'culprits' and compel them to make amends for their wrongdoing. What at first appears to be a readily identifiable solution, is, on closer inspection, rather more complicated. First, we have to establish whether there is indeed a problem; some scientists have strongly disputed this 'fact'. Even if we assume that global warming may contribute to climate change, is that necessarily a problem? Assuming that we agree that it is a problem, we have to decide whether ultimately, we value material goods over the risks of global climate change, or coping with the consequences of pollution? Second, if we accept that the rich nations of the world have contributed most to this problem this still begs the question of whether they should rectify the damage which has already been done? Is justice, in essence about righting a wrong?

At the same time the drive for just solutions raises many potentially divisive issues. For example, Dobson argues that protecting the environment might ultimately mean less development, but this is likely to have a much greater impact on the poor countries of the world. This raises the question of whether the interests which poor countries would be expected to sacrifice are of a different order to rich nations? Action to tackle environmental problems is being debated in the context of a world where disparities in wealth and awareness of those disparities is increasing. Therefore, it is clear that the issues of development, resource depletion and environmental destruction must be viewed in the context of much more profound issues of international distributive justice. In the past few decades an array of institutions, regimes and forums have grown up that, potentially, allow some mechanism to redistribute wealth, income and resources across the globe, but if these mechanisms are to succeed, all participants must accept that they are legitimate.

There have been numerous attempts to apply the basic principles of justice to global environmental problems. For example, in relation to global warming, some theorists have used the existing framework of international 'common law' to try to decide what constitutes a 'fair' and accepted level of carbon dioxide emissions. We can only skim the surface of what is already a large literature here; suffice to say that the global warming literature leans towards the view that equity requires differential obligations between rich, industrialised nations and developing nations, and transfers from the former to the latter. Collectively, the literature indicates that it is difficult to justify existing levels of international inequality. Unfortunately, there is no real consensus on how best to move towards a more equitable international order.

You might have noticed that so far our discussion of inequality and justice has been somewhat anthropocentric. That is, questions of justice have been confined to relations between human beings. Greens are, of course, seriously interested in issues to do with international redistributive justice, because they recognise that very little will be achieved unless these divisive issues are tackled head on. However, Green Thought goes beyond questions of 'who gets what'. The environment is seen to have its own value and so Greens might want to include the 'needs' of the environment and the 'rights' of other living creatures in any assessment of what is a just order. Ecocentrism is based on an ethics that recognises the interests of the non-human community, recognises the interests of future generations of humans and non-humans and adopts a holistic perspective, so valuing populations, species, ecosystems and the ecosphere as a whole.

Identity and Community

One of the problems of attempting to think about questions of justice and ethical behaviour in an international context, is that it assumes some notion of community. Communitarians say that ethical ideas are rooted in specific communities, so arguments about justice are only convincing within community boundaries. Cosmopolitan thinkers, on the other hand, get around this problem by extending the notion of community to the entire human race. Green Thought on community is distinctive because it, at once, requires us to think about community on both global and local terms. That is, as is implied by much of the previous discussion of inequality and justice, many Greens are seeking to expand the boundaries of 'community' to include all of the world's peoples and, indeed, non-human species, but at the same time, in questioning industrial society and development, Green approaches support diversity and resist the destruction of difference which is manifested in many cultures and communities.

Greens have been criticised for encouraging parochialism in their visions of community. Some Green Thought can be quite authoritarian – small scale communities run along hierarchical, conservative lines aiming at self-sufficiency because freedom and egotism create problems. However, most Greens argue that there is not necessarily a contradiction here; while social and economic problems are global in nature, they can only be addressed effectively by the construction of small scale communities and self reliant economies. Hierarchical social relations are seen as a problem. However, at the same time, we might need a degree of coercion to meet basic ecological responsibilities and guarantee human rights. However, this would be significantly less than the concentrated, coercive powers vested in the sovereign state. These same local communities might be linked in a global 'community of communities'. Greens evoke a new image of 'community' (in the sense of universal ethics) as stretching across the globe and yet intimately connected to the locality.

From a Green perspective, of course, the problem of thinking about justice and community is made even more challenging by their insistence that conceptions of community must include non-human species. In terms of Green Thought on community, Mary Midgley's book *Animals and Why They Matter* (1983) was an important milestone. Midgley argues that questions of community, morality and ethics can be extended to animals if we accept that they are sentient beings. That is, animals might not possess the capacity to reason, in the sense that we commonly use the term, but they do have feelings. However, this view of community does not make meaningful connections between humans and animals and the ecosystems that sustain them. All ethics is based on the idea that the individual is a member of a community of interdependent parts. From this we can extrapolate a land ethic – species and plant life should be preserved because it is a stockpile of genetic diversity – which allows for recreation, aesthetic pleasures as well as meeting needs, but this is essentially anthropocentric. The erosion of sovereignty might see the increasing import-ance of local identities and communities whose lives are much more closely intertwined with specific ecosystems. In order to revision community we must get away from the view of the world divided into distinctive political spaces, like states and, instead, conceptualise the Earth as being made up of integral bio-regions. Earth nationality is one diverse place, one diverse people.

Greens argue, therefore, that the realisation of a secure Green future is not only a question of revisioning community, but also entails a radically different understanding of self/identity and our relationship with 'others'. Eco-feminism has been very influential in Green Thought, particularly in relation to questions of self and identity. Eco-feminists have developed an important critique of the mind/body dualism which is fundamental to Cartesian thought, and offer an alternative conception of what Freya Matthews termed the 'ecological self'.

CONCEPT BOX

The Ecological Self

Mary Mellor (following Freya Matthews) has argued that breaking away from Cartesian dualisms involves re-examining the lower value accorded to the underside, the body, the senses, emotion, the imagination, the feminine and nature. It also involves problematising rigid boundaries and polarised conceptions of identity obtained through exclusion. The ecological self goes beyond the boundaries of mind/body, human/nature, man/woman, self/other, to a conception of the self as embedded in social and ecological communities, acting in solidarity with and caring for others, and recognising the 'other's' intrinsic value.

You will recall from earlier discussions, that Descartes has been a central figure in the story of modernity. Central to Descartes' conception of the self and modern identity is the notion that there is a clear and necessary distinc-tion between the realm of the mind – rationality and critical reflection – and the body – the realm of the passions. The identity of the modern subject – who we think we are and how we relate to others – is intimately tied up with this notion of the domination of mind over body. The subordination of the passions is seen to be essential to the construction of the rational, autonomous individual. This mind/body dualism is also fundamental to the modern world view – the subordination of nature to rational control in the interests of human

---

REFLECTION BOX

How does the eco-feminist critique of the Cartesian world view compare with the post-modern critique outlined in chapter 5? How does the eco-feminist view of the ecological self compare with standpoint feminist views of the construction of self and identity, out-lined in chapter 6?

advancement. From a Green perspective, this notion of the formation of self through processes of self/other dualisms, is inherently problematic for many reasons. Fundamentally, the construction of self and identity is tied up with the exploitation and domination of nature.

Summary

1. Environmental issues have been taken up by IR scholars in various ways and so 'thinking green' and Green Thought have shaped the discipline in various ways.

2. 'Adding in' the environment has served to enrich many existing theoretical perspectives in International Relations and furthered our understanding of a range of areas and concerns such as the state, conflict, inequality, cooperation, institutions and governance.

3. However, 'adding in' is a problem-solving approach to the environment, based on an anthropocentric world view. Contemporary environmental problems and disasters have shown the dangers inherent in adopting such an anthropocentric view. Environmental concern has developed as a result, especially since the 1960s.

4. It is possible also to identify a distinctive tradition of 'Green Thought'. Drawing upon Green Thought it is possible to construct a distinctive Green position or Green perspective on IR.

5. At the very heart of the Green perspective is a concern with the human–nature relationship.

6. Green Thought emphasises the change from pre-modern to modern world views as crucial to our understanding of environmental problems. Whereas in pre-modern times people were deferential towards/fearful of nature, modern perceptions have emphasised humanity's ability to conquer nature.

7. A Green perspective demands, then, a radical restructuring of the various facets of human organisation, from everyday practices like consumerism, to contemporary world order built on the exploitation of the natural world and the oppression or marginalisation of specific social groups.

8. While we should be careful not to overstate the similarities, Green Thought shares some similarities with feminism and postmodernism.

9. The problems of going beyond a deep green critique (that is actually putting such suggestions into practice) should not be underestimated. Nonetheless it provides a powerful critique of the contemporary organisation of

international society. Awareness not only of environmental problems but of the philosophical underpinnings of how human beings relate to nature may be crucial to the future of the planet.

Criticisms

As with other chapters, at this juncture we will outline some criticisms of both shallow environmentalism (thinking green) and Green Thought. You should be aware that there is a debate about many of the issues raised below. We offer these criticisms as a way into those debates, not as the final word on the weaknesses or flaws in Green Thought.

First, on a practical level, shallow environmentalism seems very much to be dealing with the realms of the possible; asking what action we can take to minimise the impact that human beings have on nature but within current patterns of social, economic and political organisation. Whilst this may seem sensible, the worry is that the possible (even if we take this to mean a new international economic order – NIEO) may not be sufficient to deal with the problems faced. In the North, environmental concern tended to lose influence in the 1980s and then re-emerged in the 1990s. There has since been a waxing and waning of the Green lobby. Ultimately, the environmental lobby might only promote NIMBYism and short-term problem solving.

Second, shallow approaches have tended to urge the third world to do as the first world says rather than as it did. That is, in encouraging a different (or sustainable) development, shallow approaches tend to suggest the preservation of the vast resources of the South for Northern use, whereas more radical Green Thought acknowledges the role of the North and its high consumption practices as the primary cause of environmental degradation. In this context, the clamour for sustainable development may be more correctly interpreted as an attempt to protect the existing way of doing things against a critical tide of cultural, ecological and feminist arguments than as genuine environmental concern.

Of course, these criticisms cannot be levelled at radical greens (Green Thought). However, some radical Greens, especially in North America, have been criticised for conservatism, or even authoritarianism. This is because of a concentration on the oppression of nature over other oppressions. However, there is much misunderstanding surrounding 'deep ecology' and such accusations are refuted partly by arguing that humans dominating other humans is an effect of humans dominating nature. Moreover, eco-feminism, for example, is a very influential strand of Green Thought, which seems to suggest that Greens are attuned to the complex forms of social oppression and exclusion which exist. Fundamentally, the impossibility of growth in a finite system and the lack of respect offered the non-human world by the human, necessitates profound changes in *all* aspects of our social and political behaviour.

There are, though, some very practical problems for an ecocentric position. In the real world, wars may start over water, whales may be saved through the deliberations of an international regime and children may die because of contaminated water supplies – arguably some of the more established IR perspectives such as realism or structuralism are more helpful in understanding the nature of these things. Furthermore, the dangers of actually attempting to dismantle current patterns of social, political and economic organisation are likely to be very great. To achieve such deep green futures is deeply problematical; it would require a complete reversal of the economic growth trajectory and a radically revised international system. In other words, deep ecological prescriptions frequently tend towards the unrealistic.

Further Reading

Adams, W.M. (1990), *Green Development: Environment and Sustainability in the Third World*, London: Routledge.

Brundtland, G. (1987), *Our Common Future*, Oxford: Oxford University Press. (World Commission on Environment and Development, The Brundtland Report.)

Carson, R. (1962), *Silent Spring*, Harmondsworth: Penguin.
Conca, K. (et al.) (1995), *Green Planet Blues*, Boulder, CO: Westview Press.

Dobson, A. (1995), *Green Political Thought* (2nd edition), London: Routledge.
Dobson, A. (ed.) (1999), *Fairness and Futurity: Essays on Environmental Sustainability and Social Justice*, Oxford: Oxford University Press.

Eckersley, R. (1992), *Environmentalism and Political Theory: Towards an Ecocentric Approach*, London: UCL Press.
Elliot, J. (1994), *An Introduction to Sustainable Development: The Developing World*, London: Routledge.

Hayward, T. (1994), *Ecological Thought: An Introduction*, Oxford: Polity Press.
Homer-Dixon, T. and Blitt, J. (eds) (1998), *EcoViolence: Links Among Environment, Population and Security*, London: Rowman and Littlefield.
Hurrell, A. and Kingsbury, B. (eds) (1992), *The International Politics of the Environment*, Oxford: Oxford University Press.

Imber, M. (1994), *Environment, Security and UN Reform*, Basingstoke: Macmillan.

Litfin, K. (ed.) (1998), *The Greening of Sovereignty in World Politics*, Cambridge, MA: MIT Press.

Matthews, F. (1991), *The Ecological Self*, London: Routledge.

McCormick, J. (1989), *Reclaiming Paradise: The Global Environmental Movement*, Indiana: Indiana University Press.

Meadows, D. (et al.) (1972), *The Limits to Growth*, Washington, DC: Potomac Associates.

Mellor, M. (1997), *Feminism and Ecology*, Oxford: Polity Press.

Merchant, C. (1992), *Radical Ecology: The Search for a Liveable World*, London: Routledge.

Paterson, M. (1996), 'Green Politics', in Burchill, S. and Linklater, A. (eds), *Theories of International Relations*, Basingstoke: Macmillan.

Pepper, D. (1996), *Modern Environmentalism: An Introduction*, London: Routledge.

Porritt, J. (1984), *Seeing Green*, Oxford: Blackwell.

Sessions, G. (ed.) (1995), *Deep Ecology for the 21st Century*, London: Shambhala.

Susskind, L. (1994), *Environmental Diplomacy: Negotiating More Effective Global Agreements*, Oxford: Oxford University Press.

Thomas, C. (1992), *The Environment in International Relations*, London: Royal Institute of International Affairs.

Werksman, J. (ed.) (1996), *The Greening of International Institutions*, London: Earthscan.

Conclusions

The Postpositivist Debate in IR

This concluding chapter has two main aims. First, to pull together some of the themes that have run through the preceding chapters. Second, to develop your understanding of the theoretical underpinnings of International Relations a little further, through a discussion of the so called 'postpositivist' debate. By this stage, you might feel that you have learnt enough about theory and your time would be better spent learning more about the practice of world politics. In this case, you might opt to put this book aside for the time and, perhaps, come back to this chapter later on in your studies. If, however, you are inspired to read on, be forewarned that this debate raises some quite complex questions – to do with the politics of 'knowledge claims' and the relationship between theory and practice – which are not easy to grasp immediately.

What are we studying when we study 'International Relations'? As is evident from the foregoing discussion, there is no simple answer to this question. For some scholars, the 'critical turn' in IR theory since the mid-1980s, and the proliferation of perspectives like postmodernism, critical theory, feminism and Green Thought, along with the blurring of boundaries between IR and other areas of the social sciences and social theory, is a cause of not a little anxiety. These developments could be viewed as undermining the notion of International Relations as a distinctive 'discipline' – a branch of learning or discrete area of study concerned with the high politics of war, diplomacy and foreign policy – and so weaken its claims to be relevant to policy makers.

However, it could be objected that positing that IR theory should provide a guide for policy makers to safeguard or further the national interest, presupposes an implicitly realist distinction between the domestic and the international realms. Arguably this has always been something of a fiction. The notion of a clear domestic and international/global division is difficult to sustain in the wake of economic interdependence, nuclear weapons, the growth of global telecommunications networks and changes in weather systems which necessarily affect all of the world's peoples, and are beyond the control of any single state. It may well be that other theoretical perspectives are actually more helpful to policy makers.

Moreover, liberals, structuralists and critical theorists, in a broad sense of the term, would no doubt contend that this complaint is in any case based on a narrow and partial view of IR. One could argue that there has never been a consensus on the core concerns of the discipline. Although International Relations was born out of the human tragedy of war, from the earliest times there have been debates about what its main focus should be, disagreements about how to go about studying the world and contrasting views on the purposes this knowledge could serve. Furthermore, 'politics' is not simply about the activities of government and the formulation and implementation of policy, but is more broadly concerned with the exercise of power and so embraces a variety of 'actors', processes and interests. Should not theory also be useful as a 'guide to action' to NGOs or social movements like Greenpeace, Oxfam, Amnesty International, Jubilee 2000, or the international women's movement, perhaps? (This has been the subject of a recent debate between Wallace, Booth and Smith – see further reading.)

However, rejecting realism as the dominant perspective, entails accepting that at all levels – ontological, epistemological and methodological – IR is essentially contested. We will now deal with each of these areas in more detail.

What is the Nature of the World? What Can Be Said to Exist?

It is clear from the above discussion that theoretical perspectives are necessarily partial, based on certain assumptions about the main actors, processes and issues in the study of international relations. In IR theory there may be a degree of consensus about what 'exists' in the sense that we can identify 'actors' such as states, international institutions, NGOs, social movements and multinational corporations, even if theorists disagree about the role, relative weight or significance of these 'actors'.

However, we immediately run into problems when we try to understand, say, the nature of the state, or identify the existence of structural inequalities between social groups or countries. Clearly, in all of these cases, we are not dealing so much with real 'things' directly, but with intellectual constructs – ideas and concepts which help us read or construct 'reality' and thereby gain an understanding of the material world around us. There is also disagreement about the dominant processes in international relations. For example, realists argue that conflict between states is inevitable because it is the nature of 'man' to try to dominate and oppress others; liberals hold that cooperation is an essential feature of international life; while structuralists believe that a major process is conflict between states and social classes. Inevitably, this means that there are disputes about whether we can speak meaningfully of structural inequalities, observable cycles of economic booms and depressions, real balances of power, or manifest patterns or networks of cooperation.

Moreover, as we have seen, there is something of a divide between those who view the world through an essentially state-centric prism and those who argue for a holistic approach to 'global relations'. So while realists offer a view of the world as a system of territorially bounded nation-states, Green thinkers view the 'global' as a complex array of interconnected ecosystems sustaining human, animal and plant life. While recognising the existence of 'artificial' political boundaries between territories (land/earth) and peoples, Greens argue that drawing rigid distinctions between the 'national' and 'international', obscures the interconnected and interdependent nature of all life on the planet. If we were to adopt a postmodern position, we would gain a fluid and dynamic understanding of how discourses of political identity are intimately connected to actual practices like war and foreign policy, which involve the carving up of political space on a global scale. In short, theoretical perspectives conceptualise or construct the domain of international relations in distinctive and contrasting ways.

One of the most fundamental assumptions which theoretical perspectives make is about 'human nature'. We have employed a somewhat simplistic notion of 'human nature' in this text, in the hope that it will encourage you to think about how making sense of the (social) world around us, necessarily presupposes some conception of human nature/being – who and what we are – and how we relate to others. In plain terms, if we think that 'man' is power seeking, selfish and instrumental in relationships with others, then we can apprehend that the substance of international relations or international politics is power and the pursuit of interests. Conversely, if we believe ourselves and others to be rational creatures, capable of reflection and moral development, then we begin to grasp the human capacity for cooperation in the interest of realising a better, more rationally organised world. Liberal idealism is sometimes taken to mean a somewhat utopian, optimistic and, perhaps, naive scheme to organise world affairs on the basis of principles of justice, moral right and the rule of law. However, there is rather more to idealism than wishful thinking. The desire to construct a just international order is rooted in profound philosophical beliefs about the developmental capacity of the human person or self.

The branch of philosophy that deals with the nature of existence or being is called ontology. From time to time in this text, we have referred to modernity and a distinctly modern conception of 'man'. Central to modern, Western social and political thought is the concept of 'autonomous man', which is supposed to represent all of us. 'Autonomous man' develops consciousness as a real, living, cognisant being by differentiating 'himself' from other people and from the natural world around. The modern person, then, is presented as an independent individual who has a strong sense of boundaries and distance from other people, animals and the 'natural' world.

You will recall that Greens have a very different conception of our 'nature' (our subjectivity or selfhood) and our relationship with the so called natural world. At the heart of Green Thought has been a reconsideration of the 'human–nature' relationship. Greens reject the idea that our natural environment should be conquered and subdued rather than respected and lived with. The 'ecological self' is not understood in terms of separation, difference and domination over nature, but rather in terms of connection with nature. This gives rise to a world view which emphasises the interconnected nature of human life, animals and ecosystems across the planet. This notion of the self as 'embedded' or connected is not uncommon in non-Western philosophies like Buddhism. Postmodern and standpoint feminists also critique this atomistic conception of 'autonomous man' because they see it as a gendered construct. The characteristics of this subject or self – rationality rather than passion or sentiment, for example – are associated with the masculine, not the feminine, self. Marxist inspired theory sees the genesis of human experience in social labour and the social reproduction of the species. Contemporary critical theorists do not rely so heavily on ideas about labour and social class in the formation of consciousness or identity, but rather link the formation of the human psyche, with the institutional framework of society. So we might reject the idea that 'human nature' is fixed and immutable, because people develop a sense of identity and infuse their lives with meaning through language; specifically the capacity to recount a continuous life history.

Ontology and its relationship to theory is, then, complex and we need not elaborate any further here; suffice to say that it is not possible to separate ontological questions – what and who we think exists – from how we understand the nature of the world around us, and how we construct world views or theoretical perspectives on international relations.

What Can We 'Know'?

Facts are meaningless. You can use facts to prove anything that's remotely true. (Homer J. Simpson)

The construction of theoretical perspectives leads us on to issues of epistemology. Epistemology is concerned with the nature and purpose of human knowledge. In regard to questions of epistemology, contemporary IR theory is currently in the throes of the so called postpositivist debate (sometimes referred to as the third or even fourth debate, see below). Of course, debates within IR theory do not take place in a vacuum and the postpositivist debate has to be understood in terms of its relation to a wider debate in social theory. For this reason, we have included in the further reading some key texts by authors who are not identified with IR directly, but whose ideas have been very influential. However, again our aim is to simplify as much as possible and so for our purposes we will limit our discussion to IR. Here we can broadly identify the main divisions or positions in this debate which are between those who argue that it is possible to understand the world objectively, and those who believe that interests, values and dominant power relations inevitably shape the activity of theorising and the claims that are made about the 'real' world.

Positivism is associated with the methods and epistemological claims of the natural sciences. A biochemist, for example, might study the function of bacteria in the human digestive system. In this case, social, moral or political values – whether he or she supports the institution of marriage, believes that lying is sometimes justifiable, or votes for the Conservative Party – are unlikely to have any bearing on the task in hand. There is a school of thought which argues that it is possible to gain a much better understanding of international relations by attempting to emulate the methods of the natural sciences, putting aside our own values and beliefs in an endeavour to establish the 'facts' about the world. On the other hand, it can be argued that social values and practices always have a bearing on research, influencing both what we choose to study, and how we interpret the evidence. In this view, the natural world and social world are different, because the social world is a world infused with social and cultural meanings, constructed through language which invokes powerful symbols and imagery. From this point of view, positivism is dangerous because it tends to imply that certain phenomena occur 'naturally'. For example, if we 'establish' that major wars occur at regular intervals, or in 'long cycles', we do not necessarily need to understand the motives or beliefs of those involved to understand why wars break out. Human beings become 'objects' of study, because it is assumed that a social phenomenon (in this case war) can be understood without reference to the meanings which people ascribe to social situations.

It is not uncommon for students to confuse positivism with state-centrism, but state-centric approaches are not necessarily positivist. For example, the English School (see glossary) is a state-centric approach to IR, but adherents of this school of thought do not regard the study of international relations as a scientific enterprise. Instead they argue for a more intuitive approach (things which can be known without conscious reasoning, by instinct perhaps) and draw upon philosophy, law, history and political theory in their studies.

Sometimes positivism is equated with realism, liberalism and structuralism and postpositivism with critical theories like Frankfurt School, feminism and postmodernism, but, again, this is misleading. For example, there is some disagreement about whether realism should be regarded as a positivist approach. On the one hand, classical realists were explicit about the basis on which they staked their claims, or constructed knowledge about the world. The 'Machiavellian strand' of realism claims to represent the world view of the statesman or diplomat who is forced to operate in an uncertain and dangerous world. Realism provides a guide to action based on the guiding principles of *realpolitik* in the interests of the preservation of the nation-state. In this view, the 'balance of power' is a conscious strategy, or practice, pursued by states-men, diplomats and military leaders to preserve the peace, or more accurately to prevent the dominance of one power and maximise the autonomy of indi-vidual nation-states. Clearly, realists invest value in the state, or they would not be so deeply concerned with problems of 'national security' and autonomy, and their knowledge of international relations is constructed from the point of view of the interests and affairs of the state.

On the other hand, realists clearly believe that 'threats' are real threats, the world is dangerous and uncertain, these conditions exist independently of what we imagine or what we would like to believe about the world. At different times, influential writers like Morgenthau and Carr have both insisted that the study of International Relations should eschew normative concerns with justice or rights in the interest of discovering more about the realities of power. This was taken a stage further in the 1960s, when the North American behavioural-ist school insisted that researchers adopt the exacting standards of scientific analysis and research in their studies. Behaviouralists took key concepts from realism – the state and power – but developed a positivist, mechanistic view of the workings of the international system. Positivism remains a powerful influence on the study of IR in the USA.

The Hobbesian influences on realism are also significant in this respect. Hobbes was influenced by early modern science. As we have noted on a num-ber of occasions, the rise of science was associated with the control, or sub-ordination of nature in the service of human needs or wants. Knowledge thus came to be associated with the subordination of nature and in this process the 'knower' was clearly regarded as standing outside of, rather than a part of, the natural world. Hobbes was a quintessentially modern thinker in that he posited a sharp division between 'reason' and 'sentiment' and identified reason with 'knowledge'. Feminist philosophers like Sandra Harding have challenged this division between the 'knower' (mind/subject) and the 'knowable' (nature/object), arguing that it is profoundly gendered. The so called 'objectivity' of science presupposes a scientific mind and modes of knowing rigidly set apart from what is to be known, that is nature, which is identified metaphorically with the 'feminine'. In this way, the 'masculine' by association comes to connote autonomy, separation and distance. Moreover, all 'scientific' ideology specifies the relation between knower and known as one of distance and separation. Another way of putting this is that positivism is based on the premise that onto-logical considerations – who and what we think exists – have nothing to do with epistemology – the claims we make about the world. Many social theor-ists (including International Relations theorists) would reject this premise.

For these reasons, realism is frequently subject to postpositivist critiques, but you should be aware that realists are not necessarily always unreflective about the values and beliefs which underpin their world view. The 'problem' with realism is not that it is a particular and partial construction of a complex reality – all theoretical perspectives are particular and partial constructions of reality – but that it is often presented as 'common sense' or 'objective reality' and its claims are used to marginalise or undermine the 'utopianism' of alternative positions (more on this below).

In philosophical terms, an idealist is one who holds that our pictures, or images, of 'reality' come to us through our ideas about the world. That is to say that the whole structure of 'reality' is a creation of the mind. All that exists are our ideas, or mental concepts, or mental images. We are able to construct categories and concepts which collectively give us a picture of reality and help us to understand our world because we are capable of rational thought. Idealists are, therefore, deeply reflective about the conditions under which it is possible to 'know'.

However, some liberals are influenced more by empiricism than by idealism. Empiricism holds that all human knowledge is arrived at by experience. Empiricists do not posit the existence of transcendental reason, but rather argue that we 'know' things because we are sentient beings, who observe certain acts, or events, experience particular sensations and learn, over time, how to properly interpret these experiences. So, for example, a small child might not 'know' that if she puts her hand in the fire she will be burnt, but over time she will be told of the dangers, or might let her natural curiosity get the better of her, or witness a friend's unfortunate error. Either way, the child will eventually learn that fire can be dangerous and should be avoided. However, when empiricism is applied to the study of the social world, there is a danger that it can lead to the endless recording of evidence, or the collection of data which is presented as 'fact', without much conscious reflection on what specific motives are driving a particular research project, or how the information is being interpreted and what ends it serves.

REFLECTION BOX

Structuralism

Is structuralism a positivist approach? To help you answer this question you might like to re-read the section on 'origins' in chapter 3. Also, think about some key concepts in structuralist thought like, for example, 'surplus value', or the 'world-system'. Do these imply that real, material structures exist which can be understood independently of the values, beliefs or interests of the 'knower'?

We do not have much difficulty in clearly identifying postpositivist approaches in IR theory. Critical theory, postmodernism, feminism and Green Thought are generally regarded as postpositivist approaches. However, this classification is not quite as straightforward as it at first appears. Moreover, postpositivism is not all of one kind, in the sense that there are important differences between each of these approaches.

For example, the linkage between knowledge, power and social practice is, of course, at the heart of postmodernism. Postmodernism is a postpositivist position because it rejects the idea that there are objective facts about the world that can be discovered through painstaking research and the testing of hypotheses. The claims of science cannot be seen as impartial or not influenced by the social conditions of the age. In the past, science has been used to 'prove' that people of Asian and African origin had smaller brains and were inferior to Caucasians. Similarly, some Darwinists have claimed in the past that women did not contribute as much as men to the evolution of the human species. We no longer believe these things to be true, but at one time they were accepted as 'scientifically proven' and, moreover, served to justify the subordination of women and black and Asian peoples (interestingly, Darwinism has been making something of a comeback recently and this has again opened up debates about gender differences). Furthermore, postmodernism regards the whole Enlightenment project as imbued with bias and serving to consolidate the position of powerful groups.

On the other hand, critical theorists are explicit about the connections between knowledge and interests, but do not reject Enlightenment ideals or the possibility of scientific advancement completely. Habermas was inspired to construct a theory of society, because he wanted it to serve a practical end – the self-emancipation of people from forms of domination. This does not mean that Habermasians completely reject the notion of science and scientific analysis. Why should they? If science can help us to gain a better understanding of ourselves, why we succumb to certain illnesses perhaps, or how we could transcend the limits imposed upon us by our physical bodies, by discovering the laws of aerodynamics, then why not harness the potential of science? There are certain spheres of human life where the pursuit of scientific knowledge and understanding is perfectly legitimate. The 'problem' does not lie in science *per se*, but the influence of scientism, or positivism, in philosophy and other spheres of thought which are to do with the meaning and purpose of human life.

There is no contradiction here. Critical theorists hold that there are different forms or kinds of knowledge which serve different ends or purposes. So, for example, scientific and technical knowledge is in essence about the objectification of nature in the interests of human advancement, while the social and human sciences are, or should be, directly concerned with the conditions under which human beings achieve greater autonomy, control and freedom in their lives. Critical theorists hold that knowledge about the social world is necessarily of a different kind from knowledge about the natural world. In science we might desire knowledge in order to subordinate or control the natural world, but knowledge about the human world is sought in order to foster greater freedom, rather than greater control – or at least it should be. The 'problem' is that we no longer regard science as one form of possible knowledge, but rather identify knowledge only with science. A scientific ethos had also come to dominate philosophy in the form of positivism and has become more influential in the study of the social world generally. If emancipation is to remain a project for humanity then the influence of scientism, which has given rise to a tendency to regard all human problems as essentially technical problems amenable to technical solutions, must be countered. In turn, this can only be achieved if the epistemological subject (the 'knower') is reflective and consciously aware of his/her interests, motives and to determine his/her own actions. In this way, knowledge is generated which enhances autonomy and responsibility.

Feminism is not all of one kind either. As we have seen, feminists have critiqued 'dominant' IR perspectives, particularly realism, on the grounds that they are imbued with gendered assumptions and a masculinist bias. However, there is a division between feminist standpoint theorists, who argue that it is possible to reconstruct IR theory from a 'woman's point of view', and those who embrace postmodernism. To return to our earlier point about the relationship between ontology and epistemology, some standpoint theorists argue that women's experiences of child rearing and caring for others give rise to a sense of 'self' which is embedded in a network of – mainly cooperative – relationships. The woman comes to understand her 'self' in relation to others, rather than developing a sense of selfhood grounded in abstract individualism. This has implications, of course, for how we think about many aspects of international relations, from security and power, to questions of identity and community. While postmodern feminists are not hostile to the idea of constructing different kinds of knowledge or seeing the world through different lenses, they steer clear of epistemological claims made in the name of 'women' in general. We will not labour these epistemological points any further at this stage; simply be aware that while we can usefully group together a range of 'critical theories' for some purposes, in many ways they are quite different from one another. Similar simple divisions of theories into positivist/postpositivist can disguise subtle and important distinctions both within and between schools of thought.

 REFLECTION BOX

Science and Deep Ecology

Here we have identified Green Thought as a postpositivist approach and it is easy to see why. Greens believe that far from helping human beings, scientific knowledge and attempts to achieve more and more control over the natural world have done a great deal of harm to the planet and all creatures that live on it. Greens also believe that the emergence of the modern period and the triumph of science, helped men to establish their power over women and legitimised the domination of the West over the rest of the world. Therefore, knowledge cannot be considered value-free and objective. Greens also argue for a fundamental change in how we understand ourselves and our relationship with nature. At the same time, at least some part of the Green perspective relies upon scientific evidence, of the hole in the ozone layer, for example, or the damage caused to forests by acid rain. Are these two positions compatible do you think?

What is IR Theory? What is it For?

Although we have noted important differences between postmodernism, critical theory, feminism and Green Thought, we have suggested that for some purposes they can be grouped together as 'postpositivist' or 'critical' approaches in IR. This is because they all highlight the importance of the social and historical context in which the activity of theorising takes place. Critical perspectives raise questions about the nature of theory and, crucially, what or who it is for. The central insight of the 'postpositivist debate' has been that knowledge is never innocent. It is always 'for' someone, or at least some purpose.

The so called 'inter-paradigm debate' of the 1980s (sometimes, the 'third debate') was essentially a debate about the implications of competing paradigms in IR (see box). What emerged out of the inter-paradigm debate was the insight that realism, liberal pluralism and structuralism, which were the three main perspectives in IR at the time, were not so much different interpretations of the 'real world', but ideological constructs, rooted in competing value systems and driven by different normative agendas. It was also recognised that since these perspectives constructed – rather than described – reality differently, their world views could not be compared in any meaningful way.

AUTHOR BOX

Thomas Kuhn on The Nature of Paradigms

A paradigm is a shared understanding and way of approaching problems which is accepted by a community of scholars and used to inculcate students with fundamental ways of 'knowing the world'. Thomas Kuhn, a historian of the natural sciences, believed that even in science, theory could not be seen as an activity designed to discover or establish 'truth'. Paradigms did not describe reality but rather constructed reality differently. These broad world views – fundamental assumptions about the nature of the world and how it works – were generally accepted by scholars, and once established, profoundly influenced the way that research projects were identified and carried out. For long periods of time, the central beliefs or assumptions of a paradigm are not contested and can even be used to define the field as 'not contested'. However, at particular periods in history dominant paradigms were subjected to challenge, perhaps because they were seemingly unable to explain new phenomena, or because more persuasive accounts emerged. For example, Newtonian physics had been the influential paradigm for a long period of time but was eventually displaced by quantum physics, influenced by Einstein, Bohr and others early in the twentieth century. Since paradigm shifts did take place from time to time, Kuhn argued that science should not be seen as a quest for 'truths', but more as a gradual moving away from falsity.

When Kuhn's insights are applied to the social sciences (see box), it suggests that one has to be sensitive to how disciplines have developed historically, which paradigms have been widely accepted and the consequences of this. Paradigms are not accurate representations or models of the 'real' world, but our best beliefs about 'reality' in any one historical period. As we have noted in earlier chapters, realism became influential in the study of IR in the aftermath of the Second World War and during the Cold War period to the degree that it became almost an established 'orthodoxy' – its fundamental assumptions and propositions were widely accepted and served as a guide to empirical research projects and the construction of knowledge in the discipline. So much so that for a long period of time the central beliefs or assumptions of realism were 'not contested'. Critical theorists take this one stage further by arguing that dominant paradigms (in effect realism) reflect the assumptions and beliefs about the world of powerful groups in particular historical periods, and, moreover, in some sense serve the interests of such groups. So, realism, can be seen as a world view which attempts to identify and explain certain historically contingent phenomena, like the state-system, anarchy, power politics – but which both reflects and furthers the interests of dominant states, or influential groups within dominant states. From this perspective, the ideology, or discourse, of realism, constructs a particular model of the world which then serves to justify and perpetuate the kind of social and political order it describes.

If theories are constructed from particular perspectives and are always conditioned by the social, political and historical context in which the theorist operates, this suggests that at the very least there are multiple 'realities' and multiple perspectives on the world. It is probably accurate to say that realism retained its hegemonic position in IR theory even in the face of the emergence of competing perspectives like liberal pluralism and structuralism. The existence of competing perspectives, immediately raised the question of why and how realism had established such a dominant position in IR and, in so doing, shifted the focus of enquiry to the relationship between power and knowledge.

In the face of what appeared to be a theoretical impasse, Hoffman (see further reading) argued that IR should embrace critical theory because this approach was at once materialist, historical and reflective about the ideological nature of knowledge claims. Critical theory was championed as the 'next stage' or future of IR. The postmodern response was to embrace theoretical pluralism, not because elements of world views could be combined to give us a better understanding of international relations, but because this had the effect of weakening the truth claims of powerful groups and empowering those previously marginalised in the study of IR. That is, recognition that there were numerous ways of viewing the world, many different 'lenses', which opened space for other approaches or perspectives like, for example, feminism. In other areas of the social sciences, academic enquiry has gone beyond the type of understanding which is offered within the inter-paradigm debate. In so far as IR theorists are now beginning to reflect more deeply upon the profound implications of social practices, culture and, crucially power relations, in the construction of knowledge about the world, IR theory (what Jim George has labelled the 'backward discipline') is beginning to 'catch up' with trends in other branches of social theory.

Does it Matter Which Perspective I Adopt?

If knowledge is never disinterested, impartial or 'objective', then you might conclude that all perspectives are equally valid or, conversely, equally 'wrong'.

Moreover, if knowledge is generated only within the framework of existing paradigms or perspectives, there is surely no such thing as 'correct' or 'final' understanding? You might reasonably ask, therefore, if there are any good reasons to accept or reject competing knowledge claims, or if it actually matters which perspective you adopt. Clearly, it *is* important although scholars do not agree about why it is important! Below we will try to explain why theory matters, by elucidating a little more on the politics of knowledge claims and the relationship between theory and practice.

First, choosing to adopt one position or perspective rather than another matters because it involves making judgements about what is significant and insignificant, central or marginal, enduring or ephemeral. As is evident from our discussion of feminism, these choices are not innocent, but profoundly political. Feminists claim that if we choose to focus solely on the male dominated world of states and foreign policy, for example, we effectively marginalise the study of women in IR. More importantly such analysis presupposes a public/private division and thus disguises the profoundly gendered nature of international politics. From this point of view, failing to highlight issues of gender in both the theory and practice of international relations further perpetuates unequal power relations.

Having said that, there is some disagreement among feminist scholars about what the focus of feminist scholarship should be. So, for example, liberal feminists want to 'bring in' women, by undertaking more empirical research on the status of women around the world, or perhaps by enquiring into whether the incorporation of women into the foreign policy making process, or conflict resolution negotiations, would make any significant difference to international relations. Postmodern feminists go further than liberal feminists by arguing that it is not enough to simply 'bring in' women, we need to unpack (deconstruct) existing discourses about IR to expose the profound gender bias embedded in key concepts and categories of analysis. However, they reject the idea of a 'woman's perspective' or 'feminist perspective', in the singular because they argue that 'woman' is not a single, universal category. Postmodern scholars generally are keen on the project of generating different understandings of the world by adopting different lenses or 'perspectives' on IR. However, this is because in this way we undermine the idea that there is a fundamental 'truth' to the world which we might discover. From this perspective, there are many stories which we could tell about the world and these are certainly not limited to the seven broad perspectives we have outlined in this text. Discourses of IR and the existence of competing claims also serve to undermine dominant power/knowledge relations and empower, to some degree, previously marginalised groups.

Critical theorists, especially those who follow Habermas, reject the theoretical pluralism advocated by postmodernism, and cling to the belief that while there are no undisputed 'facts' about the world and no disinterested positions, we can nevertheless adjudicate between different claims. Through discourse different claims can be assessed for their comprehensibility, truthfulness and correctness. Theory cannot, in itself, adjudicate and justify action, but it can create agents capable of full participation in decisions concerning action. The 'truth' depends upon the force of the better argument in the cooperative search for truth. In this way, the 'truth' of statements is linked in the final analysis to the intention of the good and true life.

Second, as we suggested in the introductory chapter, there are practical consequences which flow from adopting certain theoretical positions. Theory should not be seen as something which is separate from the world of international relations (the practice of international politics, perhaps, or international economic relations), but as intimately connected with that practice. The actions of 'practitioners', be they diplomats, government officials or NGOs, are informed by their underlying beliefs and assumptions about how the world works. Similarly, the prescriptive implications (in effect, recommendations) of our 'theory' might be revolutionary. That is, we might be forced to conclude that the only solution to the problems that beset humankind is fundamental change in the way societies – including societies of states – are organised, and a radical alteration in the way people behave. In the case of Greens, for example, it may require that we fundamentally rethink our relationship to the natural world and so have a profound effect on how we think about ourselves, our relations with others and our day-to-day practices. As is evident from our earlier discussion, postmodern thinkers see an intimate connection between 'theories' or, more properly discourses of international relations and actual practices. Therefore, we need to be alert to the way in which discourses justify and legitimise certain practices and how these are contested.

CONCEPT BOX

Critical Theories and Problem Solving Theories

In an influential article first published in 1982, Robert Cox made a crucial distinction between critical theories and 'problem solving theories'. Problem solving theories take the historical context as given and concentrate on providing solutions to problems which arise in that given 'reality'. So, for example, nuclear deterrence strategies are an attempt to think about the specific problems which nuclear weapons pose for the security of states. Deterrence theory takes for granted the existence of the state system and the security dilemma which arises under conditions of anarchy. In this sense, realism can be seen as a 'problem solving theory' because it presupposes a world of sovereign states and the existence of international anarchy.

In contrast, critical theory asks deeper questions, about why 'problems' arise in the first place. So, critical theory asks how did human beings come to be divided up into nation-states? How does this create perceived security dilemmas? In the specific case of nuclear deterrence, rather than asking how 'threats' can be deterred, critical theorists ask: How did nuclear weapons come to exist in the first place? How and why did they come to be perceived as a 'threat'? and so on.

Critical theorists argue that theory and practice must be seen as intimately connected. Critical theory encourages us to think critically and reflectively about how particular values, assumptions and concepts are used to describe the current social 'reality' and possible alternatives. Theories proscribe what can be thought, and consequently, courses of actions which can be taken and can be adjudged according to the degree to which they either open up or close off the possibilities for human emancipation. At the same time, as we noted earlier, our action changes existing 'reality' and so has an impact on what we and others come to think of as 'possible'. From this perspective, knowledge is generated through self-reflection, which provides the impetus to achieving self-understanding and autonomy of action and, so, emancipation.

Afterword – Is It Worth It?

If, all in all, this still seems difficult, you might take some consolation from the oft quoted remark that we become truly 'enlightened' only when we fully realise that we 'know' nothing! When studying IR (a discipline which sometimes appears to be dealing with everything) it can, at times, feel like you will never know *anything* at all; that there are simply more questions, but not any final answers. However, with perseverance, the study of IR is well worth the effort. IR raises questions about, and provides a window on, many aspects of life and, more importantly embraces peoples across the world. We hope that this book helps to open that window a little, making you aware of how your own practices impact on this world, and how ideas about the world have impacted on and influenced you. The words of Homer Simpson, or indeed anyone, will never be the same again. In the introduction to this book, we suggested that our efforts had been something akin to providing a teach yourself language book. Theory 'matters' because it provides us with a language, a vocabulary and a set of concepts through which we understand reality and frame our actions. Having now explained the basic theoretical and conceptual underpinnings of IR, it is now time for you to get on with speaking the language.

Further Reading

Banks, M. (1985), 'The Inter-Paradigm Debate', in Groom, A.J.R. and Light, M. (eds), *International Relations: A Handbook of Current Theory*, London: Pinter, pp. 7–26.

Barrett, M. and Phillips, A. (1992), *Destabilising Theory: Contemporary Feminist Debates*, Oxford: Polity Press.

Booth, K. (1997), 'Discussion: A Reply to Wallace', *Review of International Studies*, Vol. 23, No. 3, pp. 371–7.

Booth, K. and Smith, S. (eds) (1995), *International Relations Theory Today*, Cambridge: Polity Press.

Bourdieu, P. (1977), *Outline of a Theory of Practice*, Cambridge: Cambridge University Press.

Bourdieu, P. (1993), *The Field of Cultural Production: Essays on Art and Literature* (edited by Randal Johnson), Cambridge: Polity Press.

Brown, C. (1992), *International Relations Theory: New Normative Approaches*, Harlow: Prentice Hall.

Brown, S. (1988), 'Feminism, International Theory and International Relations of Gender Inequality', *Millennium: Journal of International Studies*, Vol. 17, No. 3, pp. 461–76.

Cox, R. (1986), 'States, Social Forces and World Order' in Keohane, R. (ed.), *Neo-Realism and Its Critics*, Princeton: Princeton University Press.

Foucault, M. (1980), *Power/Knowledge: Selected Interviews and Other Writings, 1972–1977* (edited by C. Gordon), Harlow: Prentice Hall.

Gadamar, H. (1977), *Critical Hermeneutics*, Berkeley: University of California Press.

George, J. (1994), *Discourses of Global Politics: A Critical (Re)Introduction to International Relations*, Boulder, CO: Lynne Rienner.

Grimshaw, J. (1987), *Feminist Philosophers*, Harlow: Prentice Hall.

Habermas, J. (1972), *Knowledge and Human Interests*, London: Heinemann.

Harding, S. (1990), 'Feminism, Science and the Anti-Enlightenment Critiques', in Nicholson, L. (ed.), *Feminism/Postmodernism*, London: Routledge, pp. 83–106.

Held, D. (1990), *Introduction to Critical Theory: Horkheimer to Habermas*, Cambridge: Polity Press.

Hoffman, M. (1987), 'Critical Theory and the Inter-Paradigm Debate', *Millennium: Journal of International Studies*, Vol. 16, No. 2, pp. 231–50.

Hollis, M. and Smith, S. (1994), 'Two Stories about Structure and Agency', *Review of International Studies*, Vol. 20, No. 3, July, pp. 241–52.

Jaggar, A. (1983), *Feminist Politics and Human Nature*, Harlow: Prentice Hall.

Kourany, J., Sterba, J.P. and Tong, R. (eds) (1993), *Feminist Philosophies*, Harlow: Prentice Hall.

Light, M. and Groom, A.J.R. (eds) (1985), *International Relations: A Handbook of Current Theory*, London: Pinter

Linklater, A. (1990), *Beyond Realism and Marxism: Critical Theory and International Relations*, London: Macmillan.

Linklater, A. (1992), 'The Question of the Next Stage: A Critical Theoretical Point of View', *Millennium: Journal of International Studies*, Vol. 21, pp. 77–98.

Maclean, J. (1981), 'Political Theory, International Theory and Problems of Ideology', *Millennium: Journal of International Studies*, Vol. 10, No. 2, pp. 102–25.

Matthews, F. (1991), *The Ecological Self*, London: Routledge.

Merchant, C. (1992), *Radical Ecology: The Search for a Liveable World*, London: Routledge.

Rosenau, P. (1991), *Postmodernism and the Social Sciences: Insights, Inroads, Intrusions*, Princeton: Princeton University Press.

Scruton, R. (1982), *A Dictionary of Political Thought*, London: Macmillan.

Smith, S. (1996a), 'Positivism and Beyond', in Smith, S., Booth, K. and Zalewski, M. (eds), *International Theory: Positivism and Beyond*, Cambridge: Cambridge University Press, pp.1–5.

Smith, S. (1996b), 'Power and Truth: a Reply to William Wallace', *Review of International Studies*, Vol. 23, No. 4, pp. 507–16.

Smith, S. and Hollis, M. (1996), 'A Response: Why Epistemology Matters in International Theory', *Review of International Studies*, Vol. 22, No. 1, January, pp. 111–16.

Smith, S., Booth, K. and Zalewski, M. (eds) (1996), *International Theory: Positivism and Beyond*, Cambridge: Cambridge University Press.

Sylvester, C. (1994), 'The Emperor's Theories and Transformations: Looking at the Field through Feminist Lenses', in Sylvester, C. and Pirages, D. (eds), *Transformations in Global Political Economy*, London: Macmillan.

Vasquez, J. (1995), 'The Post-Positivist Debate: Reconstructing Scientific Enquiry and International Relations Theory After Enlightenment's Fall', in Booth, K. and Smith, S. (eds), *International Relations Theory Today*, Cambridge: Polity Press.

Wallace, W. (1996), 'Truth and Power, Monks and Technocrats: Theory and Practice in International Relations', *Review of International Studies*, Vol. 22, No. 3, pp. 301–21.

Whitworth, S. (1989), 'Gender in the Inter-Paradigm Debate', *Millennium: Journal of International Studies*, Vol. 18, No. 2, pp. 265–72.

Wittgenstein, L. (1969), *On Certainty*, Oxford: Blackwell.

Glossary of Key or Problem Terms

Introductory Note

This list of simplified definitions is designed to aid your understanding. However it is not comprehensive. Some words are not included because they are covered sufficiently in the text itself; you should use the index to clarify the meaning of any such word you do not understand.

Actor: If the world is regarded as a stage then actors in international relations can be understood in much the same way as actors in a theatre. An actor in international relations is an entity that can be said to 'act'. This notion of an 'actor' can be applied to entities that are recognised under international law, so in this sense states are actors, but not individuals. The notion of actor might also be used more loosely to describe entities which have influence or agency (see below); in this view actors might be states, multi-national corporations, international organisations, social movements, or in exceptional cases, influential individuals.

Agency: An actor (see above) is said to have agency when they are able to exert influence, or affect the outcome of any given process or event in some way. It is perhaps easiest to contrast 'agency' with the idea of 'structure' (see structural adjustment below). For those people who believe that 'structure' is highly important in international relations, human agency is limited; actors are unable to greatly influence individual events or the general course of history, because they are constrained by the structure of the international system or world-system.

Alienation: A term used by Hegel, Marx and Freud among others, the word alienation is similar in meaning to the idea of estrangement; to feel left out or somehow apart from another person, or social group. The term can be used in a stronger sense to denote a feeling of exclusion which generates feelings of anger or antipathy towards society.

Anarchy: (This term is discussed extensively in the text itself). A term used to describe a situation in which a central government is absent. Anarchy should not be conflated with chaos or disorder. English School scholars (see below) argue that in international relations, order, rather than chaos, is possible in a situation of anarchy on the basis of informal rules which are accepted by most states, most of the time. Such rules might derive from international law (see below).

Anthropocentrism: This simply means human-centredness. In the context of environmental debates it refers to the argument that nature is a resource which exists to be exploited by humans for satisfaction of their needs and wants. As such, nature does not have rights and can therefore be used by humans as they see fit for their own ends.

Asylum: An asylum is a place of refuge. In international law/international relations, it refers to the process by which states grant asylum to citizens of other states who have a well grounded fear of persecution in their home country. Asylum seekers should be distinguished from refugees, who have been temporarily displaced from their home land (although refugees might subsequently seek asylum in the host country if they have a well grounded fear of persecution upon their return).

Atomistic: See holistic.

Autonomy: The ability to independently formulate and pursue goals. Questions of autonomy most often arise in relation to states, but can be applied to other actors (see above). It is frequently argued that autonomy is increasingly rare in a world characterised by interdependence. Autonomy should not be confused with sovereignty (see below).

Billiard Ball Model: This is an image often used to present the (classical) realist world view. The billiard table represents the world and the balls are states. The analogy/metaphor suggests that states have very clear boundaries – a 'hardshell' – and so domestic politics is not directly affected by international politics. However, states do come into contact with each other, and just as with a billiard ball hit at speed, sometimes have a big impact on each other's behaviour. In this view, international relations is, in essence, about such interactions. The billiard ball model usually allows for different sizes of balls (unlike the game) to represent the fact that some states have more power than others, and some states make a greater impact than others.

Bourgeoisie: First used to describe the emerging middle class in revolutionary France who challenged the political dominance of the aristocracy (*ancien régime*), the term is now more usually associated with Marxist thought. The bourgeoisie is the class constituted by the owners of the means of production, in contrast to the proletariat, or working class who are wage-labourers. Whether enlightened and philanthropic or downright oppressive, the bourgeoisie, according to orthodox Marxist thought, is destined to fall along with the supporting economic system of capitalism because of the latter's internal contradictions (see below).

Capitalism: A social and economic system which is founded on the principles of private property and free – voluntary – contracts. In a capitalist society, market mechanisms (the forces of supply and demand) ultimately determine the allocation of resources, the production of goods and services and distribution of 'rewards' (wages and profits). The nature of capitalism – whether it is socially beneficial and progressive or divisive and harmful – continues to be debated. For example, liberals typically claim that though based on the selfishness of individuals, this system of social and economic organisation ultimately works to ensure the greatest good of the greatest number. In contrast, socialists complain that capitalism generates social inequality, encourages materialism and rampant consumerism and is ultimately wasteful in terms of both human and natural resources.

Contradiction: A Marxist term used to express the idea that capitalism generates the contradictions which will ultimately cause it to collapse. In economic terms, the contradictions of capitalism are a tendency towards monopoly, and to force down wages, while at the same time encouraging overproduction in the drive to increase profits. In social and political terms, while ostensibly based on a system of free contract and individual choice, capitalism leads to the progressive impoverishment of the proletariat (see below). The system of economic organisation also creates the conditions in which workers are able to act collectively to throw off the chains of oppression.

Core–Periphery Model: This is the name given to the idea that the world is fundamentally divided into the haves and have nots, privileged and victimised, powerful and controlled. Basically the core–periphery model describes how the structure of global capitalism (see above) as an economic, social and political form of organisation, inevitably divides the world into winners and losers. This system operates and is perpetuated by linkages between élites in core (rich, industrialised) countries and élites in the (underdeveloped, dependent) periphery, who have shared interests in supporting a system which guarantees their privilaged position. The core–periphery model, is a stark contrast and, perhaps, an important antidote to liberal views of a free trade system or interdependent world (see chapter 2).

Deconstruction: A philosophical approach implying a thoroughgoing critique of the way in which knowledge is constructed. Deconstruction questions the idea of truth by exposing the assumptions, and presuppositions in a 'text'. It has its origins in literary studies (literary critique), and is particularly associated with the work of Jacques Derrida.

Deep Ecology: Also know as 'deep green', a deep ecological approach is one which rejects the idea of anthropocentrism (see above). Nature is viewed as alive and living creatures as deserving of respect. Some deep green thinkers even argue that we should assign rights to nature. It does not, as some of its critics claim, suggest that, for instance, anthrax spores are as morally considerable as humans. Deep ecology is a philosophy tied to bio- or ecocentrism (see below).

Deterministic: A theory is said to be deterministic when it implies that actors have little room to manoeuvre (agency); that their behaviour is predetermined (as in biological determinism) or profoundly shaped or constrained by social structures (as in economic determinism). Thus, determinism denotes the idea that human choices have little bearing on social and political arrangements which are somehow inevitable/would happen anyway.

Development: 'Development' is a good example of a 'discourse' (see below). Development began to attract the attention of social scientists in the 1950s and 1960s, at a time when many former colonies were moving towards independence and needed to simultaneously build stable political institutions and achieve economic growth and diversification. For a long time, the concept of 'Development' expressed the idea that all countries of the world follow a similar path towards industrialisation and modernity. Poorer countries, if they followed the right path or strategy would pass through a series of stages until they reached the same position as rich, developed states. Development 'experts' offered advice to developing countries based on the experience of western countries. Development towards high mass consumption societies has clearly not worked in most cases. In more recent years, the entire concept of development as economic growth and modernisation has been challenged by green and postmodernist thinkers, among others, on the grounds that it can be considered another manifestation of Western domination.

Discourse: In simple terms discourse means the way in which we use language to construct meaning or the way in which we infuse words with meaning or significance. Ordinary everyday conversations about the world are examples of discourse. Discourse is inherently social or inter-subjective. In poststructuralist thought discourse has a rather more precise meaning. Poststructuralists argue that nothing exists outside of discourse. That is to say that the only way in which we can understand our world is through the 'conversations' that we have about it. Through discourse – the use of language, symbols and imagery – we try to construct meaning. However, we are not using language to describe a real world 'out there', we are constructing that 'reality' discursively.

Ecocentrism: This simply means nature-centredness. In the context of the environmental debate, it refers to the argument that humans should not have free reign to exploit the planet's living and inert resources exactly as they please but should recognise the intrinsic value of the non-human world.

Ecosophy/Ecosophies: A nice abbreviated word used by the Norwegian deep ecologist Arne Naess and meaning an ecological philosophy.

Egalitarianism: A belief in equality as a value or principle, from which follows the idea that inequality signifies injustice.

Egoistically: This word appears frequently in international relations literature and implies that states, like human beings, are essentially self-interested and act as maximisers of their own well-being or interest.

Emancipation: In popular usage, to emancipate is to liberate or set free, as in the case of the freeing of slaves. In Western philosophy, emancipation means the achievement of autonomy, the ability to act independently. To be emancipated does not mean that one is free of all constraints and obligations towards others, only those which are deemed oppressive or unnecessarily confining.

Empirical: To be empirical is to favour modes of investigation or study which are derived from experience rather than relying on theoretical analysis and explanation. Empiricism thus denotes the belief that all knowledge of the world derives solely from experience. This should be distinguished from positivism (see below).

Empowerment: To empower is to give a person or group the capacity to act effectively to realise their own self-defined aims and objectives. Empowerment is thus distinct from liberty, which means the mere absence of unnecessary constraints, and implies some positive form of enablement, or facilitation, through perhaps access to resources or decision making structures.

English School: The term 'English School' denotes a school of thought or collection of works which explore the nature of 'international society' (see below) or the 'society of states'. Both facets of the English School are encapsulated in the phrase 'anarchical society' made famous by Hedley Bull, ironically an Australian! Though the English School is sometimes regarded as a variant of realist thought (both appear to be essentially state-centric), the intellectual influences are actually more varied, drawing upon liberal and rational strands of IR thought and other disciplines like sociology and international law.

Enlightenment: Period of human history (around the eighteenth century) when people moved from an age of superstitious medievalism to a belief in human reason and moral (and material) advancement.

Epistemology: Pertaining to knowledge. How do we know, what we know? Epistemology can be distinguished from the idea of ontology (which deals with the realm of what exists) in the sense that it concerns how we know things; what grounds we have for making knowledge claims.

Ethnocentric: Not to be confused with racism. In the broad context of international relations, ethnocentrism involves the tendency to regard one's own experience as normal, one's own way of thinking as rational and right and to suppose, therefore, that others will think similarly and will understand your motivations and actions.

Frankfurt School: The name given to a school of critical theory emerging first in Germany in the 1920s. The Frankfurt School was important in breaking away from orthodox (deterministic) schools of Marxist thought (drawing from the work of early 'humanistic' Marx, rather than the later 'economistic' work) and for developing an analysis of culture.

Genealogy: Term associated with the work of Michel Foucault. In everyday usage, genealogy means to trace back a lineage, family or origins. It has a similar usage in post-structuralism where it describes a method of study which traces back the historical origins of ideas, concepts or theories. However, unlike history, which uses sources and evidence from the past to construct a coherent account or story about the present, genealogy demonstrates the ways in which dominant ideas and concepts have been used to construct particular power relations and the ways in which dominant discourses have been contested.

Hermeneutic: A method which is about interpretation rather than science.

Heuristic: A heuristic device is one which is used to aid understanding of something more complex by allowing the learner to discover for themselves. The device may not be a comprehensive explanation in itself, but allows one to go beyond it through analysis and reason.

Holistic: A holistic approach is one which studies things as a whole rather than breaking them down into constituent parts (which could be termed an individualistic or atomistic approach). A holistic approach to the environment believes that it is linked in numerous complex ways and should be studied as such. An atomistic approach might believe it possible to study a problem, such as deforestation, without reference to broader social, economic, political and ecological structures.

Ideological: Ideology literally means the science of ideas, but has come to denote all embracing, belief systems, which relate to the nature of society, and economic and political relationships. Ideology is sometimes contrasted with 'science' or 'truth' which claims to describe a 'reality' which exists independently of our beliefs about the world. However, it is not at all clear that science, 'truth' and ideology can be contrasted in this way, since all truth claims are rooted in fundamental beliefs or normative (see below) visions, while science does not so much consist of undisputed 'facts', but rather our best beliefs about reality in any given period.

International Law: In essence international law is no different from domestic law. It governs relations between states (and other internationally recognised actors) on the basis of agreed principles and according to binding rules (such as those outlined in Treaties or Covenants), which can, in theory, be enforced through the Courts. However, international law is interesting because in the absence of centralised authority (a condition of anarchy) there is no effective government or 'police force' to enforce the rule of law. Consequently, much of what is agreed is on the basis of consensus and cooperation. Moreover, states are only bound by agreements that they actively sign up to or by principles which they can be shown to have adhered to in their relations with others – state practices (customary law). Critics argue that the lack of sovereign government means that ultimately international law is not really law (a positivist view of law as the command of a sovereign) or that lack of effective sanctions or enforcement mean that international law is not effective. However, despite the absence of a sovereign power, states do obey international law most of the time. Thus international law can be viewed as a way of expressing what states will normally do in a given situation and a codification of what it is useful for them to do (see also Laws).

International Society: The notion of International Society should be distinguished from the idea of an international system. An international system might be used synonomously with the 'state-system', the political organisation of the world into a system of states. International system also denotes the idea that states interact with each other in various ways. However, in a society, behaviour is 'rule governed'. Rules and norms of behaviour develop among states and, consequently, states come to have some notion of obligations to and expectations of each other, the most basic of which is the recognition of sovereignty.

Intersubjective: Intersubjective meaning is that established (or constructed) through the interaction of 'subjects' (see below). The idea implies that 'things' have no independent 'meaning' outside of that which is established through interaction or dialogue between conscious subjects.

Laws: The word 'laws' can be used in a scientific and legal sense. A scientific law is a regularity in behaviour (the law of gravity suggests that a cricket ball will fall if dropped); this type of law is comparable to a 'truth'. In IR there are few 'laws' of this type, although the proposition that democracies do not fight one another is sometimes held to be close to an established 'law'. In legal terms, a law prohibits, permits or insists on certain action or behaviour (murder is illegal, i.e. against the law); this type of law is based upon principle or some socially agreed notion of what is acceptable behaviour.

Marginalisation: The process whereby some are considered to be of less significance or are neglected; that is, those with little economic or political power, at local, national and global levels. Thus the third world is marginalised in the global economy and international politics, the poor are marginalised in national economies and women are marginalised in many ways in socio-economic and political terms throughout the world.

Material: Something material is something made of matter or which is 'real', tangible/has substance. There has been a long, ongoing debate in social theory about the relative importance of material forces and ideas and the relationship between the two. This centres on the extent to which human behaviour and relationships are largely rooted in or determined by material circumstances or conditions (for example, the extent to which material factors (lack of food) determine (see deterministic above) our ability to act and the way in which we relate to others). Materialism is often contrasted with idealism which holds that 'reality' is essentially a construct of the mind. In contrast, materialism holds that real material circumstances shape our consciousness (ideas) of the world.

Military–Industrial Complex: A phrase originally used by US President Eisenhower to signify the close relationships existing between politicians, business and the military which operate to keep military/defence spending at high levels. Such close relations were reinforced by the revolving door phenomenon where soldiers become politicians, politicians become businessmen and vice versa.

Misanthropic: A misanthrope is one who hates human beings; hence misanthropic. In the context of this book, some Deep Greens have been accused of misanthropism for their 'privileging' of the natural world over the human world. The counter argument is, of course, that since human beings are part of nature, privileging nature cannot be considered misanthropic.

Modernity: This is the period of history associated with a belief in the ability of reasoned thought (and especially science) to achieve breakthroughs leading to human (material – see above) progress. A belief in the possibility of modernisation (and progress) is still very prevalent today, despite wide ranging criticisms of Modern, Western thought made by postmodern and poststructuralist thinkers.

Nihilist: A nihilist is one who believes in nothing. The reason for believing in nothing is a 'belief' that society is founded on lies and that truth is therefore not possible in this context.

NIMBYism: NIMBY is an acronym signifying 'not in my back yard'. NIMBYism in an environmental context is the tendency to be concerned about environmental issues only in so much as they affect oneself; for instance campaigning for or against a bypass scheme.

Normative: In everyday usage the term 'normal' or the 'norm' is used to describe a practice which conforms to the standards of a given society. The term 'normative' can be used to describe practices which obey the laws of 'normal' behaviour, or which conform to the norms of society, deviations from which might incur some form of sanction. The realm of normative action then encompasses values, ideals and judgements; it is about what is expected of us, what we should do. In IR, the term normative is used in a similar way. An example of normative IR theory is that concerned with the role of moral codes, norms of behaviour or laws in the 'society of states'. A theory can also be considered normative if it raises, explicitly, questions or judgements which are founded upon certain ideals or moral standards, for example, theories which are concerned with inequality or justice between states, or social groups. Realists frequently claim that normative questions belong properly to the realm of political theory and not IR theory. This is because raising questions about law and morality, or inequality and justice, presuppose the existence of a political community (for example, a state) in which it is possible to make such judgements and, crucially, devise effective sanctions to punish transgressors. In contrast, realists argue that IR theory is a theory of state survival in an anarchic world, where 'might makes right'. Normative theory is also often contrasted with positivism, which claims to simply describe actions, events, or behaviour, without making judgements about whether this is 'right' or 'proper'. Whether or not it is actually possible to be 'objective' or 'value free' when studying the social world, is a matter of considerable debate (see positivism/postpositivism).

Otherness: Associated particularly with poststructuralist thought, otherness is that which is deemed as opposed to the self/that which is excluded or outside.

Patriarchal: Patriarchal society is a society in which men's dominance over women is institutionalised. Male domination is multi-faceted, and both structural (embodied in institutions like marriage and the family) and ideological through perhaps the celebration of masculine, rather than feminine traits and values.

Pedagogical: Pedagogy is the science of teaching, hence pedagogical means relating to the theory of teaching. Hence there is a pedagogical rationale behind exams in terms of the learning they are said to demonstrate.

Polemic: To be polemic is to be argumentative or controversial. In the context of this book the use suggests that a debate has been conducted at the level of insult and 'mud-slinging' rather than as a genuine attempt to discuss problems.

Positivism/Postpositivism: Positivism suggests that there are 'facts' about the world which can be established by observation and that such observation is neutral/independent or 'value free', i.e. not dependent on the 'position' of the observer as a part of the social world. While positivists carry out empirical research, positivism is not the same as empiricism (see above). Postmodernists (a postpositivist approach – see chapter 5) eschew grand theory in favour of empirical studies of specific societies. At the same time postmodernists reject the idea of value-free knowledge.

Postcolonial: If colonialism was the time when countries like Britain ruled others as possessions, the time after these countries gained independence (e.g. Zimbabwe) is known as postcolonial. Postcolonialism implies not just the throwing off of the imperialist yoke, but also that in important ways contemporary postcolonial societies continue to be profoundly affected by the colonial experience. Since the 1980s post-colonial writing has provided an important and influential critique of the West, and the constuction of postcolonial societies as 'other', that is different from and inferior to the West (see otherness above).

Praxis: The intimate connection between theory and practice used largely in Marxist writing.

Proletariat: In Marxist theory, the class of labourers under capitalist industrial production who must sell their labour to survive.

Realpolitik: A German word popularised by the policy of Chancellor Otto von Bismarck. It means a realism about what is possible and a preparedness to use force where necessary. The latter has lead to its association with 'lack of principle' or 'ruthlessness'.

Regime/s: The term regime has been around in IR theory since the 1970s and several classic definitions have emerged. Regime might be used to signify the leadership of a state (e.g. Saddam's regime). However, in contemporary IR, regime is most frequently used to refer to a set of rules and procedures concerning a given issue area which govern the behaviour of a particular group of actors – who are said to make up the regime which then makes decisions on the basis of this consensus. The International Whaling Commission is thus an example of an international environmental regime, though not an effective one. There is a more coherent international trade regime expressed in the World Trade Organisation.

Second Wave (Feminism):   Denotes the re-emergence of feminism as a radical social and political movement in the West in the 1970s.

Shallow Environmentalism: This is a view of the environment that, whilst it recognises there is a problem and that action needs to be taken, also suggests that our solution need not fundamentally alter the way human societies are organised. It suggests, in effect, that we can amend our behaviour to ensure that we live in harmony with nature so that nature may continue to provide for us.

Sovereignty: To be sovereign means to have power or control. Most often, a state (to be sovereign) needs control within its own territory and the power to act independently in the international system, although there are numerous examples of states which do not have this capacity to act (due to say civil strife), but nevertheless remain sovereign. In these cases, continual recognition by the international community of states is crucial to their survival as sovereign, independent state actors.

Structural Adjustment: The name given to policies 'negotiated' between indebted developing countries and the IMF and World Bank. Structural adjustment is a condition for receiving money. The money was needed in the wake of oil price rises and debt crisis in the 1970s and 1980s. Structural adjustment programmes (SAPs) meant countries spending less (fewer hospitals, scaling down government jobs, etc.) and earning more (growing more crops for export). The effects of SAPs have sometimes had the desired effect in terms of raw economic data, but in removing peasants from subsistence land (in order to grow for export) and in reducing social expenditures, SAPs have also had serious effects in terms of hardship for already poor groups.

Subject: In everyday usage the subject is 'who' or 'what' an account, story or narrative is about. In contemporary poststruturalist theory, the term is used in a similar way. However, the subject is that thing or entity which 'acts'. The subject is invested with a concrete identity and agency (the capacity to 'act' – see actor above). Thus discourses like realism construct the 'state' as the central actor which has concrete interests and acts to further the national interest. The study of IR is about the state. Thus in realist discourse it is the state, rather than a group or individual which is subject.

Substantive: Coming from the word substance, substantive means real, or genuine. A substantive argument is therefore one over real, important issues; a genuine exchange of ideas rather than insults and contradictions (see/compare polemic above).

Sustainable Development: Often given a bland definition such as 'development which meets the needs of present generations without compromising the needs of the future', sustainable development is highly controversial. Some critics have suggested that it is a contradiction in terms; others that it requires much more serious changes than politicians currently propose.

Telelogical: Modes of thought which construct explanations, or prescriptions for action premised on some notion of an ultimate end or desirable goal.

Universalism: A doctrine is universal when it is said to apply to all human beings regardless of creed, colour or nationality, or other 'superficial' differences.

Utopian: A utopia is a vision of the perfect social and political system. To be utopian is therefore to be visionary and to believe in the possibility of improving human society until utopia is reached. Oscar Wilde is reputed to have said that a map of the world without Utopia is not even worth looking at, though many IR scholars would disagree (see chapter 1).

World-Systems Theory: Associated particularly with the work of Immanuel Wallerstein, World-Systems Theory can be considered a variant of structuralism that conceptualises world order as being structured into a (rich, developed) core, (poor, underdeveloped) periphery and a number of intermediary or semi-perpheral states (see chapter 3).

Zero-sum: A 'zero-sum' game is one in which the answer is always zero. What does this mean? It means that if I gain something, you must lose a similar amount. Thus in war, a gain in territory by one side is automatically a loss by the other. Most closely associated with realism, not all international relations can be characterised in this way. For example, liberals hold that trade brings benefits to all and international environmental agreements suggest that all humanity will benefit from their adoption. In these cases the answer is more than zero (i.e. everyone gains) and can be called a positive-sum game.

Index